C1989 1995 4/15 15x

I0638778

ULSTER
An Illustrated History

edited by
Ciaran Brady, Mary O'Dowd and
Brian Walker

Foreword by J.C. Beckett

B.T. Batsford Ltd · London

© Ciaran Brady, Mary O'Dowd and Brian Walker 1989
First published 1989

All rights reserved. No part of this publication
may be reproduced, in any form or by any means,
without permission from the Publisher

Typeset by J&L Composition Ltd, Filey, North Yorkshire
and printed in Great Britain by
Courier International, Tiptree, Essex

Published by B.T. Batsford Ltd
4 Fitzhardinge Street, London W1H 0AH

*A CIP catalogue record for this book is
available from the British Library*

ISBN 0 7134 6239 6

Contents

List of contributors

Dr Ciaran Brady is a lecturer in Modern History, Trinity College, Dublin.

Dr W.H. Crawford is keeper of Material Culture at the Ulster Folk Museum, Cultra, Co. Down.

Mr Charles Doherty is a lecturer in Early Irish History, University College, Dublin.

Dr Raymond Gillespie works at the Department of Finance, Government Buildings, Dublin.

D.W. Harkness is Professor of Modern History at Queen's University, Belfast.

Dr Tom McNeill is a lecturer in Archaeology, Queen's University, Belfast.

Dr Mary O'Dowd is a lecturer in Modern History at Queen's University, Belfast.

Dr Éamon Phoenix is a teacher and archivist at St Malachy's College, Belfast.

Dr Brian Walker is a lecturer in Politics, and Assistant Director of the Institute of Irish Studies, Queen's University, Belfast.

Foreword

by J.C. Beckett, Emeritus Professor of Irish History, Queen's University, Belfast

The history of Ulster is part of the history of Ireland, from which it cannot be wholly separated without distortion. But it has some distinctive characteristics that justify our treating it separately, though not of course in isolation, from the history of Ireland as a whole. These characteristics arise mainly from the geographical position of the province, remote from the southern and south-eastern coastal areas where invaders from the continent and, later, from England were most likely to land. Thus, for example, Ulster was the last area to be brought under effective English control. The fact that the completion of the English conquest coincided with the union of England and Scotland under one crown gave a new significance to Ulster's closeness to Scotland; and from that period onwards we can trace a marked, though never dominant, Scottish influence on the political, social, cultural and economic life of the province.

These are the principal considerations that justify a separate treatment of the history of Ulster. But they are assumed rather than asserted in the essays that make up this volume. The editors have not tried to impose any over-all pattern on the contributors: each has been left to interpret the period assigned according to his own view of its significance. Yet despite this, the volume has a remarkable degree of coherence. Greater space has been given to the most recent periods of Ulster's history. The editors felt that the public for whom the volume is designed would wish to be brought as nearly as possible up to date on the present situation in Ulster and that this could not be done effectively in general terms. Even those who disagree with their decision will find that the concluding essays provide a perceptive assessment of the course of events during the troubled period that they cover.

Finally, I am glad to have this opportunity to congratulate both editors and contributors on the publication of this volume. It is a clear indication of the healthy state of Irish historical studies at the present time.

December 1988   J.C.B.

Editors' Introduction

History has always been a political weapon in Ulster, a powerful sustenance to ideological myth, a defence and validation of unities and continuities that did not exist, and a buttress of divisions and distinctions that were equally false. The earliest of the myths which history sustained was also the most potent. Even at the beginning of the historical record, Ulster's myth-makers, as Charles Doherty demonstrates in the opening chapter, were busy formulating a version of their province's past, which is at odds with what is known about its earliest history. History was being carefully tailored to meet immediate political concerns. Thus, the saga *Táin Bó Cuailgne* – 'The Cattle Raid of Cooley' – was a powerful piece of early political propaganda. It depicts a united Ulster led by a heroic band of warriors endeavouring to establish a superiority over the rest of Ireland. In reality, early Ulster, far from being a single political unit dominated by a single dynasty, was little more than a collection of competing statelets, each attempting to enforce a spurious claim over the others.

Yet belief in Ulster's past unity persisted and became a powerful political weapon in late medieval and sixteenth-century Ulster when it served to bolster the claims of the O'Neills to rule the whole province. In fact, as Ciaran Brady indicates in chapter three, loyalty to the O'Neills in the sixteenth century was tenuous. Politically, the province was divided into a collection of lordships, each concerned to serve its own interest and, if possible, to come to an accommodation with the English crown. It was the failure of the Tudor administration to carry through its reform programme in the province which led eventually to confrontation between the lords and the government. In the war of the 1590s the myth of Ulster unity was exploited and reinforced by the wider assertion that the province's lords were involved not just in a defence of Ulster but ultimately in a defence of Gaelic civilization and culture.

Belief in sixteenth-century Ulster as a golden age of Gaelic independence and unity was strengthened in the seventeenth century as plantation and colonization left many of the Irish remaining in Ulster resentful and hostile. The myth of the lost province sustained resistance to the plantations in the seventeenth century, entered the mythology of nationalist Ireland in the eighteenth and nineteenth centuries, and remains a powerful motivating force even today.

Yet, despite the popular belief in the purity of the Gaelic world, a recurring event in the history of the province is the arrival of new groups of settlers and their assimilation with the native population. A classic example of this process is the Anglo-Normans who, as Tom MacNeill documents in chapter two, adapted well to the rigours of the environment of the north-east. They integrated with the local community while at the same time contributing to the culture of the province through the introduction of more advanced agricultural techniques, urban development and new architectural styles in domestic and ecclesiastical buildings. Settlers from Scotland have always been attracted to the east coast of Ulster. Throughout the middle ages and the sixteenth century, Scottish people had come to Ulster to find temporary employment as mercenary soldiers or to settle permanently. In the seventeenth century this process was accelerated when the Stuart government sponsored the plantation of six counties in the province and encouraged private enterprise involved in colonizing the counties of Antrim and Down. In chapter four Raymond Gillespie shows that the new settlers, like their predecessors, integrated to some extent with the native culture and population. But by the early seventeenth century, there were also powerful forces working against assimilation.

Land, the struggle for political influence and, above all, religion contributed to an increase in tension between the two communities which was to issue in bloody conflict in the years after 1641.

The strong Presbyterian faith of many of the settlers, however, encouraged the fostering of a new historical myth strangely echoing the earlier myth of Ulster's golden age: a commonly held belief that they were the chosen people destined to inherit the province. The settlers' faith in this was reinforced by the economic development of Ulster in the seventeenth and eighteenth centuries, a process which was largely attributed to the intrinsic virtues of the hard-working settlers. As Gillespie and Crawford document, there was considerable material progress in the province during this time as the market economy expanded and many rural areas benefited from the spectacular growth in the linen industry. The economic advancement continued into the nineteenth century when Ulster shared in the benefits of the industrial revolution and Belfast gloried in its role as an imperial city in the Victorian period.

The economic and industrial success of the province strengthened popular belief in the distinctiveness of Ulster and the historic achievement of the seventeenth-century Protestant settlers. Yet the popular myth of Protestant progress ignored some of the historic realities. Industrial progress in the province was uneven and largely confined to the north-east. As Brian Walker points out in chapter six, the majority of the inhabitants of Ulster were still employed in agriculture at the end of the nineteenth century. The class and religious divisions within the Protestant population in the province were also ignored by a myth concerned to stress unity and common purpose. The dissenters of the seventeenth and eighteenth centuries resented the dominance and oppression of the established Church of Ireland, and in the nineteenth century, identities of religion and class rarely coincided as landlords, middle-class merchants and farm labourers frequently belonged to different denominations.

Despite the reality of division and disunity, by the end of the nineteenth century two popular interpretations of the province's history existed among the province's Catholics and Protestants. Although fundamentally irreconcilable, both helped to consolidate group loyalty and a sense of continuity with the past, and both interpretations were confirmed by the growth of sectarian tension in the late nineteenth century. With the foundation of the government of Northern Ireland in 1920, the Protestant interpretation received official sanction as the government gave a 'virtual endorsement' to Protestantism, a process described by Éamon Phoenix in chapter five. The establishment of the new state also gave rise to a new historiography which bolstered belief in the distinctiveness of Ulster and its economic, religious and intellectual superiority over the rest of Ireland. At the same time, Catholic popular writers continued to evoke the myth of the lost province and to celebrate the continuing efforts of successive generations to reclaim it.

The foundation in 1923 of the Public Record Office of Northern Ireland, and the establishment of the Ulster Society for Irish Historical Studies in 1936, have done much to foster a more objective interpretation of Irish history but this has not been easy given the political attraction of subjective interpretations. In chapter eight David Harkness's analysis of the history of the province since 1972 reveals that intellectual and cultural life in Northern Ireland has continued to flourish despite the troubles of the last 20 years. But it is clear that in the same period, powerful but opposing beliefs in Ulster's past have gained in intensity, and in their capacity to motivate political action.

It is easy, of course, for academic historians to dismiss popular myths as having no historical foundation, but the function of myths in validating group loyalty and unity is of central importance and needs to be more fully explored. They help to simplify the very complex story of the history of Ulster, providing a sense of continuity within a history which is full of disruption. The history of the province is one of fluid and shifting borders, conflicting religious loyalties and diverse ethnic origins. The boundaries of Ulster have changed: from the extended Ulster of the Ulaid of pre-Christian times to the more confined territorial limits of Northern Ireland, as the maps in this book dramatically illustrate. Conflicting religious loyalties have been a problem in Ulster since the seventeenth century, but it is important to stress that the simple conflict between Protestant and Catholic was neither inherent nor inevitable. Finally, the ethnic origins of Ulster people do not consist only of Scottish Protestants and Irish Catholics. Scottish Catholics settled in the province in the sixteenth and seventeenth centuries, as did many English Catholics and also English members of the Anglican church.

The history of Ulster remains intellectually problematic and politically troubled. It is for this reason that the editors did not impose any rigid guidelines on the contributors to this volume. Rather, they chose to allow the contributors to select what they themselves saw as the principal problems and issues of their period and to explore them by whatever techniques they believe to be the most illuminating. As a result there is a variety of historical styles and approaches to be found in the eight chapters: emphases change from political to social, from economic to religious history in line with the authors' views as to the most significant tendencies of the periods under examination.

The volume had its origins in a series of lectures delivered in 1984–5 to the Dublin Historical Association, a society dedicated to the aim of maintaining a liaison between the research of professional historians and the needs and interests of teachers and the reading public. The series arose from a demand from both teachers of history and the general public for an accessible and up-to-date history of the province. Though recent years have seen the publication of a number of scholarly monographs dealing with aspects of Ulster's past, the last general history of the province was published in the 1950s (*Ulster since 1800*, ed. T.W. Moody and J.C. Beckett, two series, London, 1955, 1957). It was, therefore, with the intention of producing such a volume that the Ulster Society for Irish Historical Studies decided to subsidize the publication of this collection of essays. The editors, who represent both the Dublin Historical Association and the Ulster Society for Irish Historical Studies, hope that the book will fulfil that aim and provide, for those interested, an up-to-date guide to the current state of research in successive periods of the history of Ulster.

December 1988   C.B.
                                                                        M.O'D.
                                                                         B.W.

Acknowledgments

The editors and publishers wish to thank the following for the illustrations appearing in this book:
The Belfast Telegraph (nos. 70, 71); Mr Joe Dundee (nos. 45–47); Frazer and Haughton Ltd (no. 37); Mr Barry Hartwell (nos. 12, 15, 16, 19); the Historic Monuments and Building Branch of the Department of the Environment for Northern Ireland (nos. 2, 22, 27, 28, 35) the *Irish News* (no. 55); Lensmen Ltd (no. 59); Dr Tom McNeill (no. 14); the National Library of Ireland (nos. 1, 49, 51); the National Maritime Museum (no. 20); the National Museum of Ireland (nos. 4, 7); the National Trust (no. 38); Northern Ireland Housing Executive (nos. 65, 74); the Northern Ireland Government Information Service (nos. 56, 57, 61, 63, 75); the Northern Ireland Tourist Board (nos. 18, 66, 69); Pacemaker Press International Ltd (nos. 64, 67, 68, 72); the Public Record Office, London (no. 25); the Public Record Office of Northern Ireland (nos. 52, 62); the Board of Trinity College, Dublin (nos. 33, 34); the Ulster Museum (nos. 3, 10, 11, 36, 39–42, 48, 60); the University of Cambridge (nos. 5, 8). Thanks are also due to Dr Paul Compton, Mr Nick Brannon and Mr Bryan A. Follis for their assistance.

The maps were drawn by Ian and Gillian M. Alexander. The maps on pp. 79 and 110 are based on maps by K.W. Nicholls, T.W. Moody and R.J. Hunter in T.W. Moody, F.X. Martin and F.J. Byrne (ed.), *A New History of Ireland*, iii: *Early Modern Ireland, 1534–1691*, Oxford, 1976, pp. 2–3, 198–9. The map on p. 114 is based on the map in P. Robinson, *The Plantation of Ulster*, Dublin, 1984, p. 94. The map on p. 58 is based on the map in T.W. Moody, F.X. Martin and F.J. Byrne (eds.), *A New History of Ireland*, ix, Oxford, 1984, p. 80.

The editors are happy to acknowledge a grant in aid of publication from the Department of Education of Northern Ireland and the Ulster Society for Irish Historical Studies.

1 Ulster before the Normans: ancient myth and early history

Charles Doherty

I

The finger of land that stretched from Ireland out towards Britain gradually sank beneath the waves at the end of the last ice age. Although Ireland had then become an outpost on the Atlantic coast of Europe, she was never to be isolated for long.

Archaeological research shows clearly that Ireland had a close relationship with Britain and continental Europe throughout the prehistoric period; and the north-east of Ireland had a particularly close relationship with Scotland. The underlying rocks in the northern two-thirds of Ireland are aligned north-east to south-west, stretching down from Scotland, from which this pattern has been called the Caledonian trend. Geologically Ireland and Scotland are partners, and it is not surprising that this partnership was reflected during the prehistoric and historic periods in the close relationship which existed between the peoples who inhabited these areas. South-west Scotland was colonized by court cairn builders from Ireland in the Stone Age, and there was an important trade in polished stone axeheads from the industrial site at Tievebulliagh above Cushendall.[1] Similar trading connections are to be found in the Iron Age when objects for personal adornment such as combs were imported from Scotland in the first century AD.[2] Such trading links continued into the beginning of the historical period and are further confirmed by the evidence now found in Ptolemy's map. The information on the northern part of Ireland, consisting of names of tribes, tribal capitals,

KAUKI   Tribes   O MONA   Islands

■ Reba   Towns   ◄ Logia   River mouths

English equivalents of latin names are given
where reasonably certain

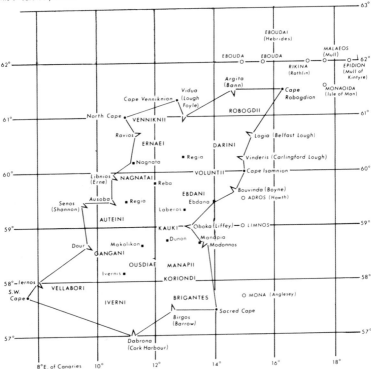

1 Ptolemy's map of Ireland, c. AD 150.

headlands, rivers, estuaries and islands, was gathered by the
Romans as a result of Agricola's military activity in
northern Britain and Scotland in the 80s of the first century
AD. It has been said that some of this material went back to
the time of the Greek navigator Pytheas in the fourth
century BC but this is in the highest degree unlikely.[3]

The northern rivers mentioned in the map are the Logia
(Lagan), Argita (Bann), Vidua (Foyle) and Ravios (Roe).
Rikina or Ricena is likely to be Rathlin. The cities are
Isamnion (Emain, Navan Port) and a Regia, 'royal seat', is

probably Clogher. The tribal names are the Robogdii in a location in north-east Antrim and north Down; the Voluntii (Uluti), the Ulaid, represented later by the Dál Fiatach in east Down.[4] These names are arcane but allow us to say that in the first century of the Christian period the inhabitants of the north-east have Celtic names and that some of these names are the same as those mentioned in later historical sources.

What do we know of these peoples? For this period we know very little beyond the names that can be deciphered. The contemporary historical documents that we have do not become sufficiently numerous or detailed until the seventh century. The first few centuries of the historical period, therefore, are seen as through a veil. One could call the fifth and sixth centuries the protohistoric period. As in the history of many other countries, where there are similar periods for which there is little contemporary information, a great deal of legend and mythology is to be found filling in the blanks in the historical record. This presents the historian with the enormous challenge of separating the thin stream of contemporary evidence from the mythology which has grown up around it.

One source which dominates the early history of Ireland is the saga, *Táin Bó Cuailgne* – 'The Cattle Raid of Cooley'. It is likely that this and related sagas had their literary origin in the Ulster monasteries of Bangor in Co. Down and Dromsnat (Druim Snechta) in Co. Monaghan during the course of the seventh and eighth centuries. The *Táin* is the main story in the Ulster Cycle of tales. It depicts a pre-historic Ulster, with its capital at Emain Macha (Navan Fort), in confrontation with the forces of Connacht and Leinster. Kenneth Jackson suggested in 1964 that its tales, although not historical accounts, reflect society in Ireland in approximately the third and fourth centuries AD and so record historical circumstances of warfare between the Ulaid (ancient Ulstermen) and the Connachta.[5] This interesting suggestion is, however, speculative.

One major problem encountered when trying to deter-mine the relationship between oral tradition and the stories written by a literary sage, is the medium by which these

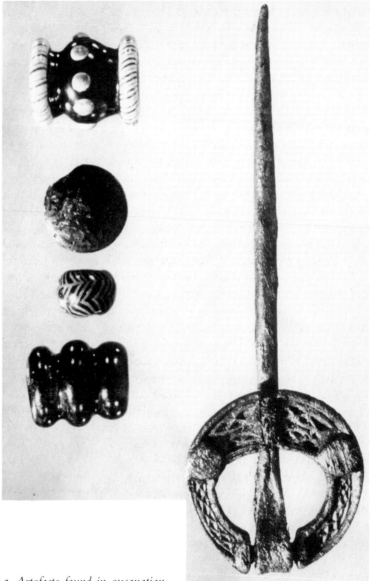

2 *Artefacts found in excavation
of a rath (fort) at Deer Park Farm,
Co. Antrim.*

stories have come down to us.[6] Do they contain genuine history? – or are they primarily mythological texts re-shaped as propaganda in the seventh and eighth centuries? They are, of course, good stories and had enormous entertainment value, but like much early medieval material they carry messages relevant to the audiences of their time. If the Ulster Cycle of tales reflects a historical situation it does so as a mere shadow. Recent work shows that in some respects it reflects the propaganda and social conditions of the seventh century, the time at which it was committed to writing, rather than those of the fourth century.[7]

We can trace the beginnings of writing in the vernacular, as distinct from Latin, to the 630s. By this stage paganism was no longer a threat to the church and so the native language began to reassert itself in a literary form and, as it was the natural medium of communication, it served as a much more subtle vehicle of propaganda. The way in which tradition can be used for particular purposes shows how dangerous it is to accept this kind of material as direct historical evidence.[8] By the seventh century, during which the *Táin* was being committed to writing, the territory of Ulaid – formerly embracing all of the north of Ireland – had been reduced to the eastern part of the province. By that time too Ulaid was divided between a number of groups, the most important of which were the Dál Fiatach in east Down and the Dál nAraidi or Cruthin in Antrim. Despite their declining political power, these groups still cherished memories of their former unity and dominance and there was much rivalry between the Dál Fiatach and the Dál nAraidi as to who represented the *fir-Ulaid* or 'true Ulstermen'. The Dál Fiatach claimed the title of the Ulaid but this was strongly disputed by the Dál nAraidi or Cruthin. In the later seventh and early eighth centuries the abbots of Bangor were generally drawn from a branch of the Dál nAraidi who exercized control over Bangor. It was natural therefore that they should have had an immediate political interest in propagating stories describing the glorious past of the Ulaid, and in glossing over the circumstances leading to the decline of the dynasty.

In the same way, Lugaid moccu Ochae, the founder abbot of Dromsnat, also founded Clonfertmulloe in Co. Laois on land granted by the king of the Loíges. In some genealogical traditions this people who were a subject group on the Leinster borders and thus of a very low political status were said to be of the same stock as the Cruthin. The monks of Clonfertmulloe reciprocated the grant of land by writing a new genealogy for the Loíges which made them descendants of Conall Cernach who features in the *Táin* as the guardian of the Ulster border. Other politically inferior peoples of Ireland had similar genealogies written for themselves, linking them to the Ulster heroes, and so giving them a respectable ancestry. It is quite clear that there was considerable prestige attached to the Ulster tales, especially the *Táin Bó Cuailgne*, and for this reason it was used as a means of raising the prestige and explaining the political irrelevance or obscurity of unsuccessful peoples by claiming that they were Ulster 'exiles'. Manipulation of the evidence was a natural means of realignment in this tribal society. For this reason we must be sceptical of the importance of this material for a knowledge of early peoples.[9]

II

The boundaries of the ancient province of Ulster are unclear. Certainly the boundaries of the present state of Northern Ireland do not correspond to any previous historical borders. Before the Government of Ireland Act in 1920 Ulster consisted of nine counties, and the ancient province at its most constricted in the twelfth century was confined to an area approximating to the two counties of Down and Antrim in the north-east. Ulster's boundaries have constantly changed throughout history and have been interpreted differently by different political groups. At each point in history ancient myth has been called upon to validate a particular point of view. In the past writers who

3 (left) *King*; (right) *Abbot: sculptures from White Island, Co. Fermanagh, 8th or 9th century.*

wished to provide an ancient basis for the present borders of the Northern Ireland state created a 'history' which may be described, without any injustice, as one of the current myths.

The main source of inspiration for this view is the Ulster Cycle of tales and in particular the *Táin Bó Cuailgne*. Because of the theme of this and related sagas there has been a temptation to relate the series of earthworks which are found in various localities across the northern part of Ireland, generally known as 'Black Pig's Dyke', 'The Dane's Cast', 'The Worm Ditch', and so on, to a prehistoric boundary of Ulster. The line of this boundary was first worked out by Rev. H.W. Lett in the last century.[10] Further work was carried out by W.F. De Vismes Kane.[11] He concluded that

> It seems therefore probable that the making of this formidable ditch dates about the year 200 of this era, if we can place reliance on these early Irish Chronicles, which of course long precede any known written history. But the identification of this chain of ancient earthworks as coterminous with the frontier of Ulster as set forth by these historic legends – a frontier which differs widely from that described by the earliest written authorities as existing in their time – seems a remarkable and unexpected proof of the truth of these traditional narrations, whether we accept their chronology as accurate or not.

Oliver Davies, writing in the *Ulster Journal of Archaeology* in 1948, suggested that these earthworks were copies of Roman frontier-works and that they 'probably formed frontiers, of the state of Ulster'.[12] But in 1955 when he returned to the problem he revealed a greater sensitivity of interpretation when he stated that 'Frontier-delimitation is a pastime better suited to the amateur politician than to a serious scholar', although he did speculate along these lines in his concluding paragraph.[13] By contrast historical geographers, in particular E. Estyn Evans have argued that in its geological structure and in its physical habitat Ulster looks toward Scotland: 'Most of the drainage of Ulster fans out northwards from a devious watershed which never lies far from the historic frontier of Ulster. This border zone is the Drumlin belt consisting of the scraping of the Ulster

4 Grianan Ailigh.

hills deposited under the ice as it moved into the central lowlands'.[14]

More recently the excavations at Navan Fort, Co. Armagh and the Dorsey, in southern Co. Armagh have placed this problem in a new perspective.[15] It would now appear that the timbers used in the 'forty metre structure' in Navan Fort and those found in the Dorsey (a structure associated with the Black Pig's Dyke) were felled in approximately 100 BC.[16] It is not unreasonable to associate the creation of these structures with the same people, or that similar forces brought them about but at present both archaeologists and dendrochronologists agree that it is essential to recover dating criteria from other sections of what is known as the Black Pig's Dyke to determine if they were erected in the same period and thus formed part of an overall plan for the defence of the north of Ireland.

The boundary of the province of Ulster is therefore unclear. For the historical geographers it is the Drumlin belt; for the older generation of archaeologists it was the Black Pig's Dyke and related earthworks. What both these interpretations have in common is the burden of the contemporary political division. To impose modern concepts of a frontier or boundary on prehistoric or early historic tribal population groups is to show lack of sympathy for what is best studied from an anthropological perspective. It may be that in the future it can be shown that there was a dominant political group which built a defensive boundary across the northern part of Ireland but it cannot, automatically, be proven by appeal to the kind of early saga and genealogical material which has been referred to above.

Some popular historians have claimed that the Cruthin were the original population group to occupy the north-east. They see in the Cruthin a pre-Gaelic people who held out against Gaelic 'invaders' from the midlands. It is also suggested that the role of the Cruthin has been played down by professional historians:

> By what amounts to a conspiracy of silence broken only by a sponsored Mythology of half-truths and religio-political emotionalism the Gaelic pseudo-historians still rule.... For traditional, historical and linguistic considerations all support the conclusion that the Gaelic settlement of Ireland was a LATE event in Irish history.[17]

For some this interpretation may serve as a means of uniting the people of Ulster by giving them a common ancestry or common interest in the past[18] but much of this theory is derived from the work of the late T.F. O'Rahilly whose historical conclusions have been questioned by archaeologists and historians. In particular, O'Rahilly's thesis on the chronology of the invasion has been subject to serious revision and, consequently, as explained in more detail below, his views on the ethnic makeup of early Ireland are no longer accepted.[19]

Such popular views of Ulster's ethnic origins have parallels in and are in part a response to nationalist myths which stress erroneously the pure Gaelic origins of Ulster's early population and the unity of ancient Ireland. Such ideas were current at the beginning of this century and are still to be found in some popular accounts.

5 *Pagan statue of the god Nuadu, from Tandaragee,
Co. Armagh.*

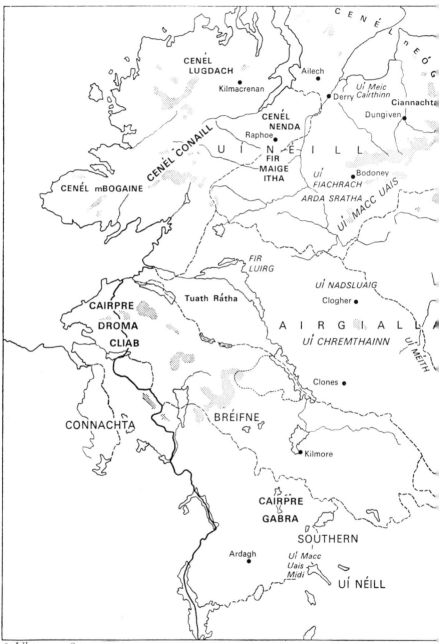

6 Ulster, c. 800

DÁL
RIATA

Coleraine

ir
hraíbe

CENÉL
mBINNIG

EILNE

Fir Lí

DÁL
Connor
nARAIDE

Antrim

Latharna

UÍ
THUIRTRÍ

Tulach
Óc

Bangor

Mag-Bile

Craeb
Tulcha

DÁL

FIATACH

UÍ ECHACH ARDA

IND

Armagh

AIRTHIR

Dromore

UÍ
ECHACH

COBO

Downpatrick

LETH
CATHAIL

MUGDORNA

Monaig

MAIGEN

CONAILLE

MUIR-
THEMNE

FIR ROIS

Louth

Mugdorna
Breg

Uí Macc
Uais Breg

Fir Arda
Ciannachta

The North c. 800 A.D.
Shading indicates 1000 ft. contour
Dotted boundaries are those of later medieval
dioceses of Raphoe, Derry, Connor, Down,
Dromore, Armagh, Clogher, Kilmore and Ardagh.
Continuous boundaries those of ecclesiastical
provinces of Armagh, Dublin and Tuam.
UÍ NÉILL DYNASTIES. **Subject tribes of
Uí Néill**
TRIBES OF AIRGIALLA. Tribes of Airgialla
directly subject to
Uí Néill over-kingdoms

Propagandist history of this type belongs to an ancient tradition. Its creation and use is not any different from ancient sources such as the *Lebor Gabála* ('Book of Invasions') which gave it birth. It is essentially the creation of new myth out of old. The *Lebor Gabála* is pseudo-history and is essentially mythological in character. It is a twelfth-century composite text in its present form, although it is likely that its core goes back to the seventh century. This type of literature came into being from the sixth and seventh centuries onwards, as the recently Christianized Irish tried to work out how they should be fitted into the contemporary histories of the world.[20] It was part of the process of an oral culture adapting to a literary tradition. In order to create a prehistory for themselves they fused the residue of their pagan myths (at least those which did not directly conflict with Christianity) with contemporary histories of the world, such as that of Orosius, and with the Bible. In this way they treated the mythological peoples, their ancient pagan gods and goddesses, as if they had been historical. Although there may be genuine historical echoes in this material it is exceptionally difficult to identify such historical strands.

At the time when such ideas were first written down, about the seventh century, there existed a multiplicity of kingdoms and overlordships throughout the country. The political relationship of one group to another was expressed genealogically. Such genealogical explanations were frequently at variance. Peoples explained their origins and their genealogical relationships in terms of their current political status. Much (if not all) of this genealogical material was manipulated, as we have seen above, as current ideology demanded.[21] T.F. O'Rahilly in his famous book, *Early Irish History and Mythology*, tried to use this material to demonstrate that the early Irish population was made up of various ethnic strands which arrived in a series of invasions in recent prehistory.

It is very likely that there may have been a strong pre-Celtic element in the population. As O'Rahilly says, there was still a memory of such diversity among the men of learning in the eighth century.[22] Such diversity in the sense of racial differences must have been a very long time in the past. Indeed the contemporary reason for assigning to peoples diverse origins was yet another means of expressing social and political relationships – of stating who owed tribute and to whom. By the seventh and eighth centuries it had little to do with racial origin. By this time the island was Gaelic-speaking and its culture, from the literary and archaeological records, seems to have been remarkably homogeneous. The battles that were taking place were not between native and invader but between tribes and dynasties for control of various parts of the island and even for dominance of the island itself.

The Ulaid were called Érainn by the genealogists. This was also the name given in Ptolemy's map for a people, the Iverni, living in Co. Cork. As a word that lies behind the name for Ireland, it was used frequently by genealogists to refer to the older population groups in the country. The heartland of the Ulaid was in fact the area of the diocese of Down.

The main population group in the Ulaid were Cruthin or Cruithni. Their territory lay mainly within the diocese of Connor and Dromore but in the sixth century they also occupied territory in Co. Derry. The word Cruthin itself is the Q-Celtic (Gaelic) form of the word *Pretani*. Greek writers used this word to refer to the inhabitants of the British Isles. This name also implies an ancient population group. Peoples such as the Loíges in Leinster and the Ciarraige in Munster were said by the genealogists to belong to this group. It is likely that the distant ancestors of these groups may even have been pre-Celtic. The northern Picts in Scotland may have been a survival of such communities into the historical period. When the Irish referred to the Picts of Scotland they used the word Cruthni. While the Picts of Scotland were called *Picti* by the Romans, the word *Picti* is never used of the Cruthni in Ireland. There is no trace of the material culture of the Picts of Scotland to be found in Ireland. If the Cruthin were ever

7 *Trumpet from Loughinashade beside Navan Fort, showing La Tène decorations (enlarged detail, below).*

the same people as the Picts of Scotland it was in the very remote past, because in the historical period there is no connection between the two peoples.

When Julius Caesar arrived in Britain in the first century BC the inhabitants he met were the ancient Britons who occupied most of the island and whose descendants are now the Welsh. Their language is called P-Celtic because of linguistic differences with the Celtic language of Ireland which is known as Q-Celtic. Since the Irish colonized Scotland and the Isle of Man the Gaelic of these areas is also Q-Celtic.

Professor F.J. Byrne has noted that there are traces of P-Celtic among the personal names of the Ulaid, but by the time of our documentary sources these peoples are speaking Goídelic or Irish. The peoples of the north-east who colonized Scotland brought the Irish language with them and this was to be the dominant language of Scotland in the middle ages.

As a far-from-ancient people of Ireland, were the Ulaid responsible for bringing an intrusive P-Celtic-speaking element into the north-east in the late prehistoric period? It is possible to argue that they formed a dominant overlordship for some time and that we are witnessing the final collapse of the regime in the opening centuries of the historical period. Yet recent studies of the La Tène culture in Ireland would seem to caution against the 'invasion hypothesis'.[23] The subject is complex and allows for no simple solutions. Therefore, it is dangerous to assign racial origins to any particular tribal group in early Ireland. Such was the degree of homogenization of the various peoples of prehistoric Ireland that by the opening of the historical period they had all gone 'native', and the pattern of internal political dynamics, which we can see operating throughout the early middle ages, had already become established.

III

The material culture of the whole of Ireland was homogeneous; the country was heavily forested. There were areas

8 Navan Fort earthworks.

which had been cleared and which had been continuously settled for a very long time. The normal type of residence was the *rath* or *liss*. This is the 'fairy fort' of the Irish countryside. Originally they were banks of earth, sometimes revetted with stone and topped by a palisade, which enclosed a farmer's dwellings. Other habitations were *crannógs* or islands in lakes. These served the same function and had the extra protection of the surrounding water. They were the dwelling places of kings and nobility. Some of them may have been more heavily fortified than others. It is likely that some of the servile communities may have lived in unenclosed settlements (archaeological traces of which are much more difficult to find), which are scarcely mentioned in the documentation. The great tribal 'capitals' or ritual centres, such as Emain Macha and Tara, of the immediately prehistoric period, had already fallen into disuse. Their past glory survived in myth and saga, and was revived on the occasions of the inauguration of kings, for they were still the focus for this least Christianized of rites.

As the Church grew in wealth and power her settlements began to dominate the landscape; not least of these was Armagh, which seemed to have taken on the mantle of Emain Macha. By the middle of the seventh century she was dominant not merely in the north, but was well on the way to being accepted as the chief church throughout the island. The Church later became extremely wealthy. The major monasteries were the centres of vast estates and the churches themselves attracted a considerable population. In the course of time they acquired urban characteristics and functioned as towns. Secular power and ecclesiastical power soon became interwoven as ambitious kings sought to control all resources within their expanding kingdoms.

The coming of the Norsemen in the late eighth and ninth centuries profoundly altered the course of Ulster's economic and political history. During the ninth century they established several encampments along the Ulster coast at Lough Foyle, Lough Neagh, Lough Erne and in Belfast Lough, Strangford Lough and Carlingford Lough. From these bases they launched an extensive series of raids throughout Ulster. The prosperous monastic centres were particularly attractive to the Norsemen. Armagh, for instance, was attacked on several occasions throughout the ninth century, three times in one month alone in 832. The Norsemen suffered a major defeat, however, in 866 when

Áedh Findliath of the Cenél nEóghain (the Uí Néill high king) plundered all their strongholds in counties Derry and Antrim and defeated them heavily in Lough Foyle. It was, perhaps, successes such as these which explain their failure to establish a major trading centre such as Dublin in Ulster. Larne, however (Ulfreksfiord in Norse), was clearly established as a town by the twelfth century and may have been of greater importance than is realized.

In this society cattle were the basis of the economy. There was no coinage before the Norse began to mint in the late tenth century, and cattle were used as the main units of value. The constant cattle-raiding which took place was the parry and thrust of politics. The economy, although dominated by cattle, was mixed. Essentially it was a society of farmers. The kings and great lords owned large estates. Lesser men were their followers. Their bond was cemented through the acceptance of a fief (cattle rent) which also indicated their inferior position. It was from among such followers that kings and lords assembled their warbands.

Already in the seventh and eighth centuries society was moving rapidly from a tribal condition towards a system of lordship as existed in other parts of Europe. This development was further accelerated as a result of the Norse impact of the ninth and tenth centuries. By this time the establishment of wealthy coastal trading posts, some of which during the tenth and eleventh centuries were to develop into primitive towns, with a strong interest in the slave trade, brought a new dimension to the economy and politics of early Ireland. Kings sought to control these centres of wealth and the ensuing competition resulted in an extraordinary consolidation of power in Ulster in which 10 or 12 lordships emerged as significant, headed by the Uí Néill (see map, p. 25). These were the only political units that really mattered by the twelfth century.

IV

Against this general background we may now return to developments within the ancient province of Ulster itself.

At the core of the present text of the *Annals of Ulster* is a document first compiled in the monastery of Iona. This was a table for the calculation of the date of Easter and was probably in the monastery from the time of its foundation in *c.* 563. Into this were written brief statements about the deaths of bishops and abbots, cosmic and earthly phenomena, the deaths of kings, battles, and items of interest to the community of Iona. This material allows us to create a picture of sixth- and seventh-century politics.

Because *The Annals of Ulster* was written from the perspective of Iona most information refers to the north-east of Ireland. In the overall picture the Uí Néill dynasty is expanding in the midlands and the north-west. This expansion was at the expense of older power groups. In the midlands the ancient Leinstermen were being pushed back towards the boundaries of the present province. In the areas of Donegal and north Meath pressure was being placed on the ancient province of Ulster and the Ulaid.

The kingdom of Dál Riata, from the Glens of north Co. Antrim, had colonized the islands and peninsulas of south-west Scotland. This is generally thought to have been under way at the opening of the fifth century. There were three main divisions of the Dál Riata in Scotland – the Cenél nGabrain, Cenél Loarn, and Cenél nÓengussa. In the course of the sixth century the Cenél nGabrain were at the forefront of attacks against the Picts. Áedán mac Gabráin, the most successful of the kings of Dál Riata, was 'ordained' king by St Colum Cille (Columba) on Iona, probably in 574. In the following year at the famous 'Convention of Druim Cett' in Co. Derry Áedán made an alliance with the northern Uí Néill king, Áed mac Ainmuirech, to oppose the Ulaid who had been putting pressure on the territories of the Dál Riata in Ireland. A further part of the agreement was that the Dál Riata homeland in Ireland would in future be subject to the high-king and serve him with its land forces but that the Scottish kingdom should be independent except for the obligation to serve the high-king with its fleet if required. During Aed's reign he campaigned against the Picts, the Miathi (a tribe in southern Scotland), the Angles, and for a time he controlled the Isle of Man. This type of overlordship in the north Irish Sea area was to be repeated at various periods in early history. However the fortunes of Dál Riata began to decline in the seventh century. After the disastrous battle of Mag Roth (Moira in Co. Down) in 637 they appear to have lost control of their Irish territory. In Scotland they were defeated by the Picts and Strathclyde Britons. By the opening of the eighth century the Cenél Loairn emerged as the dominant segment of the dynasty in Scotland, and in the following century during the reign of Cináed mac Ailpín (843–858) the Picts and Scots united to form the basis of the medieval kingdom of Scotland.[24]

To return to Ulster itself, the Ulaid, so prominent in the sagas and whose overlordship in the prehistoric period may have extended as far south as the Boyne and embraced the northern part of Ireland, were by the sixth century in much reduced circumstances but still held a tenacious pride in their former dominance in the province. Their overlordship still stretched as far south as north Louth, into the territory of the Conailli Muirtheimne, and extended east to the Isle of Man. The Ulster king Báetán mac Cairill led two expeditions to the Isle of Man in 577 and 578 in a short-lived attempt to gain control of the island. Indeed it was this interest in the north Irish Sea which led to the alliance between the king of Dál Riata, Áedán mac Gabráin, and the king of the Uí Néill, Áed mac Ainmuirech, to counter-balance the power of Baétán. This was a major considera-tion at the Convention of Druim Cett.

One of the main groups in the reduced Ulaid was the Dál Fiatach (Báetán belonged to this dynasty) whose territory lay between Dundrum Bay and Belfast Lough. Their capital was at Dún-dá-Lethglass (Downpatrick). A minor branch, the Uí Echach Arda, occupied the Ards peninsula until their obliteration by the Norse in the ninth century. The main branch of the Dál Fiatach expanded westwards towards Lough Neagh and northwards towards south Antrim in the eighth century – a territory now corresponding to the diocese of Down. Due to internal dynastic pressure a new capital was established as Dún Echdach (Duneight in north

Co. Down) in the ninth century. Like the other peoples in the northern part of Ireland in the early centuries they were under constant pressure from the Uí Néill. Their more immediate opponents in the north-east, however, were the Cruthin.

The Cruthin formed the bulk of the population in the reduced over-kingdom of the Ulaid. As mentioned above, when we first encounter the Cruthin in Ireland, they are Gaelic-speaking and there is no archaeological evidence to suggest a Pictish connection. The idea of a Gaelic invasion pushing the aboriginal 'Irish Picts' into the north-east corner has no support either historically or archaeologically. From the contemporary historical evidence it seems that the language and social structure of the Cruthin was identical with that of the rest of the Irish. In the sixth and seventh centuries the Cruthin formed a loose confederation of petty states in north-east Ireland. They were at the forefront of early battles against the Uí Néill, and occasionally provided kings of the province of Ulster, but in the *Annals of Ulster* they are never given the title *rí Ulad* ('King of Ulaid'). By the eighth century the Dál nAraidi emerged as the single dynasty ruling the remnants of the Cruthin east of the lower River Bann. They had subdued minor tribal groups such as the Bóindrige (in the kingdom of Dál mBuinne, south Antrim), and the Eilne (between rivers Bann and Bush) in the late seventh century, and exercised overlordship of the Latharnae (modern Larne) and of the Uí Derce Cein (south Antrim and north Co. Down). The northern branch that had settled in Eilne were defeated by the main line of the dynasty in 776 and disappear after the ninth century. Another branch, the Uí Echach Cobo (baronies of Iveagh, Co. Down), is linked genealogically to the main line but the link is artificial. The Dál Fiatach were always regarded as the legitimate rulers of Ulster but on occasion the Cruthin gained the over-kingship of the province and this gave rise to the claim that they were the *fir-Ulaid*, the 'true Ulstermen'.[25]

The most powerful king of the Cruthin was Congal Cáech. It is not at all clear to which tribe he belonged although later genealogists attempted to place him within the Dál nAraidi since they were later the most powerful of the Cruthin. In the law tract *Bechbretha*, 'bee-judgements',[26] Congal 'The One-eyed', was said to have been king of Tara until he was stung in the eye by a bee and thus, as a result of the physical blemish, disqualified from office. Because of internal feuding among the Uí Néill dynasties during this period it is very likely that Congal Cáech did become king of Tara for one or two years at some time between 630 and 635. His triumph was short-lived because he was defeated and killed in the great battle of Mag Roth (Moira, Co. Down) in 637. He and his allies, the Dál Riata, and the Mugdoirna (of south Armagh) were overwhelmed by the forces of the Uí Néill. One branch of the Uí Néill, the Cenél nEógain, may have fought on his behalf in the naval battle of Sailtire (off Kintyre) on the same day. They too were defeated. This serves to emphasize the fluid nature of the political situation in the north-east. It also emphasizes the fact that the Cruthin, whatever their remote ancestry, were playing a role similar to all the other participants in the complicated and complex politics of the period.

The dynastic capital of the Dál nAraidi, the group that eventually dominated the Cruthin, was at Raith Mor, east of Antrim town, in Mag Line. This power was weakened by the expansion of the Uí Thuirtri (on the western shores of Lough Neagh), and after 972 they were incapable of providing an over-king of Ulster. They soon became politically subject to the Dál Fiatach. The present diocese of Connor encompasses their traditional territory but it also includes that of Dál Riata.

In central Ulster, ranging around the Sperrin mountains, was a confederation of tribes collectively known as the Airgialla, 'the hostage givers', and various other associated groups. These were the Uí Meic Cairthinn, on the eastern shores of Lough Foyle, the Uí Fiachrach, around Ardstraw, the Fir Luirg in Co. Fermanagh, the Uí Chremthainn, around Clogher, Ind Airthir around Armagh, the Uí Meith in Co. Monaghan, the Mugdorna in south Armagh and Monaghan, and the Fir Rois in Co. Louth. There were also

other important groups, such as the Ciannachta, around
Dungiven, the Fir Chraíbe, Fir Li, Uí Thuirtri on the west
bank of the Bann, and on the western shores of Lough
Neagh. The locations suggested for these peoples are only
approximate since the extent of their territories changed
with political fortune (or more usually misfortune) during
the centuries. Some of these tribes such as the Uí Macc Uais
and Mugdorna are found in north Co. Meath, Westmeath
and Longford. These apparent outliers may have lived at the
southern-most points of the overlordship of the ancient
Ulaid as it was at its greatest extent.

It is generally agreed that these peoples were originally
under the overlordship of the Ulaid but as the power of the
Ulaid weakened they became independent for a period. It is
possible that the ritual destruction of Emain Macha relates
to the collapse of the overlordship of the Ulaid at the time,
but this is not certain.

V

What we do know is that in the fifth and sixth centuries, at
the dawn of the historical period, the main opponents of the
Ulaid were the descendants of Niall Noígiallach (Niall of
the Nine Hostages), the ancestor of the Uí Néill. The
Airgialla too found themselves opposed by the Uí Néill and
had to be reconciled with their new overlords after their
crushing defeat in the battle of Leth Cam near Armagh in
827. This new accommodation is subtly explained in their
propaganda, and in particular has been demonstrated
recently by D.Ó Corráin in regard to the cult of St Patrick.
The most important of the Airgialla propaganda was
written at the church in Armagh which lay in the territory
of the Ind Airthir, a branch of the Airgialla. The early
history of Armagh is obscure but by the 630s it had
emerged clearly as the head of the cult of Saint Patrick. In
the seventh century, when Patrick's first lives were written,
there was much confusion as to the saint's activities.
Relying on a mixture of Patrick's own writings, oral
tradition and claims of different monasteries for some

connection with him, the clerics at Armagh compiled a life of Patrick. The Armagh clerics stressed above all the saint's close association with Armagh. A rival interpretation, fostered at Downpatrick, placed great emphasis on Patrick's church in Down.

The facts of Patrick's life are of course difficult to extract from the layers of propaganda. It seems probable that when Patrick first came to Ireland as a slave, he worked near Killala in Co. Mayo. When he returned as a missionary he worked in the pagan north of Ireland as a roving bishop. His headquarters, if he had any at all, may have been in the lowly building which gives Saul, near Downpatrick, its name, *Saball*, from Latin *stabulum*, a 'barn'. In the propagandist literature, however, Patrick's association with Down in the territory of the declining Ulaid gave way to the Armagh version of his life which played down his activities at Saul. The Armagh version of Patrick's life is also strongly influenced by the anxiety of the Ind Airthir and Airgialla in general to flatter the expanding Uí Néill in order to retain their independence. It stressed, for example, the saint's association with the sons of Niall of the Nine Hostages (the ancestor of the Uí Néill) and Patrick's confrontation with Lóeguire at Tara with which the Uí Néill were associated.[27]

In the early ninth century, as a result of in-fighting for control of offices within the monastery, the Ind Airthir lost control of the abbacy of Armagh which was taken over by nominees of the Uí Néill. Such a situation required a change of strategy if Ind Airthir were to regain their control of Armagh. Having lost their independence it was necessary to gain 'favoured nation' status in relation to the Uí Néill. The result was the creation of excellent propaganda from the traditional saga of the three Collas, the cousins who had slain their uncle and thus forfeited for ever their rights to the high-kingship of Ireland. The version of this story which was composed in Armagh in the ninth century was clearly intended as a political statement of the relations between the Airgialla and the Uí Néill. The story stressed that the Airgialla were not the rivals of the Uí Néill but their friends. They held their land by permission of the ancestors of the Uí Néill and so there was no reason why the Uí Néill should be hostile to the Airgialla. The story of the three Collas, therefore, far from telling us about prehistoric Ulster, is directly concerned with dynastic and ecclesiastical politics in Armagh in the early ninth century.[28]

The origins of the Uí Néill who emerged as the main opponents of the Ulaid late in the fifth century are shrouded in obscurity, like all the peoples of protohistoric Ireland. Much of the material purporting to explain their origins is propaganda for the period of writing, and it can be seen that the different versions are relevant for particular stages in the rise of the Uí Néill dynasty. Ó Corráin has shown that the earliest genealogical lore which explains their origin places them in the company of tribes which, in the historical period, were subordinate. These are the Luigne, Gailenga and Corco'r Tri of north Connacht. It would appear that from these peoples the Uí Néill emerged rapidly as a dynasty, for by the end of the fifth century power amongst the Uí Néill had become concentrated amongst the sons and grandsons of Niall of the Nine Hostages.[29]

The Uí Néill dynasty then expanded in two directions from their base in north Connacht: northwards into Co. Donegal and eastwards into the midlands. They pushed back the Ulaid in the north, and the Laigin (the Leinstermen) in the midlands. Between the fifth and the seventh centuries the dynasty consolidated in the midlands, absorbing and subjecting various tribes in the area. Tara now lay in their recently won territories and became identified more and more with the dynasty in its propaganda. In the north the three sons of Niall – Conall, Eógan and Enda – conquered the area of Co. Donegal. From Conall we have Tír Conaill, the 'Land of Conaill', rather less than the modern county of Donegal. Enda's people settled around Raphoe but were not successful in gaining further expansion. Eógan, ancestor of the Cenél nEógain, gave his name to Inis Eógain, 'Inishowen', the area that he first conquered, and to modern Tyrone – Tir Eóghain, the 'Land of Eógan'. It was this branch of the dynasty that was eventually to dominate the north. The Cenél Conaill found themselves cut off from access to the midlands with the rise of the kingdom of Bréifne in the eighth century in the area of Leitrim and Cavan, and so their ability to gain the ascendency for any length of time was limited. From the mid-eighth century onwards the Cenél nEógain kings shared the high-kingship with the Clann Cholmáin branch of the dynasty in the midlands.[30]

We can trace the beginning of their expansion out of Inishowen across the Foyle to Magilligan's Point from the middle of the sixth century onwards. In 562/3 they defeated seven kings of the Cruthin at the battle of Móin Dairi Lothair. Their expansion continued at the expense of the Airgiallan tribes over the next few centuries. An Airgiallan territory began to emerge to the north of Lough Erne covering the area of Fermanagh, Armagh, Monaghan and north Louth. Their attempt to maintain independence came to an end in the battle of Leth Cam near Armagh in 827. The significance of this defeat may be seen in that Muiredach mac Eochada (*ard ríg* – high-king – of the Ulaid) fought on the side of the Airgialla. The Ulaid fortunes had already been in decline since the previous century when they had been defeated in the battle of Fochairt near Dundalk. It was not long until they had lost control of south Louth and the 'province' was confined to the area to the north of Louth and east of the Bann and Lough Neagh. After the battle of Leth Cam the king of Airgialla was the vassal of the Cenél nEógain kings who now centered their kingship at Tulach Óc near Dungannon where they were inaugurated. Armagh became their 'capital' – at least it was here that they were buried – and in 870 Áed Findliath, the Cenél nEógain king who was also king of Tara, had a house there.

From the second half of the ninth century onwards the Ulaid were forced to recognize the reality of Uí Néill power and on occasion joined in the hostings led by the high-kings. F.J. Byrne points out that 'They would recognise a high-king of Ireland, even a Cenél nEógain high-king, but they would not submit to him so long as he remained merely king of the North.'[31] By the opening of the eleventh century, in 1004, the Ulaid suffered a massive defeat at the hands of Áed ua Néill in the battle of Cráeb Tulcha. This took place at their inauguration site and was tantamount to wiping them out. The death of Áed is probably why such a campaign was not followed up. The Ulaid continued to survive into the twelfth century and were led by the dynastic house that had now come to the surface – that of Donn Sléibe Mac Eochada. From 1137 onwards his descendants, the Mac Duinnshléibe (Donleavy) held the kingship. By this time too the Cenél nEógain were represented by the family of Mac Lochlainn and this family in the course of the twelfth century attempted to partition the territory of the Ulaid as a means of keeping it weak. It was Donnchad Ua Cerbaill who ruled the land of Airgialla, the vassal of Mac Lochlainn, who forced Mac Lochlainn to abandon this policy. He realized only too well that his territory would be next in line for such treatment. In 1166 Muirchertach Mac Lochlainn blinded Eóchaid Mac Duinnshléíbe in an act of treachery. This caused Ua Cerbaill to withdraw his allegiance and accept Ruaidrí Ua Conchobair, king of Connacht, as his lord, thereby bringing about the death of Mac Lochlainn.[32]

With the coming of the Normans and the conquest of Ulster by de Courcy, the Mac Duinnshléibe lost further control. In the thirteenth century they were kings of the 'Irish of Ulster' but by the end of the century they abandoned the kingship and took service with Ua Domhnaill in Donegal. The Uí Néill could finally call themselves *rí Ulad* particularly with the collapse of the earldom of Ulster. In 1381 this was symbolized by the feast held for the poets of Ireland by Niall Ua Néill at Emain Macha. It may by then have been over-grown but Emain Macha still stood for the sovereignty of Ulster.

This chapter has dealt with the overall political developments in early historic Ulster. The history of the church would require separate treatment. It may have been the very prestige of the ancient Ulstermen which allowed Armagh to achieve ecclesiastical dominance throughout Ireland during

the seventh and eighth centuries. Armagh's political skill
was clear in its ability to flatter the Uí Néill, on the one
hand, while preaching the virtue of strong government in a
centralized kingship, which could guarantee peace and a
minimum level of justice, on the other. Armagh's success in
turn was the envy of the great kings as can be seen in Brian
Bóruma's 'charter' in the ninth-century Book of Armagh
and his donation to the monastery on his visit in 1005.

In early Ireland the memory of a period when the men of
Ulster dominated the island was never forgotten. Armagh
was, in a very real sense, the capital of the country, and this
was reflected in the status given to it when the church was
reformed in the twelfth century. It was only with the
coming of the Normans that Dublin emerged as a 'capital
city'. In the ecclesiastical sphere Armagh is the primatial see
for both Protestants and Catholics, and provides a very
tangible link with the memory of ancient Ulster.

Further reading

F.J. Byrne, *Irish Kings and High-Kings*, London, 1973,
paperback reprint 1987, is the standard political narrative of
early Ireland; ch. 7 deals specifically with Ulster. Kathleen
Hughes, *The Church in Early Irish Society*, London, 1966 is
the standard text on ecclesiastical history. Kathleen Hughes
and Ann Hamlin, *The Modern Traveller to the Early Irish
Church*, London, 1977 is an excellent introduction: Dr
Hamlin's contribution on the archaeological evidence is
invaluable. The book also includes a list of important sites
which may be visited (pp. 116–26).

F.J. Byrne, 'The Island of St Columba', *Historical Studies*,
v, 1965, pp. 37–58, offers a close analysis of Ulster politics
in the sixth century while his O'Donnell Lecture, *The Rise
of the Uí Néill and the High Kingship of Ireland*, National
University of Ireland, 1973, offers a full account of its topic.
A standard work on St Patrick which pays appropriate
attention to the significance of the patristic legend in Ulster

is R.P.C. Hanson, *Saint Patrick his Origins and Career*, Oxford, 1968.

The most recent summary of the protohistorical period from an archaeological perspective is Barry Raftery, *The La Tène in Ireland: its Origins and Chronology*, Marburg, 1984.

2 Lordships and invasions: Ulster 1177–1500

T.E. McNeill

This period opens with the incursion of new rulers from England, and it ends at the time when the national power of England was beginning to be reasserted in a new and different conquest. It was a time of external influence and decision, and one of disunity in Ulster. It falls into two parts, divided by the events of the fourteenth century, which was throughout Europe a time of change and dislocation. Ulster during this time was not a single political or social unit, but had inherited from earlier times a triple political division which continued through until the six-teenth century. Before the incursion of 1177, the kingdom of the Cenél Conaill had emerged to control the west, with Co. Donegal as its core. East of the Bann lay the kingdom, or group of lesser kingdoms, of the Ulaid, the people from whose name the province is called Ulster. Between these geographical areas was the overlordship of the Cenél nEóghain,[1] or Tyrone, with its subject kings, the largest in area and potential power. The establishment of the English earldom of Ulster[2] after 1177 produced a fundamental social divide between it and the remaining Gaelic kingdoms. Differences in language, the ways they held and inherited land (the basis of all wealth and power), the rights of the lords over their tenants and followers and in criminal law, all remained barriers to unity.

Despite all the divisions of the period, it was one in which the power of the great over-lords was immense. Claims to such lordship were not always easy to translate into effective power, however, for either English or Gaelic lords. The lands they claimed were not covered by an orderly network

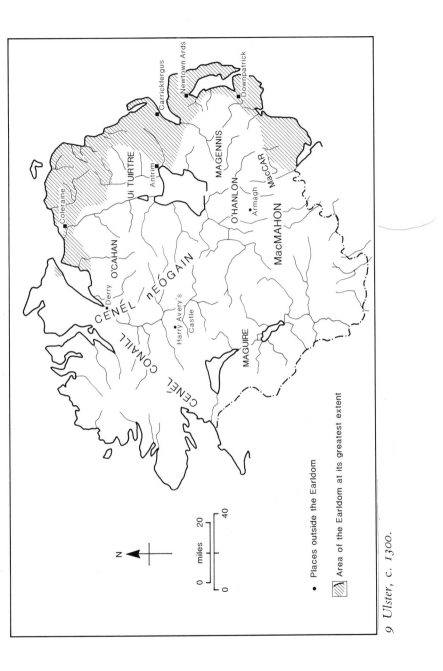

9 *Ulster, c. 1300.*

of roads or other means of physical or social control. One constant problem was how to establish men in a locality who were powerful enough to have effective control over it, but who were not powerful enough to use this as a base for rebellion. A second problem was how to harness the resources of the land effectively so that they contributed to the real power of the lord. Lands whose inhabitants paid no taxes to the lord and ignored his will were not what either English or Gaelic lords regarded as true lordships.

10 Carrickfergus town and castle, founded in the twelfth century.

I

On about 1 February 1177 John de Courcy, apparently a Somerset knight who had come to Ireland in the entourage of King Henry II in 1171, arrived in Downpatrick with a force of 22 knights and a few hundred other soldiers.[3] He had taken less than four days to march up from Dublin in winter. His small force, his speed and his sureness of where he was going, and the time of year all indicate that he was invited in, and did not conquer the country in a purely aggressive military stroke. The area of Ulster that he ruled, south Antrim and east Down, was defined by the boundaries of the kingdom which he replaced. He protected it from Tyrone, raided deep into western Ulster, and made alliances with the other small kingdoms of eastern Ulster; his knights, archers and castles were new and effective instruments of war. In 1178 he was defeated in battle somewhere in the area now known as Co. Antrim, but he was saved and was able to retreat to his castle (probably at Carrickfergus), even though he had to walk because his horses had been killed. Thereafter, he was able to unite the eastern Ulster Irish as his allies, and in his wars and alliances his actions were often those of a traditional king of Ulaid.

John de Courcy accomplished more than the shoring up of the earlier Irish kingdom. Along with him, or after him, came others. As ruler de Courcy was replaced in 1205 by Hugh de Lacy, who had full recognition from the king of England; he was formally created Earl of Ulster, and the lands under his control became the earldom. Hugh expanded them beyond de Courcy's frontiers, taking over north Antrim. In 1264 the earldom was granted to Walter de Burgh, whose son and greatgrandson succeeded him in turn; the de Burghs were resident earls of Ulster (and lords of Connacht) until 1333. During this time the area of the earldom advanced along the north coast from Coleraine to Derry. Its overall size remained small, confined to a coastal strip no more than 15 miles (24 km) deep, and excluding much of west and central Co. Down and mid-Antrim; the Co. Derry lands seem to have been barely settled.

11 Downpatrick pots (thirteenth century).

The most striking change that the establishment of the earldom produced was the founding of towns, either at established places like Downpatrick or on new sites like Carrickfergus, centred to this day around its medieval castle, church, harbour and market place. The market was crucial for at the heart of these towns, and the reason for founding them, was the creation of a self-conscious community of traders. We read from contemporary documents of the export of grain from Ulster and of ships and merchants going from Ulster to England, Scotland and France (particularly to Bordeaux for wine). In 1317, the ship, the *Grace Dieu* of Coleraine was seized by royal officials while on its way from France with a cargo of food and wine for the Earl of Ulster. The thirteenth century was one of acute shortage of land in England and Europe, and the agricultural produce of Ireland was in demand to feed the rising population. Along with the merchants of the towns came craftsmen from England such as masons and potters who supplied the settlers with goods and services of

English type; and the clerks of the Earl's household administration, who, together with their fellows of the royal government in Dublin, have left us with details of the administration of the earldom.

There were 15 places in Ulster described in contemporary documents as boroughs, but half of these were probably not towns in any modern sense of the word. One or two were founded but never developed; a number, such as Belfast and Larne, were clearly no more than small groups of families of farmers who held their land by the free tenure of burgesses. Of three others we know very little: Newtownards was under the control of the abbot of Movilla; Portrush had a mayor in the 1350s and paid tolls on fish, while we hear of men from it trading into the

12 Greencastle, Co. Donegal.

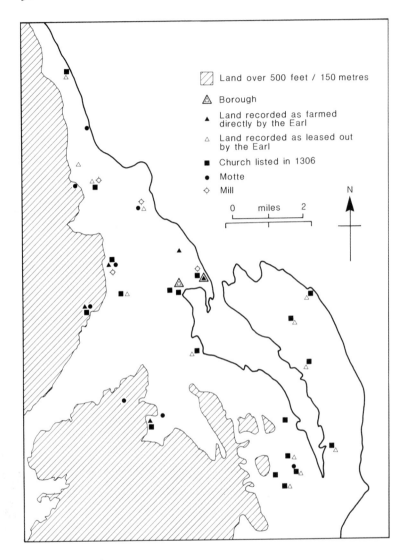

Land over 500 feet / 150 metres

△ Borough

▲ Land recorded as farmed
   directly by the Earl

△ Land recorded as leased out
   by the Earl

■ Church listed in 1306

● Motte

◇ Mill

0   miles   2

N

13 East Antrim, c. 1300.

Scottish Isles; Antrim was an administrative centre, but had 80 burgesses paying rent in 1358–9. The major towns were Downpatrick, Coleraine and Carrickfergus. Downpatrick must have been dominated by the monastic houses and cathedral, and may have simply consisted of a single built-up street along the line of the present English Street. Coleraine controlled the Bann fisheries and had a bridge over the river, fortified with towers at both ends; an Ulster example of a European type, like the majestic Pont Valentre at Cahors in southern France. Carrickfergus was the most important place in the earldom, and like Coleraine had merchants trading to Gascony for wine. It has seen the only systematic archaeological work of any town in Ulster. This has unfortunately failed to find preserved houses older than the sixteenth century, so we can deduce nothing of living standards in the middle ages. From property boundaries, however, we can see how the streets and house plots were laid out early in the thirteenth century, or even before, along the main spine of the town (High Street, Market Place and West Street) as they have remained to the present day. In both Carrickfergus and Downpatrick we can see the thirteenth-century industries of iron-working and pottery centralized in the towns, in contrast to the rural location of finds from the earlier period.

The towns were few and tiny by any standard; the population of Carrickfergus is hardly likely to have much exceeded one thousand. Society was overwhelmingly rural. The incomers, who established an English aristocracy of families, notably the de Mandevilles, Savages, de Logans and Bysets, organized the land into estates, called manors as in England. The large number of mills referred to in the surveys that have survived, and their obvious profitability, shows that the farming of these estates was largely, if not mostly, concerned with cereals, as we might expect from the needs of the market.

The estates were held by different types of tenure, thereby ranking the tenants: it was more prestigious to hold land in return for military service than for money rent. Periodic surveys, and above all, the general land survey held by the Earl in 1333, record many places and parcels of land, either farmed directly by the Earl or else leased out, particularly in south Antrim, between Belfast, Bally-galley and Antrim town, or in north Down. Frequently, the names of these lands coincides with the presence of a parish church, and an earthwork castle. The pattern appears to be one in which the Earl or his tenants farmed the land in regular estates; this, in combination with the use of the word 'manor', inevitably reminds us of the idealized English scheme of the unity of manor estate, parish and village. The emergence of such a pattern would have constituted quite a revolution in the organ-ization of the land and farming from the Irish pattern of settlement.

In organization, however, these estates were probably not the centralized farming units that many manors were in England or in the rest of feudal Europe. We have no information on the peasants who actually worked the land concerning either where or how they lived. In south-east Ireland, both documents and field archaeology bear witness to village life, but in Ulster there is no indication that villages existed. In some cases the estates seem to have been simply collections of smaller parcels of land united only in that they paid rent at the same place; they were purely administrative units, not farms. For example, the lands of Holywood, Co. Down, were part of the Earl's manor of Dundonald, but it is difficult to see how they could have been farmed from there. In some accounts, it is clear that land which was in the lord's 'demesne' (and which should therefore be farmed directly by him) was leased out, and this rent was probably paid in kind. So it is difficult to argue that these manors were the result of a large-scale change in the actual practice of farming in Ulster; indeed the Irish labourers seem to have been kept on the land deliberately by the new lords. In fact, the Irish land units and their rents were probably being reorganized with crop-sharing and a new aim: to produce a surplus to trade abroad. Thus the system was intensified and re-ordered but remained essen-tially the same in its parts, rather than being completely revolutionized, with new techniques brought to it by a newly-introduced peasantry.

This leads to the question as to how far life in the earldom could be described as English. The Earl himself clearly led the life of an English magnate in Ulster, in castles comparable to those of England and moving easily between Ulster and the English aristocracy. Richard de Burgh's children married well: one daughter married the heir of the Earl of Gloucester (the richest earl in England), while his son married the Earl's daughter; his two other daughters married into the Scottish aristocracy, one to a Stewart and one to Robert Bruce, the future king. We have no evidence of such personal connections apart from the Earl's. The towns must have struck any visiting merchant as small, but Carrickfergus at least was laid out in streets and houses like any small market town of Europe, between the castle and the parish church. The merchants and craftsmen were English and can be seen on occasions to have been immigrants to Ulster from England, usually from the north-west.

II

Life in the countryside was less English. We might expect the principal tenants of the Earl, men who held substantial estates and were counted as his barons, to live as English gentry, but they did not. The conquest of Ulster led to the construction of many earthwork castles, the so-called mottes; well over a hundred survive today. Some of these were still apparently recognized as castles in 1300, and we have no archaeological evidence that they were replaced. This was not the case in England, where they were almost certainly out of use, at least as castles, by the end of the twelfth century. Nor were the mottes themselves the same as in England. In Ulster dependent enclosures, the baileys, are relatively rare, and are confined to the borders of the earldom. They are also small in area. In England, the normal pattern of use of these castles was for the lord to

14 Harry Avery's castle, built in the late fourteenth century.

live in the bailey, in an area big enough to house his farmyard; the motte supported a tower used normally only as a refuge. In Ulster this does not seem to be the pattern. The baileys appear to have had a military function – hence their location on the borders. This leaves the lord's hall and farmyard without the protection, or enclosure, that it would seem to have needed in England. In two cases, at Clough and Lismahon, excavation has provided a partial solution, for there the hall, where the owner lived, was on the motte top. This still leaves us with the farm unaccounted for, but we have just seen that the farming system may not have been centralized; perhaps the lord had no farmyard. The situation as we picture it, of the gentry living in the thirteenth century largely off their tenants' rents, and in halls sited on the top of mottes, is certainly quite different from England, where at this time the same class of people were responsible for the emergence of the semi-fortified manor house.

The large number of castles built by the English in Ulster reminds us of the threat of war or raids, by the Irish in particular. The maintenance of stable relations with the O'Neills must have been a serious consideration for both the Earl and his tenants, in order to avoid events like the raids and counter-raids of the 1250s which culminated in the Battle of Down in 1260. Justice was dispensed by the Earl and his officers, not by royal judges, because Ulster was a liberty, where the king delegated almost all his powers to the local lord. The laws were no different from the Common Law of England, and royal justice may have produced as much corruption and more delay than private justice, but the way it worked, and might have been manipulated, must have been different.

One set of events can illustrate these points.[4] Between 1272 and 1282, after Walter de Burgh died but before his son Richard was old enough to rule it in person, the earldom was the subject of a bitter internecine dispute, which tells us much about the life of the period. The argument started over the offices of the earldom: one William FitzWarin was appointed seneschal, or chief officer in 1272, but Henry de Mandeville, who had been bailiff of the 'county' of Coleraine under Walter de Burgh, refused to give up his position. FitzWarin accused him of abuses of power, of extortion, including the fining of the burgesses of Portrush and Bushmills when they refused to feed his servants who were trying to live off their lord's tenants, and also of killing opponents and plundering their lands in alliance with Irish clans. FitzWarin's men responded; in the ensuing dispute, Henry de Mandeville was killed, and his sons accused FitzWarin of his murder. He was acquitted of the charge and the royal officials tried to reach agreement over the compensation due to him for the damage the de Mandevilles had done to his lands. FitzWarin had no trust in the Earl's justice in 1282, for he appointed Thomas de Mandeville as his steward then and William de Mandeville as his bailiff for the 'counties' of Down and the Ards. FitzWarin was able to flee to Dublin, escaping in spite of the seneschal ordering the ports and roads of Ulster to be closed, because he was friendly with the MacCartans who allowed him to go over the Newry Pass. Both sides enlisted the help of local Irish as well as English. Ulster was a border land and life must have struck an English visitor as very strange, violent and unsophisticated, if not crude, and also very Irish in customs.

The tenants of the baronage, and the lesser tenants of the Earl were both Irish and English. The documentary records are in French or Latin, the languages of the upper classes (note the French name of the Coleraine ship referred to above), but they record place names in Irish and English. Clearly at various times and places, all four languages were used in the earldom. It is easy to guess who were the main users of each, but what is totally unclear is either how common each was or how many people might have spoken more than one. It would seem very likely that very few people could have been able to live without at least a working knowledge of a language other than their own.

The structure and organization of the society and the earldom, its administration, estates and grades of the tenants, were in existence by the time of the earliest detailed surviving royal survey in 1212. We do not know how much earlier it existed or how soon after John de Courcy's conquest the English came in numbers. Judged as an attempt to make the whole of Ulster an English colony, the earldom was an outstanding failure, small in area and not very English. Within Ulster, however, it was a success; during the thirteenth century it dominated the whole of Ulster. John de Courcy raided far to the west in retaliation for raids from Tyrone, like any earlier Irish king. At intervals, the royal officials would be in charge of the earldom, because the Earl was a minor, or because the king had confiscated the earldom for some offence, perhaps. These officials also tended to do the same, again either in retaliation or else in an attempt to enforce their will on an Irish king who had angered them.

Hugh de Lacy and the de Burgh earls followed a more effective policy based on the weakness of Irish political structures and their own residence in the earldom. They waited for succession disputes to break out and then intervened on behalf of their own candidate; Richard de Burgh in particular fostered relations systematically with dissident O'Neills, so that he always had a friendly member of the family either as king or challenging for the kingship. By the end of the thirteenth century the earls were in a position to compel all the Gaelic kings of Ulster outside the earldom to maintain a force of soldiers loyal to them, but supported on the King's lands. This force, the *bonnaght* of Ulster, was both the result and means of the Earl's ability to strike quickly whenever an opportunity came. His power was considerable in England, too; in 1296, of an army of a little over 3000 who went from Ireland to support Edward I against the Scots, 1500 were under Richard de Burgh's command. Two possible means of controlling the areas remote from the power of the Dublin administration, such as Ulster, presented themselves: one was to give a local lord his head and the other was direct royal intervention. As Ulster shows the first was actually by far the most effective approach. The expedition of Richard II in 1395 and its aftermath show the royal problems. He came to Ireland with a large force, but also with his prestige. Richard tried to establish stable relations with the O'Neill of Tyrone at the cost of sacrificing the claims of Roger Mortimer as Earl of Ulster to O'Neill's homage. Ultimately, however, the combination of costs and the priority of English politics forced Richard to abandon the attempt at intervention, and hand power back to Mortimer.

The short-term disputes over the succession to the Gaelic kingdoms arose because any member of the ruling family might consider himself eligible for the position, and the earls exploited this; however, this should not hide deeper trends. The thirteenth century saw new dynasties established in several kingdoms. The battle of Caiméirge in 1241 resulted in the O'Neill line eliminating the MacLochlainns from the kingship of Tyrone. This was not only of dynastic interest but meant a shift in the power centre of Tyrone south and eastwards to the lands west and south of Lough Neagh. From about 1250 the O'Donnells controlled the kingship of Cenél Conaill, while among the lesser kingdoms, the O'Cahans were established in north Derry in the later twelfth century, and the Maguires controlled Fermanagh from 1282 onwards. These were the families who were to control Ulster until the end of the Gaelic order; the pattern remained fixed for a long time.

Institutionally there were changes. Ever since the Viking wars the power of Irish kings had been increasing at the expense of the under-kings and their tenantry. This continued through the thirteenth century, but we can pick out two developments which reinforced the process. As a result of the English invasion, some Irish kings built castles, mainly in the east (for example in mid-Antrim) to hold on to their lands, but later on elsewhere; the largest motte and bailey in Ulster is at Managh Beg, near Derry, probably the work of the O'Cahans, whose later castle at Lough Enagh is just two miles (3.2 km) away. Castles provided the Irish kings or lords with fixed points of local power against their own followers as well. More important was the practice which began in the later part of the century of hiring mercenaries, the gallowglasses, from the West Highlands of Scotland, who were billeted on the kings' followers' lands. At the same time we can see the Irish becoming involved with the economy of the earldom as well as its politics. In both cases this is clearest among the satellite kingdoms of east Ulster, like that of the O'Flynns of mid-Antrim, where coinage seems to have circulated, but some goods, especially wine, reached all parts of the earldom. Personal contacts, with the earldom or with the royal government in Dublin, must also have greatly increased the Gaelic kings' knowledge of the world outside Ireland, if not their appreciation of it.

One major institution covered the division between the earldom and the Irish and linked both to the outside world – the Church. Before the English invasion, in the earlier twelfth century, the Irish church had started on a widespread set of reforms, aimed at bringing it into line with the rest of Europe. This centred on the institution of territorial bishoprics and the introduction of European orders, notably the Cistercians, to reform the monastic institutions. Ulster had been prominent in the movement, and it continued after 1177, accommodating the church to the two nations. Before 1200 the number and boundaries of bishoprics were fixed; the last to be created was the small and poorly endowed Dromore, covering the Irish parts of Down which thus became a purely English diocese. Two dioceses crossed the division: one was Connor, where the cathedral was unofficially moved to Carrickfergus, and where the deanery of Turterye (named after the O'Flynn kingdom) was set up for the Irish areas. The other was Armagh where the division was much more equal in area and was formalized by calling one part 'the diocese among the English' and the other 'among the Irish'.

After the stabilization of the bishoprics, they were divided into parishes. In the earldom this was relatively easy; the English lords were all keen to see the organization they were used to being established, and they were all keen to see their manorial estates becoming the centres of individual, separate parishes. In Gaelic society the idea of fixed territorial boundaries enclosing the jurisdiction of a single priest was much newer and required a major reallocation of lands. By the end of the thirteenth century, however, this seems to have been introduced everywhere. The scattered small parcels of land formerly attached to the local churches were mostly assigned to the bishops (who leased them to traditional families of stewards or erenaghs). Tithes (taxes for the Church) were levied for the first time as well, and were divided between the bishops, rectors and vicars.

John de Courcy was a generous patron of the church and the greatest founder of monasteries in Ulster; apart from having religious motives, he needed the church's support politically, and it was good for his personal legend to be known as a generous dispenser of largesse. His three major foundations were the Benedictine abbey of Downpatrick, serving the cathedral in a traditional English way, and the Cistercian abbeys of Inch and Grey; Downpatrick was founded by monks from Chester, and the two Cistercian houses were subject to control by abbeys in the north of

England. John thus reinforced connections between Ulster and the north of England. The other two large Cistercian monasteries of Ulster, Newry and Assaroe (in south Donegal), were both of Irish foundation. They were both involved in the demonstration of Irish independence from the main Cistercian order's control known as the Conspiracy of Mellifont in 1227. This saw an attempt by those abbeys, founded before the English conquest, but sited in areas now taken over by them, to assert their freedom from what they saw as English control and culture. The movement ended in the enforcement of the discipline of the order; it had little effect in Ulster, for the Irish houses there were situated in lands which remained Irish and so these houses were not in conflict with their neighbours.

The physical expression of the new links that De Courcy forged came in the styles of the new churches. Grey Abbey and Inch Abbey especially are examples of the Gothic style, in its northern English guise which replaced the earlier Romanesque style at the end of the twelfth century. If Inch Abbey (as we see it now) was built soon after its foundation in the 1180s (which, given its patron and the fact that it was based on existing estates which could produce income without a lengthy period of organization, is quite possible) then it was one of the first examples in Ireland. The church of St Nicholas, Carrickfergus was new, not only in its style. It was probably intended to replace the cathedral of Connor, but Ulster had not seen a large, aisled church with a crossing tower before, apart from those in the monasteries of one of the new orders. These churches needed English masons to build them; their masons' marks can still be seen on the mouldings in the new fashions at Inch Abbey.

After de Courcy, there were few monastic foundations in Ulster and they were often the result of conversion of existing Irish houses to Continental rules, such as the Augustinian Canons, rather than true new foundations. The Friars, Dominican and Franciscan, came to Ireland in the 1220s, a new radical movement based on relief of the poor and on preaching. In their Continental origins they were urban in their interests and they followed this pattern in

15 Inch Abbey.

16 Culfeightrin Church, Co. Antrim.

Ulster at first. Both orders founded three houses in Ulster in the thirteenth century; two each in the earldom and one outside. The places they chose give us a good idea of the principal centres of Ulster; the Franciscans at Carrickfergus, Downpatrick and Armagh; the Dominicans at Coleraine. Newtownards and Derry. The Franciscan houses of Ireland were grouped into five custodies after 1325, but the Ulster ones were not all in the same one. The two houses in the earldom were in Drogheda custody, but Armagh was in Nenagh along with the other Irish houses, a division which shows the way the regular church was also organized to reflect the division of the two nations. It is from the monastic world that the most specific accusation of national discrimination comes. In 1297 the Bishop of Down was accused of joining the Archbishop of Armagh in issuing an injunction to prevent monasteries in their dioceses from admitting monks of English birth; the old Irish house of Saul in Co. Down was mentioned. The bishop denied the charge, which was not proven, and it should be noted that he was himself of English birth, while the Archbishop was Irish.

III

The fourteenth century was a time of severe dislocation throughout Europe. The population decreased to about a half its former number and there were major social and political upheavals. Ulster saw some of these. The population decline (the result of plague and famine) meant that land was available in more attractive regions, either in Ireland or England, and that the price of corn fell so that there was little to be gained from trying to grow it in unfavourable areas like Ulster. At the beginning of the century the Scottish wars of independence spilled over into Ireland and precipitated a political crisis in Ulster. Edward Bruce, brother of the victor of Bannockburn, spent three years, from 1315 to 1318, based in Ulster causing as much destruction in Ireland as he could. William de Burgh, the last resident Earl of Ulster, was killed by his own barons at

Belfast in 1333; he left a two-year old daughter as his heiress, who could hardly be expected to give a strong lead in a border earldom. Faced with the prospect of fighting hard for land of dubious value, men probably drifted away from the earldom of Ulster to the south-east of Ireland or England. Certainly during the second half of the fourteenth century, the earldom collapsed and was no longer the dominant power in Ulster.

In the political vacuum left by the collapse of the earldom a new set of Gaelic kingdoms emerged. The largest was that of the O'Neills of the Clan Aedh Buidhe (anglicized to Clandeboy), a branch of the ruling Tyrone dynasty who had been normally allied to the earls, but who were expelled from Tyrone in 1343. They moved east and took over the lands of the O'Flynns of mid-Antrim and the earldom in south Antrim and north Down. The Savages, who were the most prominent of the English families of the earldom after the de Mandevilles, survived but at the cost of giving up their lands in Co. Antrim and taking over the south-east of Co. Down. Scots moved in, in the form of MacDonnells from the Isles who settled in the Glens of Antrim; the McQuillans were probably Scots mercenaries in the late thirteenth century, but by the late fourteenth were a distinct clan with lands in Co. Down and (particularly in the fifteenth century) in north Antrim which became named after the 'Route' of their followers. The disparate histories of these groups are worth noting for behind them lies a basic fact. The earldom was not conquered as the result of a battle or single campaign by a resurgent Irish nation, but it fell apart into a set of successor lordships or family aristocracies; at least one of these, the MacDonnells of Antrim, owed its lands in the beginning to the marriage of John MacDonnell and Margery Byset, heiress of the Glens under the earldom. This transition was at least as peaceful as the movement of the Savages into their new lands.

The Savages (and the Whites) in south Down continued to proclaim their direct allegiance to the succession of heirs to the earldom of Ulster, and to the king of England; so too did the town and castle of Carrickfergus, with the result that there was always an English presence in Ulster, if only nominal at times. During the thirteenth century, the earldom of Ulster was not only the strongest military power in Ulster, it also acquired a position of political overlordship over the Irish lords or kings. The Earl was the intermediary between them and the English king, and he prevented any one king asserting his superiority over any other. With the Earl now absent, and the earldom in decline, the strongest military power was the lordship of the O'Neills of Cenél nEóghain, and it remained to be seen if they could convert this into the constitutional or political pre-eminence of the thirteenth-century earls. Certainly that is how they themselves saw it; during the fourteenth century the O'Neills made claims to be known as the kings, not of Tyrone (or Cenél nEóghain), their traditional title, but as kings of Ulster. They were never able to make this claim a reality of power or control, for a variety of reasons. Formally, they were forced constantly to admit that they had no right to it in English or Irish law. When Richard II of England came to Ireland in 1395, Niall Mór and his son Niall Óg were associated in the kingship of Tyrone. They both submitted to the English king, and called on him to arbitrate between them and Roger Mortimer Earl of March and also, by right of his wife, the Earl of Ulster, whose lordship he had in some sense to acknowledge. As for the Irish tradition, Niall Mór O'Neill held a great celebration of his power in a feast for the learned men of Ireland at the pre-Christian capital of the heroic Ulster Cycle at Navan outside Armagh, but even then the conservative writers of the Gaelic world were reluctant to concede the title of king of Ulster to him. For over 500 years it had been well known that Navan belonged to the Ulaid and, as has been shown in chapter one, the Uí Neill dynasties had no claim to Ulster in the traditional sense.

These constitutional niceties were, however, only a part of the story. Irish kings were abandoning claims to kingship in the fourteenth century anyway, and concentrating on the exercise of real power, with or without legal authority. In this area too, the O'Neills had problems. The ruling family was constantly and bitterly divided against itself. Niall Mór benefited from his father's expulsion from Tyrone of his cousins of the Aedh Buidhe line. His sons, however, were disunited; Niall Óg succeeded him but he in turn was succeeded by Domnall his nephew, the son of Henry Aimredh, a son also of Niall Mór. Domnall fought Niall Óg's son Eóghain to be king, and Eóghain succeeded him; this left the other sons and descendants of Henry Aimredh in permanent hostility to the later kings of Tyrone, the first of a series of segments of the family excluded from what they regarded as their rights to the kingship and opposing the kings in turn. In their opposition, they turned for help to others, usually to the O'Donnell kings of Donegal, whose power increased in proportion to the division and weaknesses of the O'Neills.

Opposition by these groups might not be simply personal and dynastic, but could acquire a territorial aspect as well. The O'Neills and the O'Donnells came into conflict over the land of west Tyrone as much as anywhere. Niall Mór installed his son, Henry Aimredh, in the area to hold it for him, and he is commemorated in the name of the impressive ruins of Harry Avery's castle outside the little town of Newtownstewart (see p. 54). The power which he and his sons built up there was, however, used as much as a centre of opposition to their cousins in alliance with the O'Donnells as a defence against them. Opposition came from outside the family as well. Apart from the O'Donnells, there were within the immediate area of O'Neill ambitions long-established families such as the Maguires of Fermanagh or O'Hanlons of south Armagh, who would resist the expansion of their power; Domnall O'Neill, son of Henry Aimredh, and king of Tyrone after Niall Óg, was killed by the O'Cahans of north Derry, in alliance with his cousin Eóghain.

The O'Cahans were only one of the lesser lordships of Ulster; the O'Neills, if they were to make their position supreme in Ulster, needed to control them as well. This was no easy task, for these lords had previously owed allegiance only to the Earl, if at all, and they were not keen to give up their independence without prolonged struggles. Only the O'Donnells of Cenél Conaill were powerful enough to challenge the O'Neills alone, but the others, often in collaboration with the O'Donnells or with dissident O'Neill factions, could, and did, make alliances to do this. The Gaelic world lacked the institutions which made it easy for any lord to create a superiority over another which would last beyond the immediate effects of a battle; lordship could not be inherited on either side of the relationship, lord or client, but had to be renewed continually by force.

If the control of kingdoms was difficult, so too was the control of the land itself. In the Gaelic world, there was a clear distinction between land acquired by a man's own efforts and the land he inherited, which he held only as a representative of his family, and which he could dispose of only with their consent. A king or lord of a clan might have land from a variety of sources. He would have the lands of his own immediate family, his father and direct ancestors; as king or lord he might have other land attached to the office; he might have land which he had seized from others, either enemies or dependants, and land in which he had succeeded in intruding other members of his family, such as sons. A lord had rights, often very powerful ones over the lands of his followers. He had the right to rent but much more besides. To support himself he exacted levies of food; theoretically he collected these in person by travelling around his lands, but lords exacted these yearly whether they went to the land or not. He was entitled also to call on his followers to support his servants, often by quartering them on the country. Refusal to provide these levies meant that the lord could seize the land, as he could if fines were unpaid. None of these exactions was fixed, and they could vary from place to place, or from tenant to tenant, according to the relative bargaining strengths, in the present or the past. With these lands were intermixed the lands of the church. They too were subject to payments to abbeys or bishops; in particular the twelfth-century reforms had brought most of the scattered lands of smaller monasteries and churches under the bishops, who leased them to lay stewards, or erenaghs. These lands all claimed to be exempt from the exactions of the lay lords, a claim usually disputed by the lords.

IV

It is easy to see the later middle ages in Ulster as a time of continuous violence and war. Our sources undoubtedly help us to take this view. The collapse of the earldom deprives us of the detailed administrative records which show the finer detail of how life was actually led, especially in lay society. Annals play a large role in our knowledge, and they give us a picture like that of the headlines of the modern press; politics and above all wars and deaths are their regular offering. Our picture of Ireland as a whole during this time is also coloured by the views of the clerks of a royal government in Dublin faced by a country which paid less and less attention to its wishes, and which they describe as falling into a state of Gaelicized chaos and degeneration as a result. That resources were dwindling is clear from the example of the dioceses of Down and Connor which were united in 1442, while Dromore was usually administered together with it in the fifteenth century. While it is easy to fall in with this picture, it would be wrong not to test it critically.

The registers of the archbishops of Armagh are the best guide that we have as to how life carried on apart from high politics. As with all documents, they are written for a purpose – to record the acts, claims and decisions of the archbishops as guides or precedents in later actions. They are overwhelmingly concerned, therefore, with problems and not with occasions when life ran smoothly. They have an added interest in that in Ulster they relate to the Irish areas of the country. Their concerns are mainly with ecclesiastical affairs, often with disputed claims to church appointments, but also with those of authorities in any society: sex, violence and property rights. Laymen in Ireland had never accepted that they should have only one wife during their lifetime, and the clergy had never accepted

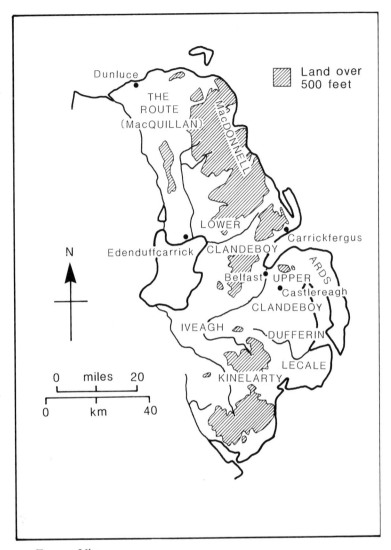

17 Eastern Ulster, c. 1500.

the principle of celibacy. Both issues set the representative of the church at odds with his flock. His intervention was required in individual acts of violence, such as the reconsecration of churchyards if they had been polluted by the shedding of blood, or as an arbitrator. Property rights involved him in the continual defence of church lands against the encroachments of the lay lords, attempting to exact dues from ecclesiastical property despite its recognized immunity from attacks. None of these problems would have surprised any prelate in Europe, except the relaxed attitude of Irish society to sex and marriage.

What is more impressive is that the machinery of the Church continued to function. Lay lords did not succeed in taking over the church lands wholesale. The parish system of the thirteenth century continued in Gaelic Ulster through to the sixteenth century, and we are able to use the various inquisitions of the plantation period to learn about its functioning and its lands. The archbishops seem never to have been prevented from visiting Armagh when they wished, although they were normally resident in Louth, where their lands were concentrated; after 1346 they were all Englishmen. When they were in Louth, the local Irish clergy carried on the administration in their name, and there seems to have been no problem of communications between them. They were disobeyed but so were they also in the English parts of the diocese like Meath, and so too were prelates right across Europe. There is no reason to believe that the circumstances of the archbishops of Armagh were sufficiently bad as to be described as chaotic.

One group of cases will illustrate the nature of the lay life as portrayed in this source.[5] In both June and July 1428 Arthur Magennis, head of the Co. Down clan, was involved, along with his followers, in stealing cattle and money from churchmen in Dromore and Dromara, and in October 1428 some Magennises and O'Hanlons occupied Newry abbey lands. Magennis was threatened with excommunication on all three occasions if he neither made restitution nor compelled the members of his clan to do so. The penalty may not have been very effective, but it was all the Archbishop could do to protect church property. On the other hand, in May 1429, the vicar of Carlingford was ordered to admonish John White of that town, because he had unjustly imprisoned the wife of one of the Archbishop's tenants, until she paid 10 shillings that Arthur Magennis owed him. The Archbishop was trying to use the only procedure open to him to protect churchmen and their property (and no other country would have given him much more) and he used it as far as he could without any particular national axe to grind, in Irish and English areas alike.

The fifteenth century saw the construction of many small castles, the tower houses, in many parts of Ireland; they were particularly numerous in those areas where the English lordships of the thirteenth century had been replaced by Gaelic lordships (at least 250 surviving in Co. Galway and 400 in Limerick). These towers seem to represent the creation of new centres of local power by a new class of minor lords. We can see something of the same development in the south-east of Co. Down, in the lands of the Savages and Whites. It is difficult to know whether we should take these as evidence of the military insecurity of the times or whether we should argue that the lords' ability to pay for them is a sign of their stability. However, if we compare the Co. Down towers with those elsewhere in Ireland, we can see how those commissioned by the Ulster lords were less elaborately planned and embellished, but they were built to provide a measure of military effectiveness; many in Meath or Tipperary preferred to put their money into elaboration of domestic arrangements or fancy turrets, rather than real warlike defences. Interestingly, in the Gaelic kingdoms of Ulster, there seems to have been no proliferation of local fortifications. The O'Cahans appear to have needed centres only at Enagh (on the east bank of the Foyle) at Limavady and possibly at Dungiven: the Clandeboy O'Neills had only three castles, Shane's Castle, and one each at Belfast and (later) Castlereagh.

Tower houses became the normal castles of the aristocracy, but we do not know more precisely than within the fifteenth century at what date this became so, and therefore we do not know when tower-building was established. Nor are towers universal. Henry Aimredh O'Neill at his castle

18 Dunluce Castle, Co. Antrim.

19 Fifteenth-century tomb of Cooey-na-Gall O'Cahan, Dungiven Priory, Co. Tyrone.

near Newtownstewart, and O'Doherty at Elagh, Co.
Derry, built castles which seem to adapt the idea of the
thirteenth-century gate house to the self-contained tower
concept, while the MacQuillans, and later the MacDonnells,
probably built, but certainly occupied and adapted, the
complex castle of Dunluce, Co. Antrim. The later fifteenth
and early sixteenth centuries also saw a phase of refurbish-
ing *crannógs* (artificial islands in lakes) probably as military
centres and refuges.

No discussion of buildings can overlook the church
monuments of the period, in particular the fine O'Cahan
tomb at Dungiven priory, traditionally of the late fourteenth century. First-class work such as this (whose
craftsmen either came from Iona or went on to work there
later), and the lesser towers and friary architecture of the
period serve to remind us of the possibilities for patronage
during the period. The results deployed a variety of skills
and traditions, involving English, Irish and Scottish craftsmen either directly or through the indirect transmission of
their ideas.

V

It remains to pick out some themes from this long and
complex period. First to be considered is the nature of the
various invasions that occurred. The invasion which
resulted in the earldom is often seen as the start of a colony
in the modern sense, but the differences need to be stressed.
None of the earls was acting as a servant of the English
state, or even of the English king against the Irish; they set
out to win land for themselves where they intended to live
and found dynasties and not to merely serve for a time
before returning to England. The men and women who
came to join the earls in Ulster undoubtedly produced a
new order there, with new methods of harnessing the
agricultural wealth of the land. These immigrants adapted
to life in Ireland, in particular to life on the border of the
English part of Ireland, establishing a compromise society.
The second invasion was Gaelic, and led to the expansion of

Irish kingdoms after the collapse of the earldom. Such conquests were continuous throughout Gaelic history, often resulting from rapid increases in numbers by Irish aristocratic families, whose members (all entitled to a share in the family lands) stuck closely together.

In places such as north Antrim, successively occupied by the English, MacQuillans and MacDonnells, there was continuity of settlement at a number of places on the estates. For example at Ballylough a Savage manor (hence the parish church nearby at Billy), a MacQuillan tower house and an estate were let by the Earl of Antrim to a lowland Scot. The estate organization continued, and because the farming and farmers seem to have survived the English conquest, we may suggest that they also survived the MacQuillans' arrival. Rarely did a major influx of people displace the former inhabitants *en masse*, but often one aristocracy replaced another.

The story of the MacQuillans, as told in the *Annals of the Four Masters*[6] between 1433 and 1444, will give an idea of this problem, as well as illustrating the sensationalism of the *Annals*. In 1433, O'Neill of Tyrone, allied with the MacDonnells, drove the MacQuillans out of Dufferin, their home in County Down, in spite of their being helped by the O'Donnells; the *Annals of Ulster* go further and write: 'only a few of his [i.e. the MacQuillan himself] people escaped with him.' They went to Meath where they were quartered on the English tenantry. In 1434, they fought for one O'Donnell in a rebellion in Tyrconnell against the O'Donnell (their ally of the year before) who was allied to the O'Neill of Tyrone, their enemy of 1433; in 1422 we find the MacQuillans fighting O'Cahans, but it is not said where. In 1444, they are back in County Down, helping the O'Neill of Clandeboy to defeat a raid by the O'Neill of Tyrone. Two things stand out: the *Annals'* exaggeration of the defeat of 1433, and the mobility of the MacQuillans, perhaps a hundred fighting men and their immediate dependents, not a whole nation of people. These groups could move easily around the country as the circumstances and fortunes of war dictated, taking over lands and being forced out of them at times. The story also illustrates the unstable nature of both enmities and alliances in the short term.

The second theme follows from the first: can we see evidence of real nationalistic or even racial antagonism between the English and Irish at this time? Two documents are usually cited to support this, the Remonstrance of Domnall O'Neill to the Pope in 1317, and a sermon of Archbishop FitzRalph of Armagh in 1349. The first is a highly partisan work, produced to justify O'Neill's support of Edward Bruce in his campaign in Ireland; it is worthless even as an objective account of generally held Irish feelings (some of O'Neill's claims would have been denied by other Irishmen), let alone a true statement of contemporary conditions. FitzRalph's sermon was, of course, a sermon, a call to repent from evils committed, and delivered in the year of the Black Death which he saw as a judgement on man; again this is hardly the place for calm objectivity. We know of a great number of cases of conflict between English and Irish men in the period, but we know of as many cases of co-operation. The earldom was a border society with many points of contact with the Irish. The earls' families certainly intermarried with the Irish, and we have seen how it was marriage that brought the MacDonnells to Ireland. In their wars both sides at all times allied across the divide; de Mandeville and O'Flynn against FitzWarin in 1278, or O'Donnell, MacQuillan and the English of Meath against O'Neill of Tyrone in 1433. Economically the two sides had clear dealings with each other, and we must assume that the reason for Carrickfergus surviving as a lonely English outpost in the Clandeboy O'Neills' land throughout the fifteenth century was because its merchants were useful to the Irish. Many of the cattle hides and horses, which were exported from Ireland to Europe in the fourteenth and fifteenth centuries, came from herds owned by Gaelic lords; O'Neill was reported to have 3,000 horses in 1397. The Irishness of some archbishops of Armagh does not seem to have hampered them in Meath or the earldom of Ulster any more than the Englishness of the others did in Irish areas.

In the sixteenth century the O'Neills of Tyrone became the major force in Irish resistance to the claims of the Tudor monarchy, and in the thirteenth century western Ulster was the largest area of Ireland unoccupied by the English. However, we should not just see the O'Neills as bastions against all foreign influence throughout the middle ages; notwithstanding the Aedh Buidhe O'Neills' pro-English leanings, the true position was more complex. The O'Neills learnt from the English in their economics, but also in their military and political power, their mercenaries and castles; their treatment of the lesser lords in the fourteenth and fifteenth centuries was not based on traditional Irish ways.

This brings us finally to the legacy of the period. Although Ulster was not in chaos and ruin at the end of the fifteenth century, its politics were unstable. The power of the O'Neills was enough to prevent anyone else building up a strong kingdom, but insufficient to control or unite Ulster. Succession disputes in all the Irish kingdoms offered continual opportunities for intervention, as the earls had shown. Disputes over lands and land rights were endemic. The events of the middle ages had also left two outside powers with bases in Ulster, and claims to be met: the highland Scots, particularly the MacDonnells, and the king of England, since Edward IV was also Earl of Ulster. The level of violence could only be kept to acceptable limits as long as neither of these chose to enter the closed system of politics in Ulster and as long as the O'Neills failed to attempt to assert their full power.

Further reading

A. Cosgrove, *Late Medieval Ireland, 1370–1541*, Dublin, 1981, is a brief overall introduction to the period. It concentrates on political narrative, but one chapter discusses the various regional groupings of Ireland.

A. Cosgrove (ed.), *A New History of Ireland, Medieval Ireland, 1169–1534*, vol. ii, Oxford, 1987, is a very long, multi-author compendium, based on a conservative account of political history, with separate chapters on economic, social and cultural matters. All the material is written from a Dublin-based, all-Ireland perspective with no concession to regional differences.

R. Frame, *Colonial Ireland, 1169–1369*, Dublin, 1981, is the twin volume with Cosgrove's *Later Medieval Ireland*; it benefits equally by its brevity. It is thematic and does not confine itself to political narrative, but discusses social and economic isues.

T.E. McNeill, *Anglo-Norman Ulster*, Edinburgh, 1980, is confined entirely to Ulster, with no attempt to bring in material from outside the province, and covers only to *c.* 1400. It attempts to use all the evidence available for the period, and so concentrates on social and economic issues, rather than on political narrative.

K. Nicholls, *Gaelic and Gaelicised Ireland in the Middle Ages*, Dublin, 1972, is the first book to deal with the subject, and remains unreplaced. It concentrates on political structures, and is inclined to over-emphasize the shifting nature of the Gaelic world.

K. Simms, *From Kings to Warlords*, Woodbridge, 1985 follows up Nicholls's book, concentrating on Ulster in particular. Its theme is the replacement of kingship by landlords in the Gaelic political structures, but it is hampered by a relatively narrow range of evidence.

J.A. Watt, *The Church in Medieval Ireland*, Dublin, 1972, surveys the main developments in the Church, secular and monastic. It is not confined to Church affairs alone, but tries to place them in their social context.

3 Sixteenth-century Ulster and the failure of Tudor reform

Ciaran Brady

I

Sixteenth-century Ulster has traditionally been presented as both the symbol and the actual cockpit of that prolonged military and cultural confrontation known summarily as the Tudor conquest. With its primitive pastoral economy, supporting only a poor, semi-nomadic population which eked out existence in unrelieved misery under the tyranny of its tribal lords, Ulster was seen to represent in ideal form the fundamental characteristics of Gaelic society. Warring, the raiding of neighbours, and the suppression of dissent among their own people were, it is supposed, the principal occupations of the province's nobility. Through war they maintained their power at home and through it also they jockeyed for a place of influence in the province as a whole. Inability or unwillingness to use violence would ruin a chieftain, consigning his dynasty to the ranks of the powerless and the oppressed. And so the ceaseless pursuit of feuds and rivalries was understood to be the mode of politics in Gaelic Ulster, ensuring that its economy would remain stagnant, chaotic, poverty-stricken.

It is not surprising, then, that Ulster should have been regarded as 'the very fostermother' of all the rebellions against the Tudor attempt to revive English rule in Ireland. And indeed throughout the sixteenth century the province's apparently chronic turbulence was seen to present a mounting series of challenges to the crown culminating at length in the great war waged by the chieftains of O'Neill, O'Donnell and Maguire between 1593 and 1603.

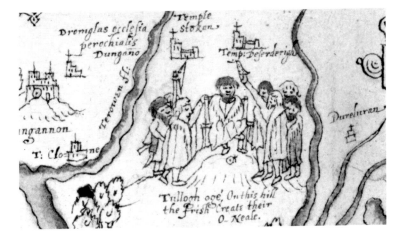

20 Inauguration of O'Neill.

All of this makes for a simple and neatly consistent story: as the most Gaelic of Ireland's provinces, it seems natural that it was Ulster which provided the most uncompromising resistance to royal government in Ireland, and natural too that, having once been defeated there, the Gaelic system should never again be an obstacle to the advance of English rule. Yet the persuasiveness of this account rests upon certain dubious assumptions. First, it is now clear that the image of Ulster as a sink of irredeemable barbarism is wildly exaggerated. Though underpopulated and under-developed in comparison with much of western Europe, Gaelic Ulster, we now know, possessed a reasonably stable and wealthy economy. Although climatic conditions determined that pastoralism should predominate, there existed a not inconsiderable arable sector within the agricultural economy. Wheat, barley and especially oats were grown. Flax too was cultivated and there is evidence of some modest linen manufacture in the province. Ulster's surplus of cattle, sheep and horses, moreover, permitted a flourishing trade both with other parts of the island and with Scotland, France and Spain. Towns were few but not non-existent. The cathedral town of Armagh served as a major provincial centre before it was sacked by the English army

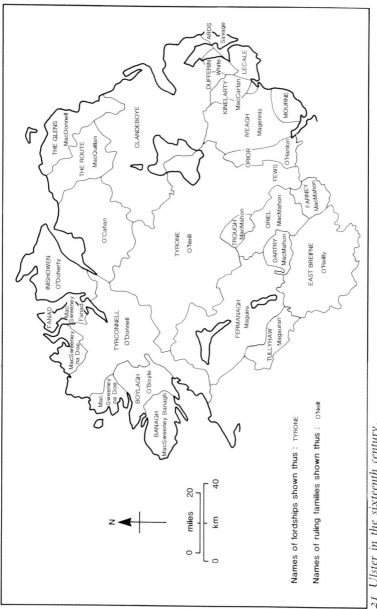

21 *Ulster in the sixteenth century.*

Names of lordships shown thus : TYRONE

Names of ruling families shown thus : O'Neill

in the late 1550s while other settlements like Lifford, Dungannon and Cavan town showed signs of substantial growth in the later sixteenth century, and Carrickfergus maintained and consolidated its position as the principal port in the province. Again, rural society was far more stable than has often been assumed. Booleying (the practice of driving the cattle-herds to the uplands in summer) was limited to poorer areas and even where practised involved only a portion of the population. Instead the community was organized under a sophisticated and carefully graduated system of land allocations which regulated the terms of proprietary possession within the ranks of each sept.[1]

At the same time, however, important processes of change were at work within Ulster society. Historians have noted the extent to which the proliferation of ruling lineages through multiple marriages generated a powerful downward pressure by which weaker families were dispossessed and forced into the ranks of the landless. Yet these same dominant groups, in their descent from political power, laid the foundations of a strong freeholding class within each territory which, while renouncing any right to overlordship, was able to defend its own position from the claims of any who would be their overlord. Although the operation of these related processes has already been demonstrated in several of the principal lordships of late medieval Ulster, their particular consequences and their general effect upon the character of the province's politics remain as yet uncertain. But it is already clear that, even before its renewed encounter with English government, Gaelic Ulster was a complex, varied society experiencing important political and social developments in its own right.[2]

The persistent disregard of the autonomous history of Gaelic Ulster in the sixteenth century is due largely to the undependable source materials upon which traditional accounts have been based: that is, the letters, reports and formal treatises of the Elizabethan soldiers, civil servants and adventurers who visited the province in the very last years of the century. The evidence of these late Elizabethan commentators is seriously biased in several different ways.

At best they supply an account of Ulster in only the most unusual and extreme conditions. The poverty, brutishness and anarchy which they describe are the symptoms of a society in the throes of total war – on the point indeed of collapse; and can hardly be regarded as representative of conditions in the province before the great rebellion began. Again, these men who were hazarding their lives and fortunes in an exceedingly bitter war could not have been expected to have observed the political and social mores of their enemy with objectivity and respect: an insistence upon the barbarity of their opponents served to justify the viciousness with which they themselves were prosecuting the war. There remained, however, a rather more subtle element of bias in their writings. Though it has often passed unnoticed, their sustained emphasis upon the unalterable primitiveness of Gaelic Ulster constituted an implicit – and sometimes explicit – critique of the belief that such a society might be reformed peacefully and gradually from within. And as such these writings, far from offering a simple, if unsympathetic, description of things as they were, formed part of a radical polemic against conventional contemporary views upon the reform of Ulster. For it was precisely upon such confidence in the possibility of Ulster's political reconstruction that orthodox Tudor policy towards the province had been based.[3]

II

Between the early 1520s and the early 1590s almost every Tudor viceroy acted upon the assumption that despite Ulster's political and social problems a satisfactory settlement could be reached between the native lords and the Crown without recourse to outright confrontation. A new conquest, it is true, was sometimes affirmed to be the ideal solution to the Ulster problem. But in practice almost everyone was agreed in discounting it as too costly, too difficult to organize and too uncertain in its outcome. It was moreover considered by most to be unnecessary, for the Kildare Geraldines (Fitzgeralds) and other Anglo-Irish lords had already shown that it was possible to establish reasonably stable accommodations with the Ulster lords by means of persuasion, diplomacy and patronage. Thus, despite occasional day-dreams of glory and some outbursts of temper, the peaceful reform of Ulster rather than its reconquest became a standard objective of Tudor government in Ireland. There were, of course, considerable differences of opinion as to how this aim might be reached, and over time a notable development in strategic thinking took place. The first English governors to replace the Geraldines in the 1530s sought simply, and generally without success, to assert their authority in Ulster by the same combination of patronage and intimidation through which the house of Kildare had operated in the province. In the 1540s, however, Lord Deputy St Leger adopted a bolder approach, abandoning the manipulation of Geraldine and anti-Geraldine interests and proposing a new political alignment based upon loyalty to no great lord other than King Henry VIII, now made sovereign of all the inhabitants of Ireland by act of parliament in 1541.[4]

Within this new political framework the great lords were formally to surrender their lands and rights of lordship and have them regranted in their entirety by the crown. All who did so would from henceforth be regarded as loyal subjects of the Irish king. They would be made peers of the realm, showered with personal gifts and lavish grants of crown land, and promised military and diplomatic support whenever necessary. In return they were merely to oversee the gradual introduction of English laws and inheritance customs into their territories. St Leger's scheme was immediately welcomed by both the greater and lesser Ulster lords. But it was in one major respect dangerously weak. The deputy had no means other than the drive of self-interest to ensure that the lords would honour their pledges, and was therefore powerless in face of a chieftain like Shane O'Neill who simply rejected the obligations which his predecessor Conn Bachach had entered into on being made Earl of Tyrone. Yet the experience of St Leger's successor, the Earl of Sussex, whose repeated campaigns against Shane

22 Tullaghoge Fort, Co. Tyrone, inauguration place of the O'Neills.

in the 1550s and 1560s ended in failure, showed equally that military force alone was insufficient to bring the recalcitrant to heel. And it was only under the administration of Sussex's successor, Sir Henry Sidney, that a solution to this strategic impasse was devised in the form of a policy known as 'composition'.[5]

Under 'composition' the crown's authority was to be asserted in Ulster by means of a large occupying army whose purpose was not to set about a conquest, but to act in the way of the great overlords themselves, by the exaction of food, hospitality and other tributes. Having thus established his authority the army's commander would then offer to commute his demands into a fixed and far less onerous annual payment. At the same time each of the lords was to be encouraged to offer a similar 'composition' of his own dues which, once agreed upon, would be guaranteed by the English garrison. 'Composition' thus promised benefits to everyone. The great lords would have their rights protected by the crown, their vassals would be freed from the arbitrary extortion of the lords' private armies, and the crown would collect a modest revenue which would

23 Sir John Perrot, Lord Deputy of Ireland, 1584–1588.

enable it to maintain a military and administrative presence in each province.[6]

Sidney's own attempt to implement composition in Ulster and elsewhere in the late 1570s failed through lack of support in London. But in the following decade the strategy was revived by the energetic viceroy, Sir John Perrot, in a series of tours of Ulster between 1584 and 1587. Paying special attention to the O'Neills, Perrot negotiated a temporary division of Tyrone between the current chieftain, Turlough Luineach, and the surviving heir of the first earl, Hugh, baron of Dungannon. Dungannon, he realized, was both ambitious and subtle, but he had been a strong supporter of the crown in the past and remained the best available hope of introducing legal and social reform among the O'Neills. Thus, to confirm his conviction that the future

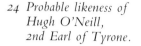

*24 Probable likeness of
   Hugh O'Neill,
   2nd Earl of Tyrone.*

lay with Dungannon, Perrot had him created second Earl of Tyrone by parliament in 1585.

Elsewhere Perrot confirmed and renewed previous surrender and regrant agreements with O'Donnell, O'Reilly and Magennis, made new ones with Maguire and MacMahon and persuaded each of the lords to permit the introduction of a small English garrison into their territories. He appointed the lords to new commissions for shiring, settled boundary disputes by inquisition, and introduced sheriffs in Breifne (Cavan), Tyrconnell and Fermanagh. In each of the agreements the rights of the freeholders were expressly reserved, and in Breifne and Monaghan Perrot began the delicate task of standardizing relations between the chiefs and their vassals by means of composition.[7]

Perrot's project marks the culmination of half a century's attempts on the part of the English government to secure the peaceful reform of Ulster. The process had not been without disruption, delay and disappointment. But confidence in its ultimate success had always been high and seemed in the mid-1580s to have been fully justified. Yet within a decade such optimism would be exploded by the outbreak of the most serious rebellion which the Tudors had ever faced in Ireland, in which the chieftains of Ulster joined in unprecedented unity under the leadership of the man from whom Perrot had expected so much, the new earl of Tyrone.

III

Such a disastrous outcome to all of the reformers' efforts was
by no means predetermined. But in retrospect it can be seen to
have been due to the confluence of three related factors which
had been developing steadily throughout the later sixteenth
century toward a crisis which no one could have anticipated.
The first and most obvious of these factors was the
delicately balanced state of many of the lordships into which
the government's reform programme was to be introduced.
A second was the unexpected emergence of Scottish settlers
and temporary migrants as a power to be reckoned with in
Ulster. But a third, and ultimately the most serious, was the
mounting incapacity of the Dublin government to maintain
itself amidst these different challenges as an effective and
coherent policy-making agency in its own right.

The benefits offered by reform to the native Irish at all
social levels were considerable. The adoption of inheritance
by primogeniture offered chieftains the opportunity of
establishing a political dynasty of their own, regardless of
the claims of familial collaterals, and of appropriating as a
hereditary right the extensive demesne lands and seigneurial
dues which were normally attached to the chieftainship. But
the benefits of primogeniture were also to apply to all the
current heads of non-governing family groups. Amongst
the most influential freeholding families of each lordship,
therefore, there existed a powerful constituency in support
of the proposed transformation. This potential consensus
between the chieftains and groups within the principal landholding families was reinforced by the second major
element in the reform policy, the proposal to standardize
seigneurial dues. For freeholders great and small, composition promised relief from the oppressions of the lords'
private armies; but for the lords themselves royal recognition of their rights obviated the need to maintain these
armies which were the most serious drain on their revenues.
'Idle swordsmen' whose sole function in the past had been
to extract all the wealth of the countryside would now be

made redundant, or forced to turn their hands to profitable labour.

It was, of course, from these redundant swordsmen and from the disappointed or betrayed dynastic collaterals that the most vigorous opposition to reform could be expected. Those lords who leaned toward reform, then, were in the early stages of the process compelled to maintain a delicately balanced attitude, alternately renewing their commitments to the crown and indulging in the conventional politics of war-making, faction and coercion. Such an attitude was, in the short term, logical enough. But the long-term strain on the native lords of attempting to maintain, even in a most minimal fashion, their dual role as supporters of the crown and defenders of the traditional interests of the Gaelic aristocracy created serious tensions which manifested themselves in varying ways within different lordships. In Monaghan, where disputes over the chieftainship were chronic, the efforts of successive nominal lords to maintain good relations with the crown resulted in a further decline of the prestige of the chieftainship amongst the MacMahons themselves. By the mid-1580s the ability of the MacMahon chieftain to exercise any authority beyond his own family lands was defunct. Elsewhere the efforts of more powerful chieftains, like O'Reilly and Maguire, to control opposing political interests by permitting members of their own immediate families to represent them, produced deadly internecine strife within the ruling group as the chieftains' power waned and a new generation came of age.[8]

The situation was even more critical in Tyrconnell where dynastic strife was sharpened in the later sixteenth century by the unusual weakness of the chieftain Hugh Dubh O'Donnell. Having seized the title upon the sudden death of Calough O'Donnell in 1566, Hugh never enjoyed the support of Calough's own family, and his failure to impose his authority upon them led to a further decline in his credit among the freeholders of the lordship and even within the ranks of his own family. His attempts to defend his position by means of a marriage alliance with the MacDonnells of the Western Isles only deepened his troubles, for although his wife Iníon Dubh brought him a substantial private army as her dowry, she soon insisted that Hugh's son by their marriage, Hugh Roe, rather than Domnall, the acknowledged heir by an earlier marriage, should become the next O'Donnell.[9]

The most severe strains imposed by the policy of reform were experienced however in Tyrone. For O'Neill the advantage of commutation on the one hand was considerable: the demesne lands of the chieftains were extensive and the seigneurial claims of O'Neill in Tyrone and elsewhere in Ulster even more so. Yet such major claims to influence were subject to serious challenge from a number of directions. The crown was naturally cautious about conceding such provincial claims in their entirety, though successive English governors were willing to grant far greater extra-territorial powers to the O'Neill than might have been expected. A more serious challenge came from the lesser lords of the province such as Maguire, O'Reilly, and MacMahon who denied somewhat disingenuously that such payments as they made under duress to O'Neill were his by right, and were supported in their claims by the O'Donnells who themselves hoped to exercise some countervailing influence in the province.

Difficulties of this kind were not, of course, entirely insurmountable. Since both the crown and most of the native lords were prepared to concede some kind of provincial role to O'Neill, the question of his provincial status was open to negotiation and compromise. But the ability of the O'Neill to conduct such diplomatic manoeuvrings was severely curtailed by the instability of the dynasty itself. In the mid-1550s the first earl of Tyrone had been deposed by his own disinherited son Shane who sought to have the royal agreement renegotiated in his own interest. Shane soon asserted his authority in Tyrone itself. But he still faced serious opposition to his *coup* both from the other Ulster lords and the Dublin government. To meet it he organized Tyrone for war, arming the peasants and hiring ever-increasing numbers of mercenaries. His strategy was strikingly successful. He subdued O'Reilly, Maguire and MacMahon, imprisoned O'Donnell and frustrated all attempts of the Dublin government to defeat him. But the sudden collapse of Shane's war-state upon his death at the hands of the Scots in 1567 produced an immediate power-vacuum in Tyrone. Shane left no successor. His own sons were still too young to take his place while Hugh, the baron of Dungannon, had been driven into exile in the Pale where he seems to have been brought up by the Hovenden family in Dublin and later spent a brief period, probably with Sir Henry Sidney, in London. In these circumstances the chieftainship was seized by Turlough Luineach O'Neill, a man who had but a modest claim by inheritance, but who had served as one of Shane's principal commanders.

To begin with Turlough benefited greatly from the absence of any real competition, but by the mid-1570s serious opposition had begun to appear. The sons of Shane O'Neill began to reassert their influence, usurping the chieftain's right to collect the seigneurial dues of the lordships. By 1579 they had forced Turlough to nominate one of their number as his successor. By then, however, Turlough had been obliged to confront a quite different challenge to his position on the part of the baron of Dungannon.

Restored to a small part of his inheritance after Shane's death, Hugh had, through the support of the English government and through a judicious series of diplomatic alliances with the freeholders of Tyrone and lords of Ulster, gradually established himself at the centre of a powerful provincial network opposed to Turlough. And in 1579 he

25 Turlough Luineach O'Neill: an unsympathetic drawing by Barnaby Googe, 1575.

too extorted from the embattled chieftain a promise that he should be the next O'Neill. Thus in Tyrone as in most of the other lordships a serious succession struggle seemed unavoidable in the decade ahead. The pervasive instability of Ulster's internal politics in the late sixteenth century accounts to some degree for the sluggishness of the Tudor reform plan. But its progress was even more seriously impeded by a step which each of the beleaguered lords took to maintain their positions, the importation of Scottish mercenaries or galloglasses.[10]

The seasonal hiring of galloglasses was, of course, traditional in Gaelic politics; but in the mid-sixteenth century the role of the Scots in Ulster changed dramatically. Each of the embattled O'Neills imported Scots in ever increasing numbers. Shane owed his ascent to power to the large number of mercenaries which he had hired and in the 1560s he sought to consolidate his links with Scotland by negotiating a permanent alliance with the earl of Argyll. Turlough Luineach's authority was supported almost entirely by the 8,000 Scots he acquired as part of the dowry of his wife Lady Agnes Campbell while the sons of Shane depended heavily on the support of the Maclean who sent them over 5,000 men in the 1570s alone. The O'Neills' conduct compelled the other Ulster lords, particularly the O'Donnells, to make correspondingly increased demands for Scottish professionals and so their numbers continued to escalate: a recent investigation of the subject has conservatively estimated the number of Scots employed in Ulster between the late 1560s and early 1590s at 25,000. This militarization of the province was self-perpetuating: once hired, the army had to be found work in the manner of war-making and cattle-raiding even when the original issues for which it had been summoned had ceased to be relevant. If the Scots could not be supplied with business, they would surely generate some for themselves. Thus chieftains who had originally benefited from the use of Scots soon found themelves prisoners of a system of dependence and fear from which there was no easy escape.[11]

The Scots, however, altered the character of Ulster's politics in a more fundamental manner. For in addition to

26 Cattle Raid, *woodcut by John Derrick, 1581.*

those temporary military migrants an even more significant group had begun from the middle of the century to settle permanently in the Glens and the Route of Antrim. For some time the MacDonnells of the Western Isles had interfered periodically in the affairs of north-east Ulster. But following their failure to withstand the encroachments of the Edinburgh government into the Isles they began to become more seriously concerned with Ireland. By the late 1550s they had settled in large numbers in Antrim, overrunning the MacQuillans and the Savages and destroying the claims of the O'Neills of Clandeboy to be overlords in the area. Despite repeated and frequently bloody attempts of the English government and of the O'Neills to dislodge them, the MacDonnells clung on and in the mid-1580s forced Lord Deputy Perrot to recognize them rather than the Clandeboy O'Neills as the real power in the north-east.[12]

The permanent settlement of the MacDonnells produced a series of reverberations of varying force. Most immediately, it disrupted the local balance of power, as several lesser lordships simply disappeared and the Clandeboy O'Neills were driven close to disintegration. None of the Irish of the north-east, therefore, was in a position to react positively to the reform proposals of the crown, even though many of them had once been willing to. The confusion in Antrim, however, presented equally serious problems to the O'Neills of Tyrone. Though they had grudgingly acknowledged a pact of mutual non-interference with the Clandeboy O'Neills, the establishment of the MacDonnells altered their attitude considerably. Shane O'Neill characteristically aimed at their total expulsion. Yet his death at their hands forced his successor to reconsider. An attitude of undifferentiated hostility, Turlough realized, might result in the general alienation of the highland lords upon whom he was so dependent, or it might produce a realignment of native lords in opposition to O'Neill under a Scottish leadership. For this reason his general and not unsuccessful policy toward the Scots was ambivalent and assiduously divisive, alternately proffering firm friendship toward the MacDonnell leader, Sorley Boy, and ceaselessly intriguing to sow dissent amongst the ranks of the Scots themselves. By these means Turlough managed to contain but never to resolve his Scottish problem. Yet his constant distraction in this area added greatly to his own insecurity and so further reduced the possibility that he might peacefully be persuaded to adopt the crown's proposals for reform.

It was, however, upon royal government itself that the Scottish settlement was to register the most severe effects. For the crown, the destabilization of the north-east was not merely a serious local problem, but an event laden with international implications. Fuelled and often manipulated by the generally Francophile government in Edinburgh, the migration posed a potentially serious danger, giving opportunity to English enemies to stimulate a troublesome diversion at least and to mount a full-scale invasion at worst. It was this awareness of the larger diplomatic implications of the issue that underlay the crown's determination to expel the Scots entirely. In the 1550s and 1560s the government organized major and increasingly costly official campaigns to stem the inflow of settlers. When these efforts had failed, to the disgrace of all involved, the government sought to contain the migration by sanctioning private enterprises such as the ill-fated colonial scheme of Sir Thomas Smith in the Ards and the extraordinary charter granted to an independent adventurer, Walter Devereux, Earl of Essex, who was to expel the Scots and settle the entire country at his discretion.[13]

The effects of the crown's increasing commitment to the forceful expulsion of the Scots were several. In the first instance it significantly increased the degree of military power which the government was obliged to display in order to maintain its influence in the province. Some demonstration of willingness to resort to force had always been recognized as a necessary exemplary accompaniment to the crown's preferred object of peaceful negotiation. But in their efforts to expel the Scots, English commanders deployed a measure of violence which contrasted greatly with their declared intent of reaching a peaceful agreement with the Gaelic Irish. The most notorious example of such conduct was provided by the Earl of Essex in the 1570s whose ferocity toward the Scots and their Irish accomplices increased proportionately as his chances of success declined. But a similar ruthlessness was also displayed by Sussex in the 1550s and even by Perrot before he conceded defeat in the 1580s. Such salutary effects as these demonstrations might have entailed were, however, diminished by the fact that they were all in the end futile; and increasingly, in its travails to obtain control of the north-east, royal government projected for the Ulster Irish the uninspiring image of an unstable, erratic and ultimately ineffective force.

The ineffectiveness of military action was of more immediate consequence, however, to the governors themselves. In the end, whether they tried either to confront the Scots, like Sussex and Perrot, or to seek some compromise with them, like St Leger and Sidney, their failure to contain the migration led only to their discredit and hastened their recall. But even before then such enforced preoccupation with what their superiors perceived as a larger international problem greatly distracted the governors from the pursuit of reform in Gaelic Ulster, forcing them frequently to renege on old agreements, to suspend current negotiations and to ignore fresh overtures.

The viceroy's distraction with the north-east did not

merely result in stagnation: it also induced regression. As the governors were obliged to suspend their commitments to reform, they often delegated responsibility for Ulster to dependable subordinates who were required to do no more than retain some military and political presence for the crown in the province, and to fend for themselves as best they might. The two most important outposts of this kind were those of Captain William Piers in Carrickfergus and Marshall Nicholas Bagenal in Newry. Both men's success in discharging these minimal requirements was considerable. Each survived dangerous times in the 1550s and 1560s and by the 1570s each had established himself as a significant influence in the local politics of the province. Piers was a close ally of Sir Brian MacPhelim O'Neill, the Lord of Clandeboy; Bagenal was a patron of Magennis, Lord of Iveagh. Yet the very extent of their personal success was in itself an obstacle to the revival of centrally controlled reform. Piers was extremely hostile to any move that threatened the interests of Sir Brian MacPhelim. He intimidated the viceroy from interfering in Clandeboy in the 1560s and his intrigues on Sir Brian's behalf caused Essex to arrest him on a charge of treason in 1575. Bagenal was equally protective of his clients. He opposed all attempts at a settlement with Turlough Luineach who claimed the overlordship of Magennis; and most notoriously he determined to subvert Perrot's Ulster project even at the risk of his own office. The presence of these men in Ulster did not provoke universal hostility amongst the native lords, who were habitually predisposed to adapt to the realities of power. But their very independence seriously compromised the sincerity of the central government's claims to be committed to reform and so correspondingly reduced the enthusiasm of the Ulster lords for any significant change.[14]

For almost fifty years, then, the genuine efforts of both native lords and English governors to discover a mutually satisfactory means of converting Ulster to English ways had been frustrated by the interaction of three disruptive factors. The unusually unstable condition of several of the Ulster lordships, especially Tyrone and Tyrconnell, made it clear that peaceful internal reform would be a far more intricate operation than its earlier proponents had hoped. The intrusion of the Scots, at once encouraging and encouraged by the province's progressive disorder, presented a further obstacle, diverting both the government and the lords, and forcing both to adopt aggressive postures which in turn gave rise to mistrust as to either side's real intent. Such difficulties, however, only exposed the essential weakness of the government's commitment to reform. For though it had shown no lack of good-will or strategic inventiveness, the Dublin administration displayed a disturbing tendency toward entropy, often interrupting its reform programme to deal with individual problems, such as the Scots or Shane O'Neill, by force, or simply losing executive drive in face of criticism, lack of finance or just unexpected difficulty. The very body, that is, which had seized the initiative in the advance of political change in Ulster had thus seriously undermined its own credibility by demonstrating a repeated incapacity to sustain its undertakings. It was in these circumstances that Sir John Perrot introduced his ambitious and demanding programme of reform by 'composition'.

IV

Perrot's scheme, as we have seen, was sensitively conceived and introduced. But it was, like so many other Tudor essays in reform, abortive. Frustrated by criticism at Court, by the Scots and by the obstruction of Marshall Bagenal and his allies, Perrot abandoned Ireland, hoping to return with stronger backing. He never did: instead his replacement, Sir William Fitzwilliam, connived at his disgrace, and Perrot was arraigned (without justification) on a charge of treason. His fall left many supporters in Ireland exposed and vulnerable,[15] but none more so than those Ulster lords who ·had embrace his plans for composition. For those who had considered establishing fixed relations with their freeholders were now faced with increased demands for autonomy from these groups without the guarantee of their own rights and privileges which the composition was to have granted them. Moreover, the garrisons which were intended by Perrot to sustain the lords and relieve them of their onerous private armies now became dangerous independent agents, scouting for their own interests, while the lordships' swordsmen had already been put on notice that their own lords could no longer be trusted to maintain them. Worst of all, however, the entire affair coincided with the onset of acute succession crises in Breifne, Monaghan and Fermanagh upon the deaths of their respective chieftains, and with the sharpening of dynastic struggles in Tyrone and Tyrconnell as competitors anticipated the imminent demise of Turlough Luineach and Hugh Dubh O'Donnell.[16]

After all this it is hard to see how any English governor could have acted with sufficient authority to stem the deepening crisis. But such steps as Fitzwilliam took served

27 *Strangford Castle, tower house restored in the sixteenth century.*

only to hasten a final conflagration. Though he was neither an advocate of confrontation nor an opponent of reform, years of experience in Ireland had made him sceptical of any preformulated projects, whatever their contents. Instead Fitzwilliam favoured the purely conservative aim of maintaining order in Gaelic society by allowing the natural balance of power to emerge in each lordship over time. All of his apparently wilful and contradictory acts in Ulster in the early 1590s can be explained in terms of this simple principle. His suppression of the MacMahon chieftainship and partition of Monaghan was merely a belated recognition of the real distribution of power in the lordship. His calm acceptance of – and possible connivance at – the escape of Hugh Roe O'Donnell and Pilib O'Reilly, both swordsmen whom Perrot had imprisoned as implacable opponents of composition, was similarly based upon a clear appreciation of their strength in their respective lordships. And it was this same attitude that explains Fitzwilliam's apparently irreconcilable policies in allowing Tyrone to consolidate his power amongst the O'Neills while also encouraging the Bagenals of Newry in their vigorous opposition to any extension of Tyrone's influence in south Ulster. Elsewhere the deputy contented himself simply with replacing those of Perrot's garrison commanders whom he could dismiss with unknown clients of his own, or with permitting those whom he could not remove (like Sir Richard Bingham, the man whom Perrot had placed in charge of the composition in Connacht) to expand their operations at their own will.[17]

Despite their conservative intent, however, Fitzwilliam's disjointed cluster of decisions served to give, in the explosive atmosphere of the early 1590s, a final confirmation to the already disillusioned Ulster lords that the Tudor pretension to peaceful reform was at heart vapid, a hopeless aspiration at best, and at worst a mere pretext for the management of affairs by power alone. The effects of his ill-considered actions were experienced throughout the province, but they registered most acutely in the highly unstable lordships of Tyrconnell, Fermanagh and Tyrone.

The release of Hugh Roe O'Donnell precipitated a final

struggle for power in Tyrconnell. During his absence Iníon Dubh had defended her son's interests by having his most serious rivals murdered. But even as the prospective chief, Hugh Roe could make no compromise with reform by composition. Lacking significant influence with the major O'Donnell freeholders but possessed, thanks to his mother, of a powerful military retinue, he recognized that composition would destroy his claim to leadership in Tyrconnell. He could retain power only by committing himself, as Shane O'Neill had done, to an indefinite campaign of external aggression and expansion in which the military commanders would be pre-eminent. The adventures of Fitzwilliam's new commanders in Ulster and, more importantly, the intervention of Sir Richard Bingham in north Connacht provided him with an ideal opportunity for attack. And so Hugh Roe grasped at the chieftainship by reasserting the O'Donnell claim to Sligo.[18] In Fermanagh, meanwhile, where the newly succeeded chieftain, Hugh, faced both formidable groups of semi-independent free-holders and serious political opposition in the person of his cousin Conor Roe, the activities of Fitzwilliam's Captain Willis, supported by Bingham's brother George, provided a suitable *casus belli* for the chieftain to rally the military forces of his territory and to join with O'Donnell in alliance against the English.

The forging of this axis of radical resistance in the west posed a serious threat to all Ulster lordships; but it precipitated the most severe disturbance in Tyrone where the question of internal reform had also become inextricably linked to an imminent succession struggle. The new Earl's success with Perrot and Fitzwilliam had considerably strengthened his claim to the lordship; but it had also produced immediate difficulty. For as his potential became clear, so his enemies gathered to forestall him. The

28 *Narrow Water Castle, Co. Antrim, tower house built in the 1560s.*

MacShanes, still seeking power in the manner of their father, made open war against him, and Turlough Luineach's sons, Turlough Brasselagh and Henry O'Neill, and other powerful interests among the O'Neills who had hoped to see the end of all claims to overlordship, refused (with the encouragement of the Bagenals) to grant him support. The Earl attempted to cope with the dual threat partly by violence – he had two of the MacShanes hanged in a dramatic public execution – and partly by diplomacy – he married a daughter to Henry O'Neill and in a famous coup eloped with the sister of Sir Henry Bagenal. But the two strategies were mutually difficult to sustain, and as the Bagenals and the freeholders remained unreconciled and the swordsmen grew increasingly alienated, Tyrone seemed destined to lose his long-sought position as mediator between Gaelic Ulster and royal government exactly when he was on the point of attaining it. It was at this stage that O'Donnell, the O'Neills' ancient enemy, and Maguire, his formerly recalcitrant vassal, appealed to Tyrone to lead the swordsmen's revolt.[19]

It is impossible to determine at what point Tyrone made his decision to ally with the western rebels. It is arguable that he did so as soon as he allowed his brother Art to join Maguire in 1593; but Tyrone himself served, albeit half-heartedly, with Bagenal against Maguire in the same year, and though he was in close contact with Maguire and O'Donnell he continued to negotiate for a settlement with the government throughout 1594. Even after his attack on the government's Blackwater fort and his proclamation as a rebel in 1595, Tyrone rejected his allies' demands to escalate the war and strove with some success to achieve a cease-fire. The promise of Spanish aid early in 1596 seemed to harden his determination, but even then his strategy of 'deluding parleys' continued. He risked much in submitting in person to Lord Deputy Russell and Sir John Norris, and when Lord Deputy Burgh (1597) refused to parley with him, he opened negotiations with the Earl of Ormond instead.

Yet any emphasis upon the ambivalence of Tyrone's position in these years would be misplaced. For from the outset, the objectives for which he strove were altogether different from those of his confederates in rebellion. Throughout he was concerned to show that Ulster would be reconciled to English rule only by the strong guiding hand of the one who was both chief of the O'Neills and the Earl of Tyrone. It was for this reason that he strove, even at some personal danger, to remain in communication with the Dublin government throughout the 1590s and that he refused, despite ample opportunity, to carry the war into the Pale. Thus his famous encounter with the Earl of Essex in September 1599 was no mere Fabian ruse but a sincere and clearly impressive attempt to explain his position to a figure who, it then seemed, had both the interest and the political influence to confirm his claims. But the plausibility of Tyrone's assertions was steadily eroded by the progress of the rebellion itself. Its early successes prompted a series of imitative rebellions within each of the remaining Ulster lordships in which those who had accepted and those who had rejected reform joined battle for the control of their territory. Amid deep division in Ulster, Tyrone thus found himself at the head of the group who would never be reconciled to change and committed to the destruction of those who had already embraced it. His position became even more difficult when the rebels' spectacular defeat of a large English army at the Yellow Ford in August 1597 precipitated widespread rebellion in Munster and Leinster. Though he delayed identification with their cause for long, Essex's disgrace and the appointments of Lord Mountjoy as viceroy and Sir George Carew as president of Munster made it clear to Tyrone that the crown had now rejected any possibility of a compromise peace. With all hope of maintaining his unique intermediary position now lost, Tyrone allowed the rebellion in Ulster to become a war for all Ireland. Ruined by success, he surrendered to the arguments of O'Donnell and Maguire, and accepted the urgent necessity of securing Spanish intervention. Ironically, therefore, the débâcle at Kinsale in December 1601 offered a welcome deliverance to Tyrone from a war which he could no longer hope to win, whatever happened. Not surprisingly he was the first of the rebels to sue for peace.

The terms of the treaty eventually concluded at Mellifont in March 1603 were remarkably lenient.[20] Pardoned and restored to all his lands, Tyrone was even permitted, against the terms of the old composition, to retain the O'Cahans as his personal vassals. But for all its moderation Mellifont could not restore the *status quo ante* 1594. Even in defeat the surviving rebels remained unreconciled to social reform for the same political and economic reasons that had provoked their rebellion in the first place, while many of those who had once supported change had either been engulfed by the rebellion or left thoroughly disillusioned by their experience in the past nine years. Although reconciliation with the Ulster lords remained the official policy of government no one was willing to pursue it.

The extent of this change of climate could be seen most clearly in the operations of the Commission for Defective Titles established by the government in 1606. Ostensibly intended to resolve the legal and tenurial uncertainties which had driven many Ulster lords into rebellion in the preceding decade, the Commission was from the outset exploited by the Dublin administrators as a means of further weakening the claims of the lords over their vassals and tenants. The maintenance of the lords' political and social status, which had been such a concern of the Elizabethan promoters of composition, was thus silently abandoned; and the most vulnerable Ulster chiefs found themselves facing an even more deadly challenge than the one which had driven them to rebellion in the past. Even Tyrone himself was under attack, as the government encouraged his principal remaining vassal, O'Cahan, to sue for independence.

Under such conditions Tyrone's hopes of reviving his role as mediator between Gaelic lords and English reformers were exceedingly slender. That they existed at all was due largely to his influence with King James, which had been established through his remarkable relationship with Mountjoy (now Earl of Devonshire and absentee Lord Lieutenant of Ireland). By this means Tyrone succeeded in having his dispute with O'Cahan referred directly to London to be heard by the king himself. But his chances of winning this test case dwindled rapidly with Devonshire's fall from grace and sudden death in April 1606. In these circumstances the decision of his old unstable allies, O'Donnell and Maguire, to renounce all pretence of loyalty by going into exile in the Spanish Netherlands rendered Tyrone's situation impossible. Their unsolicitated invitation to him to join them compromised the Earl irredeemably, and ensured that whether he accepted or refused he would be regarded by the government as a party to their conspiracy. Thus on 4 September 1607 he joined them on their flight into exile, as he had joined in their rebellion, simply because there was nothing else for it.[21]

Further reading

Lord Ernest Hamilton, *Elizabethan Ulster*, London, 1919 provides a stimulating introduction to the period. Written with great verve, prejudice and wit, the book displays a fascinating tension between the author's pronounced Unionist bias and his equally strong distaste for the Tudor government's treatment of the Scots. Hiram Morgan, 'The end of Gaelic Ulster: a thematic interpretation of events between 1534 and 1610', *Irish Historical Studies*, 26, 1988, pp. 8–32 covers many of the issues discussed in this chapter, from a different perspective.

The social and economic history of sixteenth-century Ulster remains in a rudimentary state. Suggestive indications of important internal changes have been made by G.A. Hayes McCoy, 'Gaelic society in Ireland in the late sixteenth century', *Historical Studies*, iv, 1962, pp. 45–61 and N.P. Canny, 'Hugh O'Neill, earl of Tyrone, and the changing face of Gaelic Ulster', *Studia Hibernica*, x, 1970, pp. 7–35. But the most pioneering work has so far been done by medievalists: see K.W. Nicholls, *Gaelic and Gaelicised Ireland in the Later Middle Ages*, Dublin, 1972 and his *Land, Law and Society in the Sixteenth Century*, Dublin, 1979; see also Katherine Simms, 'Guesting and feasting in Gaelic Ireland', *Royal Society of Antiquaries of Ireland, Journal*, cviii, 1978, pp. 67–100. Important late developments in one

Gaelic lordship have been traced in P.J. Duffy, 'The territorial organization of Gaelic landownership and its transformation in Co. Monaghan, 1591–1640', *Irish Geography*, xiv, 1981, pp. 1–26. An immediate impression of 'the face of Ulster' can be derived by consulting G.A. Hayes McCoy, *Ulster and other Irish maps, c.1600*, Dublin, 1964.

The political framework of Ulster in this period is also under-researched, although again Katherine Simms, *From Kings to Warlords*, Woodbridge, 1985 provides the essential medieval background. Ulster's political history has largely been written through the biographies of its leading figures. For Tyrone, Sean O'Faoláin, *The Great O'Neill*, Dublin, 1943 is compelling but over-romantic and seems strangely more outdated than Robert Dunlop's earlier essay for the *Dictionary of National Biography*. Shane O'Neill has merited an awful novel also entitled *The Great O'Neill*, Boston, 1939 by E.B. Barret, but the sheer ambition and near success of this great war-lord have yet to be fully examined. For Hugh Roe O'Donnell there is Paul Walsh's introduction to Lughaidh O'Clerigh's contemporary panegyric, *Beatha Aodh Ruadh O Domhnaill*, 2 vols., Irish Texts Society, Dublin, 1948–57. Scholarly studies for the lesser lordships have been rare. But for Fermanagh and Monaghan see Peadar Livingstone, *The Fermanagh Story*, Enniskillen, 1969, and *The Monaghan Story*, Enniskillen, 1980, the latter being better researched than the former. For Cavan, there is Ciaran Brady, 'The O'Reillys of East Breifne and the problem of surrender and regrant', *Breifne*, xxiii, 1985, pp. 233–62. On Scots settlers, George Hill, *An Historical Account of the MacDonnells of Antrim*, Belfast, 1873 remains the best available account; the role of the professional soldiers is examined in G.A. Hayes McCoy, *Scots Mercenary Forces in Ireland*, Dublin, 1937. Cyril Falls, *Elizabeth's Irish Wars*, London, 1950 covers the military side of the Nine Years War; its diplomatic ramifications are discussed in J.J. Silke, *Kinsale: the Spanish Intervention in Ireland at the End of the Sixteenth Century*, Liverpool, 1970, and F.M. Jones, *Mountjoy (1563–1606): the Last Elizabethan Deputy*, Dublin, 1968.

4 Continuity and change: Ulster in the seventeenth century

Raymond Gillespie

In so far as any historical era can be said to have ended on a specific date, the Tudor conquest of Ireland was brought to a successful conclusion on 30 March 1603 when the most powerful magnate in Gaelic Ireland, Hugh O'Neill, Earl of Tyrone submitted to Lord Mountjoy, the queen's Lord Lieutenant, at Mellifont Abbey in Co. Louth. Mountjoy had succeeded where a long succession of by then discredited viceroys had failed. Exultant, he wrote to the new king's principal secretary of state, Robert Cecil, in April 1603 saying that Ireland was 'now capable of what form it shall please the king to give it'.[1] Mountjoy did not live to see how his prediction fared. He died in 1606 and a year later the principal signatory of the Treaty of Mellifont, Hugh O'Neill, left Ireland with some of the other Irish lords for continental Europe. Even if later events had taken a different turn it is unlikely that Mountjoy's wish could have been fulfilled. He had been carried away by the fruits of victory and the next hundred years was to demonstrate just how far from accurate was his analysis.

The experience of seventeenth-century Ireland was of a society in transition, not just in central government as Mountjoy envisaged it but in a much wider sense. The social norms of Gaelic Ireland, already changing slowly in the sixteenth century, were rapidly dismantled and replaced with English standards of social order. Terms such as 'leaseholder' and 'freeholder' became the normal descriptions of a man's place in the social order rather than the older vocabulary of Gaelic Ireland. The economy became increasingly commercialized and Irish trade expanded and

29 *Plantation village at Ballykelly, Co. Londonderry. Note the variety of house types: timber-framed; stone; and mud-cabins.*

diversified. A local government system, based on new geographical units such as the county, was developed and became increasingly widespread from the middle of the sixteenth century. Regions were defined on the basis of changed economic realities, thus replacing the old native lordships. However, the old order was not entirely obliterated. Old ways of describing territories, such as the province, the townland or *ballyboe*, and the barony, were incorporated into the new order. Nor were old rivalries removed from the country by the new divisions. The traditional division of the country into north and south, the *Leath Modha* and *Leath Cuinn* of the poets, persisted. From an anonymous tract probably by Owen Roe O'Neill, which circulated widely on the Continent during an attempt to plan a Spanish invasion of Ireland in the 1620s, comes this description:

> Ireland is divided into two parts, the north part where it may be hoped to make the real diversion and the part which lies over against England ... where the English garrisons are and the greater number of Irish catholics and religious. These latter although they [are] Catholics are related to the English and united to them.[2]

Similar sentiments were expressed by the Catholic Archbishop of Armagh, Oliver Plunkett, in 1672 when he noted that 'Ulstermen and Leinstermen have never agreed and will not in the future either and the same is true of the Munstermen and Connachtmen. Connachtmen and Ulstermen will easily agree as will Munstermen and Leinstermen.'[3]

The history of Ulster in the seventeenth century is no exception to this pattern. Here the emergence of a new type of society, within the region, was based on the combination of old and new elements. At the beginning of the seventeenth century much of the distinctiveness of Ulster which resulted from the social, political, cultural and economic arrangements of the medieval period remained. Ulster was a region which had previously had little contact with the administration in Dublin. In early sixteenth-century maps, for example, Ulster still appeared largely blank although some of the blanks had been filled in during the reign of Elizabeth as a result of the military campaigns fought in the province. The isolation of the province from the central government was well demonstrated in 1608 when the attorney general, Sir John Davies, and the Lord

30 Sir Arthur Chichester, Lord Deputy of Ireland, 1605–1616.

Deputy, Sir Arthur Chichester, visited Ulster: Davies reported that 'the wild inhabitants wondered as much to see the king's deputy as the ghosts of Virgil wondered to see Aeneas alive in hell.' In contrast to the other provinces, the power of the great Gaelic lords in west Ulster had remained largely intact until the late sixteenth century, and their moral authority persisted to some extent well into the seventeenth century. In 1603, for example, Davies recorded that 'the better sort of the province of Ulster did refuse to accept the king's commission of the peace until they received warrant from the Earl of Tyrone to do so.' Such sentiments survived to a degree, as we shall see, almost to the end of the century.[4]

Despite the experience of colonization, warfare, and dramatic economic change in the seventeenth century, the distinctiveness of the indigenous Ulster community was still apparent to commentators in the closing years of the century. George Storey, an officer in the Williamite army, noted in 1691 after the war that the Ulstermen who had fled to Kerry and Clare began to return home, 'which was a little odd to see', since it was a long journey, they had no assurance of regaining possession of their own farms, and the risk of retaliation from settlers was real. In contrast, land in Munster was cheap and available 'but', Storey noted, 'the reason of this is plain, for there is so great an antipathy between the Ulster Irish and those in other parts of the kingdom, as nothing can be more, and the feuds amongst them greater than between either and their injured protestant neighbours.'[5] The experience of the native Irish was not unique. From the earliest stages of the plantation scheme many settlers found they had more in common with their Gaelic Ulster neighbours than with settlers in other parts of the country.

I

In some ways, the plantation scheme which was devised for Ulster, to fill the power vacuum created by the flight of the chief Gaelic lords in September 1607, can be viewed as a radical departure. The Dublin and London administrations were at a loss to know how best to deal with Ulster after the flight. They were unwilling to establish a plantation on the lines of the sixteenth-century Munster settlement because of the difficulties encountered there. Thus, it was only after protracted negotiations over a period of two years, and the personal intervention of King James I, that the plans for the future of the province were crystalized in the form of the *Orders and Conditions of the Ulster Plantation*.

Under the scheme land tenure was to be dramatically reorganized and the escheated (confiscated) lands of the native Irish lords were to be granted to English and Scots settlers and servitors, who were ex-army officers and government officials. The new landowners were bound under the terms of the scheme to introduce settlers as their tenants, build castles and towns and act as agents for the introduction of English law, the Protestant religion, and 'civility'.

This plan created an environment where land was cheap and the authority of the English crown weak. Consequently men who felt their opportunities limited in England and Scotland saw in Ulster a chance to make profit or reverse declining fortunes. To such men migration to Ulster was an attractive proposition, and the movement of population which resulted from the scheme to plant the six Ulster counties of Armagh, Cavan, Donegal, Fermanagh, Londonderry and Tyrone was very significant by standards of the time. By about 1630 there were about 14,500 adult male settlers in Ulster, or when one takes account of the families some would have brought with them, about 24,000 newcomers in all.

Such a dramatic increase in population had widespread repercussions in almost every area of activity and the economic impetus of rapid population increase in the early part of the century was a very important determinant of the way the province developed during the seventeenth century. Improved labour supply, for example, was one factor influencing the development of Ulster's economy in the seventeenth century. While the population had risen significantly, it was still low in relation to the resources available. Furthermore, the socially selective processes which had operated in selecting the migrants meant that they tended to be without much substance and so much of the income from their Ulster estates had to be ploughed back into their lands. One consequence of this was a low level of disposable income and hence a relatively weak domestic market, so much of the produce of Ulster was exported. Exports of goods from Ulster increased dramatically in the early seventeenth century. Valued in constant 1616 prices, Ulster exports increased by about 150 per cent between 1616 and 1626 although the type and rate of increase varied from port to port. The numbers of live cattle exported from the medieval port of Carrickfergus increased by about 94 per cent between these dates but the newer

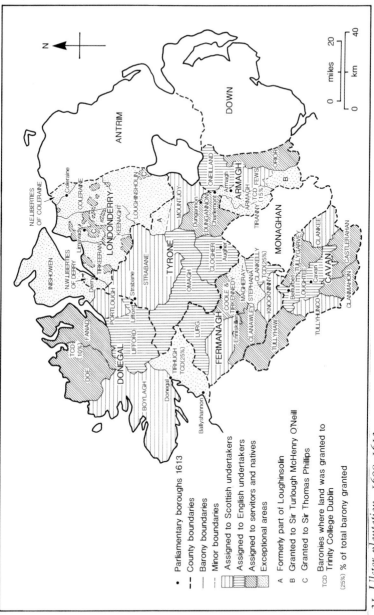

31 Ulster plantation, 1609–1613.

Parliamentary boroughs 1613
County boundaries
Barony boundaries
Minor boundaries

Assigned to Scottish undertakers
Assigned to English undertakers
Assigned to servitors and natives
Exceptional areas

A   Formerly part of Loughinsolin
B   Granted to Sir Turlough McHenry O'Neill
C   Granted to Sir Thomas Phillips
TCD   Baronies where land was granted to Trinity College Dublin
(25%)   % of total barony granted

ports of Bangor and Donaghadee increased their cattle exports almost tenfold. Ulster's exports consisted mostly of the traditional mainstays of the economy, grain, live cattle, and linen yarn. The trend of the early seventeenth century was to expand the already existing agricultural base with a dramatically increased labour force rather than to encourage the innovation of new products in any quantity.[6]

The increase in exports had also been prompted partly by improved marketing structures. Gradually, the Ulster economy moved away from a situation where surpluses were redistributed through payments in kind to local chiefs to a system by which surpluses were sold through markets and fairs, and cash came to play a much more important part in the economy. Over 150 markets and 85 fairs were licensed in the province between 1600 and 1640. Contacts with the wider markets were established with the growth of the port towns such as Belfast, Derry and Coleraine, and the establishment of rudimentary merchant communities there. We must not, however, overstress this early development as the great age of commercialization was still to come in the latter part of the century. Many of the early Ulster towns did not become market towns. Rather they fulfilled the role of suppliers of services to the surrounding countryside and were occupied by tradesmen such as tanners, carpenters and smiths. Moreover the rate at which the commercialized economy spread, as represented by the activities of towns, varied greatly in different regions and among various ethnic groups. By the 1660s the settlers, who were more used to the market economy than the native Irish, tended to live nearer than their native counterparts to the market towns.

The influx of new settlers in the early part of the seventeenth century prompted revolutionary changes in the nature of landholding, and the emergence of a new type of landlord which had significant social consequences for all groups within the province. With the exception of counties Antrim and Down, where the colonization was an informal one, the settlers had come to Ulster as part of a government-sponsored plantation scheme. Part of the object of the scheme was that the new settler landlords would act as agents of the crown in promoting the rule of law, and developing the economy so that Ireland could be governed without cost to the English crown. But the migrants that came to Ulster were not mere agents of the crown. They were also concerned with private gain, and soon found themselves caught between the two roles of 'civilizer' and 'profit-maker'. The result was that many settler landlords were more concerned with ensuring their own position than carrying out government instructions, and many of the regulations of the plantation were not adhered to. In Antrim and Down the situation was much the same but since they did not have formal rules for the settlement the breach of the spirit of the settlement did not appear as flagrant to the administration.

The arrival of a new type of landlord had important social repercussions. Older Gaelic concepts of the social hierarchy and the factors which positioned a man within it had to be abandoned in the face of tenurial change. A man's genealogy was no longer relevant as a measure of status when many new settlers had acquired positions of influence through the acquisition of cheap land, despite their lowly backgrounds. What now determined a man's status in Ulster was the size of his landholding and the tenure by which he held it. A tenant's status and economic position depended on his landlord and on the terms on which the landlord was prepared to let him occupy his holding. Such terms would be set out in a legally binding contract – a lease.

A landlord had to be able to attract reliable tenants to his estate in order to develop it, but on the other hand he also had to defend his tenants' rights. Thus landlord-tenant relations became a central question in the province, Much of the creative energy of the settlement of seventeenth-century Ulster went into trying to create structures within which landlord-tenant relations could be regulated satisfactorily. Scottish or English tenures could not be transferred without change to the Ulster environment, but were adapted for use in Ulster. The English-style copyhold tenure for lives was effectively turned into a perpetuity lease by making it renewable forever, allowing new lives to be inserted in the lease on the death of one of the previous lives. Where no such formal relationships existed a more informal one often obtained whereby the landlord offered the existing tenant first refusal, at the end of the term of a lease, for a number of years. This custom became known to late seventeenth-century commentators as 'tenant right'. The right of renewal was sometimes divorced from the lease itself and could be sold separately from the interest or unexpired term. Innovative developments such as these contributed to Ulster's distinctiveness by the end of the century.

II

While many of the innovations of seventeenth-century Ulster were radical departures from the sixteenth-century practice, some, at least, merely accelerated trends discernible by the end of the sixteenth century. Many of the chief Irish magnates were already in financial difficulties by the end of the century and were taking steps to try to improve their positions. Some were already selling land to English and Scottish settlers, particularly in counties Antrim and Down, which thus saw an influx of settlers although they were outside the area included in the formal plantation scheme for Ulster. In this way newcomers such as Sir Hugh Montgomery and Sir James Hamilton acquired extensive estates and began introducing settlers.

Not all of those who became new-style landlords in Ulster were outsiders. Some of the native Irish lords were equally opportunist in seeking to profit from the economic difficulties of their neighbours. For example the weakness of the native lords of north Antrim, the MacQuillans, enabled the MacDonnells, who had interests there which dated back to the fifteenth century, to expand. Other Gaelic lords were gradually recognizing the economic advantages of the English system of landlord-tenant relations and a commercial economy, and were attempting to develop their estates in that direction. Hugh O'Neill, Earl of Tyrone, viewed by

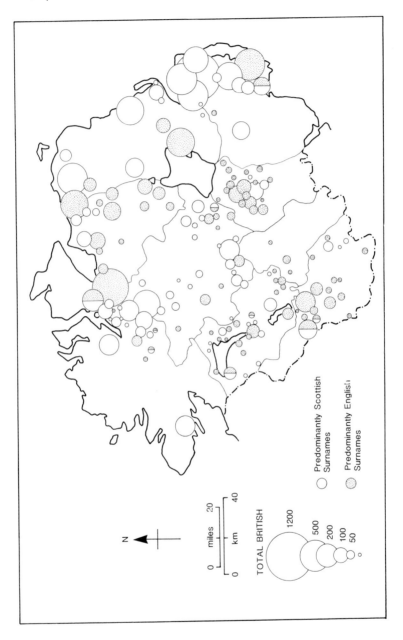

Predominantly Scottish
Surnames

Predominantly English
Surnames

N

miles

km

TOTAL BRITISH

1200

500

200

100

50

32 English and Scottish settlement in Ulster c. 1630.

some as the staunch defender of the old ways of Gaelic Ireland, was in fact attempting just such a transformation of his territory in the 1590s, but was meeting resistance from the sublords within his lordship.[7]

Change was already under way before the arrival of the large numbers of settlers who came to Ulster under the terms of the *Orders and Conditions of the Plantation of Ulster.* This situation may explain, in part, why so few of the Gaelic poets of Ulster, who can be regarded as spokesmen for the elite of Gaelic society, reacted strongly against the newcomers in the early seventeenth century. With the Gaelic lords in decline, and even in the aftermath of the upheaval of the flight of the earls, many poets castigated not the newcomers but rather the native lords themselves, whose vanity and excessive ambition they blamed for their downfall.

While those who departed for the continent had thereby abandoned the attempt to adjust to the new political, social, and economic circumstances which prevailed in the early seventeenth century, some of the literati themselves became part of the new order. Poets such as Lughaidh Ó Cléirigh and Eochaidh Ó hEodhasa accepted grants of land in the plantation scheme. Others, such as Fear Flatha Ó Gnímh retained their traditional role as poets but changed the traditional themes of their poetry to meet the new circumstances and the changed priorities of their new patrons.[8]

In some ways the collapse of the old order could be interpreted by these poets as part of the natural process within Gaelic society whereby one dynasty was ousted by a new and more powerful overlord. While some poets lamented the change, which meant a decline in their personal status, some others went as far as to welcome the head of the new order, James I, as the new high king. But while some poets continued to go about their professional task of legitimizing change by presenting it in traditional terms, there was at least one vital difference between the old dynasty and the new which could not be glossed over – the religious difference.

While the decline of the old Gaelic elite could be, and

indeed was, explained within traditional terms of reference as God's revenge on a proud people, it became increasingly evident over time that the Dublin government's persistent attempts to suppress Catholicism could not be similarly interpreted.[9] The close connection between the literary elite and the Catholic clergy may have heightened the awareness by the poets of the threat to Catholicism. What could not be glossed over by the poets as an acceptable change became a source of controversy, and this increased the likelihood of religion becoming an issue which divided native and newcomer. This does not mean that compromises could not be reached between Protestant and Catholic at local level. Indeed many such agreements were made on difficult issues such as mixed marriages and the baptism of children.

The discontent created by religious differences could probably have been contained, but when religious tensions were fuelled by other sources of discontent they became an explosive issue because religion came to be interpreted by many as a touchstone of loyalty. Such a situation arose in the early 1640s when the Catholic clergy in Ulster were intensifying their efforts and there was serious economic distress at the same time. A series of poor harvests in the previous two years, a downturn in trade and a food shortage made worse by the quartering of soldiers in Ulster all made for discontent in the province. This, combined with an unstable political environment caused by the legacy of Thomas Wentworth's viceroyalty, resulted in local frustrations boiling over in 1641 in what can best be described as a loyal rebellion. Initial conservative aims to put the leaders of the rising in a strong position for negotiating with the London administration were not achieved, and the rising became more radical and more widespread the longer it went on. Continental involvement with the arrival of Owen Roe O'Neill in July 1642 gave the rising new vigour, and the outbreak of civil war in England in August made it part of the war of the three kingdoms.[10]

War dragged on sporadically for ten years, with disastrous consequences for Ulster. Economic disruption was wide-spread, especially as a result of the need to support various armies in Ulster, and the main engine of economic growth in the early seventeenth century, population increase, failed with the mass exodus of settlers from Ulster. More than half of the original settlers fled back to their homes and even more were carried off by plague in the early 1650s. Landlords' estates were left untenanted, crops unharvested and rents unpaid. For those who remained, crippling Cromwellian taxation worsened the situation further. Viewed from the perspective of the early 1650s the outlook for the Ulster landlords was bleak.

III

From the middle of the 1650s the Ulster economy began to recover from the crisis of the 1640s. William King, later Archbishop of Dublin, recalling his youth noted that 'In the year 1658 the County of Tyrone was beginning to be cultivated after the war and my father removed there.' His reminiscences are confirmed by the contemporary comments of George Rawdon, the agent on the Conway estate around Lisburn, who noted people leaving Antrim and Down to settle in west Ulster. Landlords' rentals began to improve. The Brownlow estate in Armagh, for example, which had a rental of £728 in 1635, and had fallen to £437 in 1655, had recovered to £488 in 1659.

The 1650s were, however, a crucial decade for the development of Ulster. Although most Ulster landowners had remained royalist throughout the war, seeing the king as the best guarantee of the *status quo*, they were permitted to compound for their estates under the Cromwellian regime and so little Ulster land was confiscated for the payment of soldiers. The only large estate seized was that of the Catholic Earl of Antrim, who was regarded as being in collusion with the rebels, but even this confiscation was reversed under the Restoration land settlement. Despite this apparent continuity in ownership the fate of landlords under the Restoration was nonetheless very different from that under the early Stuarts. In the early years of the seventeenth century the influence of the Dublin administration in Ulster had been relatively weak. The ambition of the settler landowners had manifested itself in a desire to keep central government as far removed as possible from their newly acquired estates. In this way they could avoid royal taxation and unwelcome enquiries into the means by which they had acquired possession of their lands and how they had exploited them. The gentry of the late seventeenth century lacked the power their predecessors had enjoyed. Increasing indebtedness and the effectiveness with which the Cromwellian regime had imposed its authority on the localities meant that the great power blocks of landholders of the early seventeenth century were effectively broken.[11] Consequently, Ulster society moved towards a more 'English'-style community as the structure of the county emerged to replace those based on great power blocks of settler landlords. Furthermore the late seventeenth century saw the disappearance of many of the issues of contention between the centre and the localities, the most important being the quasi-feudal dues which had been demanded by early Stuart government.

The 1650s saw the resumption of migration by people from Scotland and England to Ulster to take advantage of low rents after the war. This migration continued for the rest of the century. Such movements of population were particularly significant in the 1670s when the Covenanter disturbances in Scotland encouraged migration to Ireland. Again in the 1690s harvest failures in Scotland were an important reason for increasing migration to Ulster. In northern England, tenurial innovations encouraged some to seek their fortunes in Ulster, where conditions seemed more attractive than at home. Perhaps the most significant group to become involved in the late seventeenth-century settlement in Ulster was the Quakers. Many Quakers left England in the aftermath of the Quaker Act of 1662 and the Conventicle Act of 1664 which punished them for their refusal to take oaths. Many went to Ulster because family relations or other Quakers were already established there, having acquired land through their involvement in the Cromwellian army or through the activities of the leader of the Quaker community in Ireland, William Edmundson.

Through this sustained immigration the population of Ulster rose even more dramatically in the later part of the seventeenth century than it had done earlier. In 1659, the Ulster population was probably no more than 250,000. By 1708 it stood at about 480,000. This represented an increase of 1·8 per cent per year, and was well above the normal range of pre-industrial population growth. This immigration continued into the beginning of the eighteenth century, although as time passed, and the population of Ulster rose, the opportunities of cheap land and rapid social advancement there decreased. By the 1680s the beginnings of emigration from Ulster to other areas, especially America, can be discerned as settlers began to look for new outlets for advancement. The eighteenth century was to see this trickle grow to a flood as conditions in Ulster became less attractive to the ambitious.

The distribution of the increased population of the late seventeenth century was, at best, uneven. As with the earlier settlements the greatest density of population tended to be nearest the ports of entry. For Counties Antrim and

33 House and fort at Omagh.

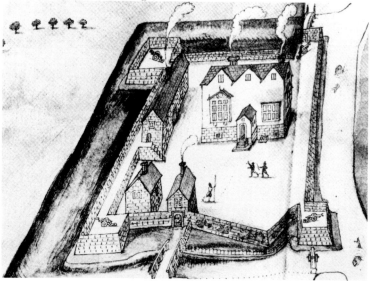

34 *A ferry carrying men and a horse across the Foyle at Derry.*

Down, Belfast was the main port of entry. Through Belfast came a large influx of settlers, mainly English, into the Lagan valley area. To judge from their surnames they had come mainly from northern England. Meanwhile Derry formed the main point of entry for the north west of the province with mainly Scottish settlers moving into east Donegal, north Tyrone, Co. Londonderry and north Antrim. The south and west of the province, relatively little settled in the early seventeenth century, were the last to be settled and consequently their labour supply, the main force for change, was lower and so that region tended to lag behind other areas in terms of economic development.

As in the earlier part of the century this growth in population brought about considerable economic change. However, the results were rather different from the earlier experience. While the earlier phase of economic activity had mainly expanded the output of the traditional economy, the later development saw much more change and diversification in the economy. One reason for this was that the external economic environment was different. The cattle acts of the 1660s had effectively killed the trade in live cattle and forced many of the Ulster inhabitants, like those of Munster, to move into processed cattle products, such as butter, barrelled beef and hides. Unlike Munster, which traded mainly with the colonies of the New World, the Ulster market was on the Continent, especially in France. This growth in trade with a wider world was accelerated by the establishment of stable merchant communities, mainly Scottish, in the ports of Belfast and Derry. Merchants, such as George MacCartney in Belfast, were attracted to Ulster in the 1650s by the need to supply the army. Later, in the 1690s, others arrived for the same reason. Seeing that there were ongoing opportunities for profit, many remained.

A second factor differentiating the later part of the century from earlier developments was the speed of population growth from a higher base. A higher population meant that there were more people who had to realize sufficient surpluses from their farming not only to survive but also to pay their rent. There were other external factors also which had a direct economic impact. Trade with continental Europe was notoriously unstable, being affected by war and rumour of war. Production was also hindered by adverse climatic conditions. Whereas between 1603 and 1641 only three major periods of harvest crisis can be identified (1603–4, 1629–31, and 1640–1) at least six such periods of failure can be identified in the 30 years between 1660 and 1690.

The implications of such economic crises could be serious in certain circumstances. Rather than being merely a temporary economic setback, the difficult years of 1687 and 1688 provided the backdrop for a political and religious crisis: the attempt of the new king, James II, and his Irish Lord Deputy, Tyrconnell, to undermine the emerging Protestant ascendancy in Ireland. The matter came to a head on 7 December 1688 when the gates of Derry were closed against the Catholic Earl of Antrim's regiment. A few days later, on 23 December 1688, James II fled for France, and Ulster and Ireland became drawn into a wider crisis over the kingship which stretched into 1691. The war in Ulster was sporadic, being concentrated in three areas. Trouble at Derry lasted into July 1689 when the siege was finally relieved. In the south-west of the province the Enniskillen force held out against Justin MacCarthy, inflicting a significant defeat in July 1689. In the east of the province the arrival of Marshal Schomberg at Bangor in August 1689 paved the way for William III's landing at Carrickfergus on 14 June 1690. William's march south to the Boyne drew much of the military action away from Ulster and this enabled the recovery from the effects of war to begin there sooner than in other parts of the country, where war continued late into 1691.

Not all years of economic crisis coincided with political instability, but all produced problems for landlord and tenant at local level. In times of economic crisis many

35 Castlecaulfield, built by Sir Toby Caulfield in the early seventeenth century.

landlords found it to be in their own best interest to assist tenants on their estates to ensure they had a surplus to pay rent even in the worst years. Some landlords encouraged the production of cider and at Lisburn, ironworks, soap works and potash making were started. One of the most important of these initiatives by landlords was the development of the linen industry as a domestic industry. While the production of linen yarn had always been important in Ulster, and the production of narrow bandle linen (in pieces approximately 12–15 in. (30.5–38 cm.) wide) was also practised, the production of fine linens which emerged in Antrim and Armagh was a new development. In one case, at Lurgan, the local landlord, Arthur Brownlow, encouraged the production of linen by providing a guaranteed market. He bought up all the linen brought to market by his tenants, and resold it later to merchants, making a considerable profit.[12]

This diversification of the economy, especially in the east of the province, emphasized the need for improved marketing structures since profits could only be made if the produce could be sold to a wider market. As a result, towns such as Lisburn grew in importance and their market places were repeatedly expanded and enlarged throughout the century. Shops selling luxury goods also became more prominent, especially in the smaller towns. Port towns, but especially Belfast, grew rapidly as a result of the increased economic activity so that by the end of the century some contemporaries regarded Belfast as the second largest port in the kingdom after Dublin. Such a view was not correct, but their perception illustrates the impact which the rapid growth of Ulster towns, relative to other areas, had on the contemporary mind. More importantly these towns began to form a network of trading centres which rapidly became interdependent. The growth of Lisburn, for example, was dependent on the growth of Belfast since Lisburn acted as an inland centre for the Belfast merchants to which produce from their agents in the smaller inland towns could be brought.

Much of this activity was the result of co-operation

between local landlords and the merchant communities of the port towns. In some areas of the province, especially the south and west, economic progress was hampered where one or other element in the equation was lacking. The lack of substantial port towns and a settled merchant community meant that marketing structures in the south and west were still little developed at the beginning of the eighteenth century. The importance of merchants was underlined by the experience of a Donegal settler, Henry Cunningham, who tried to fulfil the role played by landlords elsewhere by buying up cattle and butter locally, with the intention of acting as mediator between his tenants and the merchants. However, he could not find any merchant to sell to locally and was forced to ship the goods to Dublin at his own expense, losing heavily in the process. It is apparent, therefore, that the economy of Ulster was not uniform but varied considerably from region to region. It was not merely the presence of settlers which automatically encouraged economic development. The dynamic of economic change was more complex than that. What was clear by the end of the seventeenth century, however, was that Ulster had indeed developed a distinctive regional economic structure with a number of sub-regions, such as the Lagan valley, the relatively underdeveloped south-west region, and Derry city and its Foyle valley hinterland. The eighteenth century was to see the consolidation of this economic process as some of the seventeenth-century developments, such as the weaving of fine linens, were further exploited.

IV

By the late nineteenth century the distinctiveness of Ulster as a region within Ireland had acquired a particular political significance in addition to its economic, social and cultural characteristics. It became necessary to explain why the province was Protestant, politically loyal to the crown, and economically prosperous. The solution adopted by ninteenth-century historians and commentators was to explain these features as being the result of the Ulster plantation of the early seventeenth century which had brought Scots Presbyterians imbued with a Calvinist work ethic to Ulster, creating a haven of civility which marked it off from the rest of the country. The denial of episcopacy and the assertion of the importance of conscience, it was argued, along with the democratic rule of the kirk session, gave them an independence and stoicism lacking in the rest of Ireland. As W.D. Killen, the historian of Irish Presbyterianism, wrote of the settlers in 1867, 'their settlement in Ulster, where they constitute the large majority of the population, has rendered that province so remarkable a contrast in point of wealth, intelligence and tranquility, to the other parts of Ireland.' This picture of the early settlement which such commentators painted was heavily coloured by hindsight. The cohesion and distinctiveness which they saw had never really existed within the early settlement.

A case in point is the supposed dominance of the Scots in the settlement. It cannot be denied that Scots migrants played a major role in the settlement of Ulster, but their dominance was only achieved over a long period. The evidence of the surnames on the muster roll of *c.* 1630 suggests that Scots outnumbered English by about 1.4 to 1, but by the early eighteenth century that balance was closer to 2 to 1. This decisive increase in the proportion of Scots in the Ulster population, especially following the new influx of migrants in the 1690s, was noticed by a number of contemporaries. The anonymous author of the Jacobite tract, *A Light to the Blind, c.* 1711, observed of Ulster landlords that

> their tenants for the most part were Roman Catholics until after the battle of the Boyne in the year 1690 when the Scottish men came over into the north with their families and effects and settled there, so that they are now at this present the greater proportion of the inhabitants of Ulster.[13]

If anything, most contemporaries tended to overestimate the numbers of Presbyterian Scots in Ulster. In 1660, for instance, one commentator estimated that in Ulster there were 5,000 English, 40,000 Irish and 80,000 Scots, which represents a gross distortion of the real situation in which the native Irish were numerically superior.[14] This over-estimation of the numbers of Scots arose, in the main, because of fears of their religion: Presbyterianism. By the late seventeenth century Presbyterianism had become the main divisive force in Ulster society. This was partly because of its dominance within the Protestant population. By the beginning of the eighteenth century, Ulster was the only Irish province where Protestants outnumbered Catholics by three to two, and the majority of the Ulster Protestants were Presbyterian. They posed a greater threat because they possessed an organization through the synod of Ulster, the presbytery and the kirk session which could rival that of the established church, and the Presbyterians themselves claimed to be the 'church of Ireland'. Their organization was a powerful instrument of control, being drawn from the community rather than being imposed from without. By contrast, within the Catholic community, the Counter-Reformation was in retreat in late seventeenth-century Ulster. The number of Catholic clergy was falling and apart from a short period during the episcopate of Oliver Plunkett, there were relatively few ordinations to the Catholic priesthood. The quality of the Catholic clergy also left much to be desired, and some late seventeenth-century texts, such as *Comhairle Commissarum na Cléire* ['The Advice of the Commissars of Clare'] and *Comhairle Mhic Chlamhe Ó Achadh na Muillean* ['The Advice of Mac Clare from Aughnamullen'] reveal a growing discontentment among the laity with the quality of the clergy. By 1704, the Catholic clergy of Ulster were on average older than in other parts of the country, fewer on the ground, and less likely to have received a continental education.[15]

However, Presbyterians as a subversive body were more difficult than Catholics to deal with. In the eyes of the Dublin administration Catholics were demonstrably disloyal because of their allegiance to the papacy and their record of disloyalty to the king, which was openly revealed in the rebellions of 1641 and 1689. The Presbyterian case was less clear cut. They were, after all, Protestant, and gave allegiance to no other temporal power besides the King. Furthermore, the Restoration government, after 1660, was too narrowly based to ignore a substantial Protestant group in what was a strategically important part of Ireland. As a result, government policy towards the Ulster Presbyterians tended to fluctuate wildly. In 1672 tacit recognition was given to the Presbyterian church by the payment, admittedly initially in secret but later made public, of a *regium donum* or royal bounty to the clergy. However, both the threat and actuality of persecution were rarely far away. As Viscount Mountjoy wrote from Newtownstewart in Tyrone to the Duke of Ormond in 1683 'they [the Presbyterians] complain much to one another of the great persecutions their brethren in Scotland are under and seem to apprehend the like here which makes them talk much of going in great numbers to Carolina.'[16]

Just as the nineteenth-century commentators gave great weight to the numbers and influence of the Scots Presbyterians in the settlement of Ulster, so too they tended to misunderstand the nature of seventeenth-century Ulster Presbyterianism. They assumed the church organization of their own day extended back unbroken into the early seventeenth century. This was not the case. In the years before the 1640s such a structure did not exist. The colonial experience of Ulster in the early seventeenth century meant that accommodations and compromises had been made on liturgical and theological matters and points of church government between the Calvinist Church of Ireland, which was short of clergy, and the Presbyterian church. The differences were often seen as of minor significance and Calvinist Church of Ireland clergy, such as Archbishop Ussher, had little difficulty in appointing them to the Church of Ireland, turning a blind eye to their method of ordination and induction. There was, however, a more radical wing of Presbyterianism championed in the early seventeenth century by men such as Robert Blair, the minister at Bangor, who was not only a rigid Calvinist but also a strong supporter of Presbyterian church government.

The move towards a more Arminian theology, and greater efforts to make the Church of Ireland effectively the only church in the country in the 1630s, united the two groups within Presbyterianism.

The 1640s brought the radicals to the fore with the arrival from Scotland of an army sent to crush the Irish who had rebelled in October 1641. With the army came covenanting chaplains, such as Patrick Adair, who played an important part in establishing a rigid system of Presbyterian church government, beginning with the first presbytery at Carrickfergus in 1643. Not surprisingly splits began to appear in the Presbyterian ranks as moderates, such as the third Viscount Ards, defected to the Church of Ireland. With the arrival of Henry Cromwell as lord deputy in the 1650s a policy of conciliation toward the more moderate Ulster Presbyterians emerged.

The latter half of the century saw the development of a more Presbyterian structure with session, presbytery and later synod, such as would have been recognizable to nineteenth-century commentators. It was, however, by no means certain in 1660 that this structure would triumph over a Calvinist form of congregationalism, given that local churches were often unwilling to surrender their power to a wider structure.[17]

The development of Ulster Presbyterianism in the seventeenth century was a complex phenomenon, and cannot be used as a simplistic explanation for how Ulster society developed over the century following the start of the Ulster plantation. For a full understanding of the evolution of the society we must look far beyond the mere infuence of diverse religious groupings. Likewise we must look further than the ethnic origins or allegiances of Gaelic, Scottish or English groups in seventeenth-century Ulster society. The history of the development of the province transcends these individual elements. Both the forces making for continuity and the economic, social, and political dynamics of change must simultaneously be taken into account. The Ulster plantation of the early seventeenth century and the later migration of settlers were certainly not the only influences on the development of a distinctive Ulster society in the seventeenth century.

V

The distinctiveness of Ulster's non-settler society at the end of the century was due to a combination of the survival of some elements of the old Gaelic order and the transformation of others. According to Archbishop Oliver Plunkett in the 1670s, the native Ulstermen, though tenants to new landlords, continued to recognize their old lords and to contribute to their upkeep, the native Irish having 'great affection' for the old families.[18] Traditional social and cultural practices also persisted in that certain functions continued to be assigned to particular families in semi-hereditary fashion. The Catholic clergy continued to be drawn from certain families and attempts by the church to interfere with such arrangements were resisted. An attempt to appoint a Westmeath man, Dr Tyrell, to the see of Clogher, for example, brought strong protest from both local clergy and laity.[19] The continuity of tradition had important social consequences within native society.

But there were also dramatic changes within native Irish society in Ulster during the century. For example, the English language gradually replaced Irish as the predominant language of Ulster. Yet the dialect evidence indicates that the English spoken in Ulster continued to be heavily influenced by Irish language words and phrases. In the field of literature the traditional bardic verse did not survive the disappearance of its traditional sources of patronage but new styles of poetry came to the fore in its place. A geographical adjustment also occurred in that the centre of literary activity moved from its sixteenth-century focal point in the west of the province to a new location in the south-east during the course of the seventeenth century. An interesting combination of ideas and values from both native and newcomer was clearly revealed in the native literary tradition by the end of the seventeenth century. Thus, for example, Brian Maguire, one of the most important patrons of scribal activity in Ulster in the first decades of the eighteenth century, was described in traditional Gaelic terms by one of those scribes as being hospitable to poets, musicians, the religious orders and the poor, while it was noted also that he supported this scribal activity 'for the benefit of the county'. The values of the preservers of the Gaelic literary tradition had merged with the settler values of the county community.[20]

Cultural change was paralleled by economic change. William Brooke commented of the barony of Oneilland in north Armagh in the 1680s that the Irish 'we have amongst us are very much reclaimed of their barbarous customs, the most of them speaking English and for agriculture they are little inferior to the English themselves.'[21] Such an observation demonstrates the degree of assimilation which had taken place between native and newcomer in matters such as tenurial customs and agricultural practices. The assimilations in this area were not all one-way since the settlers adopted at least some of the agricultural practices of the natives, such as ploughing by tail, because they were well suited to the Ulster landscape.

Such adaptations varied over space and time and were, of course, not exclusive to the native Irish population. The experience of the Gaelic Irish community during the seventeenth century, of retaining some older cultural features while evolving new ones, in response to new social, economic and political pressures, was shared by the settlers who came to Ulster. By the end of the century there were few settler families in Ulster which had not become integrated into their new society through an extensive network of intermarriage. Arthur Brownlow, the late seventeenth-century descendant of a settler of English origin who held estates in the Lurgan area of north Armagh, is a good example. His grandfather was from Nottingham, his grandmother was native Irish, and his father was an Old Englishman from north Louth. Two of his three stepfathers were New English. Of his uncles, two were Old English and one New English, and he himself was married to the daughter of a Dublin official. Of his uncles, one had supported Cromwell and the other two were on the side of Ormond. Thus, within one family was contained almost the entire experience of seventeenth-century Ulster. Many settler families in Ulster had also become office holders with the Dublin administration, as privy councillors, members of parliament or at a more lowly level as county sheriffs or justices of the peace. They were no longer mere settlers or newcomers, but had attained positions of standing within society.

Among the settlers other factors also forced their increased identification with Ulster. Financial difficulties stemming from the crisis of the 1640s and the heavy taxation of the 1650s forced families to sell large amounts of land. This meant that they had to choose whether to sell their Ulster land or land they had previously held elsewhere in England or Scotland. Some, such as the Trevor family, took the first option and sold their Ulster land. Others made the second choice and so their economic and social base became totally concentrated in their Ulster properties. Gradually in this way settler families came to identify more and more with the province.

Family and local histories came to be written, emphasizing the distinctiveness of the Ulster branches of their families. The histories of the Montgomery and Hamilton families are the best examples of this development. Other Ulster settlers such as Arthur Brownlow began to take an interest in the history, geography and geology of the Ulster landscape and Ulstermen were prominent in the establishment of the Dublin Philosophical Society. Others took an interest in local music and customs and many of the patrons of the Irish harper, Turlough O'Carolan, were the settler families of the province.[22]

Perhaps the clearest indication of this trend of assimilation is to be found in the admission registers of the University of Glasgow. In the early seventeenth century the sons of Scottish settlers in Ireland attending Glasgow University had no nationality ascribed to them in the registers, as was the practice with Scots attending the University. From the 1660s, however, they tended to be described as 'Scoto-

Hibernicus' and their New English counterparts as 'Anglo-Hibernicus'.[23] It had become clear to the authorities at Glasgow that the Ulster settlers had lost at least part of their original identity and had acquired a new one. Both Scottish and English migrants to Ulster had adjusted to altered circumstances as they arrived in what one settler described as 'this our new land'. They did not simply transfer Scottish and English customs and beliefs without change to their new Irish home. Rather they modified their mode of living to suit their new environment. The older inhabitants of Ulster had likewise adapted to the changing environment of the late seventeenth century. As we have seen at the outset, George Storey could recount first hand evidence that the various religious groups in Ulster preferred to live among each other within that province than to live elsewhere.

In the remaining provinces of Ireland alternative accommodations had been made between groups which allowed for the different balance between native and newcomer, and the varied pace of economic, social and cultural change. Within Ulster, as elsewhere, it was the mixture of old and new within each group and the accommodations they had reached with each other which gave the province the distinctive character which was later to be noted by many of the eighteenth-century travellers who ventured there.

Further reading

The history of early seventeenth century Ulster, especially that of the plantation, is ground well worked by historians. Philip Robinson's *The Plantation of Ulster*, Dublin, 1984 is essential reading for anyone interested in the early seventeenth century. For the two non-escheated counties of Antrim and Down there is Raymond Gillespie, *Colonial Ulster*, Cork, 1985. A specialized but important book is Michael Perceval-Maxwell, *The Scottish Migration to Ulster in the Reign of James I*, London, 1975, and the Londonderry settlement is dealt with in T.W. Moody, *The Londonderry Plantation*, Belfast, 1939. There is almost no work on the English settlement, the exception being R.J. Hunter,

'English undertakers in the plantation of Ulster', *Breifne*, iv, 1973–5, pp. 471–500. None of these works replaces George Hill's *Plantation of Ulster*, Belfast, 1877 as a source of local material and a detailed account of the plantation scheme. The 1640s have been dealt with from a military point of view in David Stevenson, *Scottish Covenanters and Irish Confederates*, Belfast, 1981 but there is, as yet, nothing published on the social and economic developments of the mid-seventeenth century. An important essay for the late seventeenth century is W. Macafee and V. Morgan, 'Population in Ulster, 1660–1760', in Peter Roebuck (ed.), *Plantation to Partition*, Belfast, 1981, pp. 46–63. Also important is J.C. Beckett, 'Irish–Scottish relations in the seventeenth century' in his *Confrontations: Studies in Irish History*, London, 1972, pp. 26–46.

A number of special themes have been investigated in detail. Towns are dealt with by R.J. Hunter, 'Ulster plantation towns, 1609–41', in D.W. Harkness and M. O'Dowd (eds.), *The town in Ireland*, Historical Studies, 13, Belfast, 1981, pp. 55–80; Raymond Gillespie, 'The evolution of an Ulster urban network, 1600–41', *Irish Historical Studies*, 24, 1984–5, pp. 15–29. The standard work on Irish Presbyterianism is still J.S. Reid, *History of the Presbyterian Church in Ireland*, 3 vols., Belfast, 1867. A good modern introduction is R.F.G. Holmes, *Our Irish Presbyterian Heritage*, Belfast, 1985. The Reformation to about 1630 is dealt with by Alan Ford, *The Protestant Reformation in Ireland, 1590–1641*, Frankfurt, 1985, ch. 7. For the strange career of one bishop see Raymond Gillespie, 'The trials of Bishop Spottiswood, 1620–1640', *Clogher Record*, 12, 1987. The Counter Reformation in Ulster has not been investigated in any detail. Likewise, there is no comprehensive study of the fate of the native Irish and their reaction to the plantation but one revealing case study is presented in Raymond Gillespie, *Conspiracy: Ulster Plots and Plotters in 1615*, Belfast, 1987.

5 The political economy of linen: Ulster in the eighteenth century

W.H. Crawford

Ulster, the most northerly province of Ireland, is sur-
rounded on three sides by sea and separated from Scotland
by only some 20 miles. Half of its surface lies more than
three hundred feet above sea level while there are also
extensive lakelands and bog. Little of the land is naturally
fertile. Yet during the eighteenth century much land was
reclaimed and brought under cultivation by an increasing
population, and pasture gave way to tillage. By 1800, Ulster
was the most densely peopled of the four provinces of
Ireland so that its population of two million in 1821 almost
equalled that of the whole of Scotland. Contemporaries
believed that Ulster had also become the most prosperous
province. So much economic expansion could not have
been achieved by agricultural improvements alone, in spite
of a major transfer from pasture to tillage. The real
responsibility lay with the success of a single industry, the
domestic linen industry. Its very prosperity had far-reaching .
consequences for the future of the province. It created a
merchant class and financed industrial development. It was
responsible for the initial creation and subsequent development of many market towns. Throughout the countryside
the fact that the industry depended on yarn handspun from
flax cultivated by local people, disseminated cash right
down to the bottom of the socal structure so that even small
farmers could rely on a supplementary source of income to
maintain the viability of their holdings: this was to prove a
not unmixed blessing to Ulster society. Yet the relative
prosperity of the poorer classes in Ulster was evident to
every traveller.

36 Brown linen market at Banbridge.

I

In 1700 Ireland exported one million yards of cloth, and by 1800 the figure was 40 million yards (36.6 million metres), in addition to supplying an expanding home market. Why was the linen industry so successful in Ulster in 1800? Much of the answer lies in the timing of the industry's development in Ulster on commercial lines. Whereas Irish society outside Ulster evolved along traditional lines so that local craftsmen could continue to meet the demand for textiles in Ireland, Ulster society was unstable and disorganized but enterprising and ready to experiment. The sudden influx of population into Ulster in the second half of the seventeenth century had compelled the immigrants to engage in a variety of occupations to earn their living. Their landlords had encouraged such enterprise in the hope of securing their rents. The new linen industry developed on the basis of local production of linen yarn that had been exported to Lancashire for very many years, and from the arrival among the immigrants of weavers experienced in producing for the commercial market. The new industry appeared at a time

37 Hillmount bleach green.

when the demand for cheap textiles was growing fast in Britain.[1] Dublin merchants, in their search for goods to sell, provided capital and skill to promote Ulster linens until the Ulstermen were able in the long run to make their own capital and business contacts.

When the industry needed to expand production, especially in the 1730s and 1740s, it was able to obtain extra supplies of yarn from counties such as Roscommon and Sligo. Its own entrepreneurs adapted the technology of woollen tuck mills to mechanize the mills on their bleachgreens with rubbing boards, wash mills and beetling engines all driven by waterpower: their technology was introduced to Scotland in the mid-1730s.[2] In the second half of the century the finishers of the linens were quick to adopt new bleaching materials and methods so that the output of a major bleachgreen was increased by a factor up to ten.[3] Through-out Ulster many landlords organized their market towns to attract both drapers and weavers. As demand increased throughout the century the industry expanded in its search for weavers as far as Co. Mayo. Farmers took up weaving in their spare time while the women of the family spun the yarn; farmers also employed journeymen to weave for them by providing them with the necessities of life. Agriculture became an adjunct of the domestic linen industry.

It is difficult to conceive what eighteenth-century Ulster would have been like without the linen industry. Much of the province was still in its primeval state, mountain or bog, while the climate, especially in the west, could rarely ripen crops like wheat, peas and beans. It would have been able to support an increasing population at no more than bare subsistence level, vulnerable to years of shortage. The first half of the eighteenth century reads like a catalogue of woe with tales of famine and food shortage and epidemics among both men and cattle: fear of the future and resentment against rents and tithes too high to be paid from farming, drove many to listen to tales of a promised land across the Atlantic and induced some to uproot themselves. A pamphleteer in 1740, writing on the eve of the worst decade in the century, recorded:

> ... But the scarcity of bread (especially in the North) by the badness of the seasons and crops for several years past, and the loss in two years, viz '28 and '33 by shaking winds has reduced the case of multitudes very mournful before the present year, and contributed much of the distress in it. Nay, for above a dozen years past, we could scarcely be said to have plenty ... [4]

In contrast to this pessimism was the optimism displayed by contemporary commentators about the districts where the linen industry was flourishing. One pamphleteer in 1732 reckoned that 'the lands of Ulster, though naturally very coarse and for the most part the worst in the kingdom, yet by help of this manufacture are come to be valued almost equal with the best.'[5] Walter Harris, in *The Antient* (sic) *and Present State of the County of Down* (1744), a volume designed to be the model for a series on all the Irish counties, decided 'the staple commodity of the country is linen, a due care of which manufacture has brought great wealth among the people. The Northern inhabitants already feel the benefit of it, and are freed from much of that poverty and wretchedness too visible among the lower class of people in other parts of the Kingdom, where this valuable branch of trade has not been improved to advantage.'[6]

In the early years of the industry weavers had prospered under the patronage of landlords: most of them were craftsmen weaving finer linens and living in those towns and villages that administered and serviced the compact estates created by the plantation scheme. Because the structure of linen marketing was primitive in the early years of the eighteenth century many weavers' families supplemented their incomes from farming and their success attracted farmers to weaving to improve their economic status. Landlords were anxious to accommodate these weavers on their estates by offering them long leases of smallholdings convenient to the major market towns. In 1739 a commentator had remarked on 'the happy success which this method of dividing the land into small partitions and encouraging the cottager and the manufacturer has had in enriching both landlords and tenant'.[7] On the expiry of

38 Derrymore House, a late eighteenth-century thatched house, built by Isaac Corry, MP for Newry.

leases of lands held by middlemen or by substantial farmers
who had profited by subletting their lands to weavers,
landlords in the major linen-weaving districts seized the
initiative by leasing farms directly to these weavers who
occupied the land. The result was that by the closing decade
of the eighteenth century on several estates in the 'linen
triangle' (the district lying between Belfast, Dungannon and
Newry that specialized in the weaving of fine linens)
thousands of weaver/farmers leased land directly from the
owners of the estates. Leases to Protestants lasted for three
lives while those for Catholics ran for 31 years; although
this distinction did not disappear until the 1793 Catholic
Relief Act, it had never been of much significance because
landlords readily renewed leases to such weavers on the
termination of the leases.[8]

II

The security of tenure that these weavers enjoyed was
coveted by many occupiers of land in other parts of the
province but their hopes were often disappointed. Outside
the linen triangle earnings from the coarser linens were
lower so that landlords were not tempted quite so much to
take weavers on as direct tenants instead of leaving them
as subtenants to the farmers. Even landlords who tried to
obtain security of tenure for subtenants were outmanoeuvred
by the tenants. On the Abercorn estate in north-west
Ulster, for example, the landlord in 1771 instructed his
agent to pressure the tenants into giving subtenants a form
of lease that might be renewed to them directly when the
main lease expired. The agent reported later the same year
after only one success:

> It is plain by all their agreements that they guard against that,
> for they set five or six years short of the tenure they have.
> Besides they bind them under a penalty, and sometimes by
> oath, to give up peaceably when their term is expired and that
> they are not to petition or otherwise apply for any tenant right.
> Was I to lean to either side it would be to that of the under
> tenant who generally labours with great industry, and pays

exorbitantly for his earnings and improves much more land I
am sure than the immediate tenant, and if he was found on the
land at the end of the lease I would wish him to be continued.
But if he bargains and obliges himself to give it up, I think his
pretension [i.e. claim] is the less. The case of such is certainly
hard; they must, if not by the merest chance they become
tenants themselves, go on with much hardship and lose the
fruits of their labour ... [9]

During an economic depression two years later the same
agent was forced to report that tenants were more reliable in
paying rents than the subtenants. In the long term the
tenants solved the problem in their own favour by refusing
to grant subleases, while permitting their undertenants to
remain. This solution amounted to the creation of a specific
'cottier' status where the undertenant obtained, in return for
his labour, no more than a yearly occupancy of a 'dry cot-
take' on which crops, especially potatoes and perhaps flax,
were planted, or a 'wet cot-take' which included also
feeding for a cow or two. He was to have no security of
tenure against the very tenant farmer who insisted on his
claim to tenant right against his landlord.

It was the struggle for holdings that was responsible for
both subletting and subdivision. In a rural society characterized by family farms, subdivision was the commonest
strategy for transmitting property to posterity. In certain
sections of the Ulster community partible inheritance was
practised among the males of a family while in others all the
children shared in their father's property. It was the
involvement of all the members of a family in different
processes in the domestic linen industry that encouraged
families to hold together into adulthood: then all the
individuals had to be provided with portions. Subdivision
of a farm by successive generations would soon have
reduced the family group to beggary if participation in the
domestic linen industry had not provided a supplementary
source of income. It is likely therefore that subdivision was
both a consequence of the prosperity of the linen industry
and a pressure on individuals to take up spinning or
weaving to make ends meet. Dependence on the domestic

39 Spinning and reeling linen yarn, 1783.

linen industry to maintain such tiny farms was dangerous for the future of the society because any reversal of the process was bound to be painful. Emigration to the American colonies provided a potential safety valve, but until the later decades of the century it attracted mainly single men rather than families.[10]

A related phenomenon was the colonization of the marginal lands. This provided an opportunity to land-hungry families to carve out holdings for themselves instead of remaining undertenants. Estate rentals and leasebooks indicate that rents of marginal land began to rise from a very low base only after 1750 when arable land was becoming scarce. Attention to the potential of the more sparsely populated districts had been drawn by the new technology of the bleaching industry based on the use of water to power wash-mills and beetling-mills. In search of water supplies men moved into the marginal lands. This was especially true of the Callan valley south of Armagh city. According to a document dated 1795,

the manufacture gaining strength, about fifty years ago they began to push their improvements into the mountains which separate the low country from Louth, and by the assistance of turf fuel being convenient, and good constant rivers for feeding bleachyards and working machinery, they were enabled to extend their improvements into the mountains. And many wealthy farmers and manufacturers were induced by the low price of them – about a shilling to half a crown an acre – to take farms, lime and burn them although the limestone quarries were distant from the centre of the mountains, measuring from the quarries at Armagh or those on the Louth side towards Dundalk, at least eight or nine miles either way ... [11]

The successful colonization of the marginal lands in south Armagh encouraged families elsewhere to move to the uplands so that new townlands were marked out on the mountainside, divided among tenants, and converted into farms by hard labour.[12] The crop that made feasible the cultivation of marginal land was the potato. Whereas land for grain, crops and flax had to be well prepared, rough 'scraw' or top sods could be levered up and turned over with the native 'loy' into 'lazy beds' resembling broad drills. The potato not only produced a better crop than grain on poor land but it also broke up lea ground and cleansed it of weeds. The other attraction of marginal land was an unlimited supply of turf to provide cheap fuel. As land became more scarce and expensive in the lowlands more of the poorer people migrated to the mountain valleys and the shores and islands of the loughs and converted them into the farmsteads seen across much of Ulster today.

Capital for the development of marginal land came from the linen industry in the form of increasing demand for food and linen yarn for the linen triangle. As early as the 1720s northerners were buying yarn in Co. Sligo and it was recorded that 'about the year 1735 the inhabitants of the North growing too numerous for its produce, in their visits for yarn bought wool in this country, soon after beef and mutton, and corn was sometimes exported from Sligo.'[13] By 1770 Sligo was part of the Ulster economy and many Ulster people had moved there in search of land. An agricultural revolution from pasture to tillage was recorded for Co. Monaghan in 1739 so that it was supplying 'some of the neighbouring counties with bere [cereal resembling barley], barley, and oatmeal.'[14] Later in the century it was said that absentee landlords from Connacht found that their rent remittances were sent to them in bills of exchange drawn on London merchants by Ulster linendrapers and used by them to purchase ponies from Connacht for their businesses.[15] Oatmeal was transported to Ulster from many other parts of Ireland: during periods of scarcity this led to local outcries.[16]

III

The tremendous explosion in the population of Ulster was in its relatively early stages when a census was taken for the Irish House of Lords in the mid-1760s as part of an inquiry 'into the state of Popery' in Ireland.[17] The project was entrusted to the local gaugers, or excise men, in 1764 but the results seemed so defective that it was given in 1766 to the clergy of the Church of Ireland. However defective these returns may be, they do distinguish between Protestants and Catholics. They can be used to map both population density and religious affiliation throughout the province.

To focus attention on the practical implications of population density it is more effective to measure not the number of people per square mile but the number of acres of land per family. This reveals that as early as 1766 the size of family farms in the whole mid-Ulster region and in much of the Foyle basin was already less than 30 acres (c. 12 hectares) and in a few parishes was smaller than 12 acres (4.9 ha.). At this time, therefore, there still existed a balance between the linen manufacture and agriculture since 30 acres of land could provide a decent living by contemporary standards, farmed by traditional methods. An increasing population after this date was compelled to turn to the linen industry to supplement its income. The marginal lands – mountains and bogs – are clearly distinguished: in the west, Donegal, and in the north-east, the Antrim plateau; the Sperrins running south through the centre of the province to Monaghan; and the heavy soils of Fermanagh and Cavan.

40 High Street, Belfast, 1786.

Cavan was to become much more densely populated, with hosts of cottiers working and weaving for the weaver/ farmers: it became part of the linen country. Fermanagh, on the other hand, never became a significant weaving county although it produced much yarn for weavers elsewhere. Notable at this time was the relatively low population of west Donegal, especially in comparison with the eastern side of Inishowen whose economy was linked with that of north Londonderry and Antrim around the ferry at Magilligan, for sales of both yarn and barley. The major problem for those colonizing the mountains was that they could not share in the prosperity of the linen industry because they could not produce crops of quality flax on their poor lands. They were forced to concentrate on rearing young stock to sell to the lowlanders and their major cash crop became barley that was always in demand by distillers.[18]

   One of the most important factors in opening up the marginal lands for colonization was the development of communications. Even in the first half of the eigheenth century Ulster benefited from two major projects. The most spectacular and one of the earliest feats of its kind was the construction of the Newry Navigation linking Lough Neagh with the sea at Newry by 1742. Although Parliament was disappointed in its intention that the canal would provide cheap Irish coal for Dublin, mid-Ulster was opened up to the influence of Dublin while the canal saved many thousand lives by enabling great quantities of grain to be carried into the heart of the province during the hungry Forties.[19] About this time too the linen country benefited from the construction of many miles of turnpike roads under the sponsorship of the local landlords.[20] These roads were essential to cope with the traffic generated by the linen industry but until the 1765 Road Act permitted grand juries to tax the occupiers of land to provide for the construction of roads and bridges, county funds could not meet the challenge. The 1765 Act itself was the government response to the Hearts of Oak agitation against the earlier system that had required every landholding to supply six days of free labour to mend the roads in each parish. Yet so radical and far-reaching was the 1765 act in its implications for society that it encountered severe opposition, culminating in the Hearts of Steel agitation in the early 1770s. In essence, it placed responsibility for the construction and maintenance of major roads and bridges on the county grand juries and provided capital from a county cess or tax. As the collection of this tax became more efficient and the prosperity of the province increased, the funds available to the grand juries enabled them to execute a great programme of road- and bridge-building. Most impressive was the series of three timber bridges thrown across the Lower Bann (Toome, Portneil, and Agivey) and the great timber bridge built across the Foyle at Londonderry by the American firm of Lemuel Cox of Boston in 1791.

In Ulster, road projectors were encouraged by two acts passed in the 1771–2 session, the first permitting Ulster parishes to raise an extra parish cess to maintain minor public roads and the second enabling grand juries to raise money 'for the making of narrow roads through the mountainous un-improved parts of this Kingdom'.[21] New roads opened up land for development and increased its value while they made possible the transport of lime and other commodities essential for its exploitation. Too little notice has been taken of the great expansion of the road network in this period. Because the law ensured that roads could be made only between market towns or between market towns and the seacoast, road building stimulated the development of the whole urban network and diffused prosperity through the byways.

It was said of Co. Tyrone, for example, at the end of the eighteenth century that it was as well supplied with market towns as any county in the kingdom,[22] and yet many of these towns had been created, or revived, only in the eighteenth century. They owed their creation to energetic landlords anxious to secure some of the prosperity generated by the linen industry. Although neither linen nor cloth paid tolls, these markets and fairs attracted buyers and sellers of other goods as well, especially oatmeal for food and candles for light. As early as the 1740s linendrapers were making it known that they would attend regular well-organized weekly markets in preference to the haphazard seasonal country fairs.[23] In response landlords provided market-houses and tried to ensure that markets were properly conducted while some offered premiums or inducements to attract buyers and sellers. Such concern could make all the difference between the success or failure of a market. The whole atmosphere of this period is caught in a letter from Nathaniel Nisbitt of Lifford in Co. Donegal reporting in his capacity as agent to the Earl of Abercorn in April 1758:

> We had the 17th inst at St Johnstown a very fine market for the first; there was about £100 worth of green [unbleached] linen bought, a large quantity of yarn; there were also several other sorts of goods, such as suit the markets of this country; our next is the 15th of May for we were obliged to make it the third Monday in the month, to steer clear of other markets; I would allow neither cockfight, nor horse race, though the people of the town were for it, as all towns are indeed, but I satisfied

them by saying that an inch gained by honest industry was worth a yard otherwise, and that we did not want to gather idle folk at all . . . [24]

This letter contains one of the earliest references to a monthly market in Ulster – later to be known as 'the fair day' – and illustrates how the date in the month was selected. St Johnston (or Altacaskine) had been granted a patent in 1618 for a Monday market and two fairs in the year on Easter Tuesday and the Tuesday after Michaelmas respectively. At the time this letter was written the fairs had increased to four, a common occurrence in Ulster at that time. Although St Johnston had been incorporated as a borough, it had not been able to sustain a weekly market and this letter records the efforts of the Abercorns to found a monthly market that would take advantage of the increasing prosperity of the district. To create a reputation for the conduct of the markets, the agent had refused to permit either cock-fighting or horse-racing, both of which

41 Harp festival in the Assembly Room, Belfast, 1792.

sports were associated with the traditional fairs. These monthly markets got their greatest fillip from the expansion of the cattle trade after 1760 and they extended rapidly through the bleaker countryside of Counties Tyrone and Donegal. Successful markets attracted shopkeepers and tradesmen while a professional class began to appear in many of the larger provincial towns. This was reflected in their domestic architecture, notably in Belfast, Newry, Armagh, Dungannon and Londonderry.[25]

Although the sudden flowering of towns and villages all over Ulster was one of the most notable characteristics of the late eighteenth century, it has to be admitted that in almost every instance they were no more than market towns with primitive organs of administration. Only the city of Londonderry appears to have had an effective corporation with wide-ranging powers that could be adapted to meet changing economic and social circumstances. Even the corporations of the boroughs created in the seventeenth century had been neutered by the practice of packing corporations with non-residents who could be relied upon to maintain the landlords' control over the boroughs' parliamentary seats. The legality of this practice had been confirmed by the Newtown Act of 1747 and case-law in the courts recognized the rights of these self-perpetuating oligarchies. For local administration, therefore, the boroughs had to rely on corporation grand juries which had no legal status, manor courts held by the landlords, or parish vestries or a combination of all three.

The legal limitations of these courts rendered them a potential source of political trouble in the closing years of the century. In Belfast, for example, the sovereign was the nominee of the landlord but he had to act as clerk of the markets, chief magistrate and coroner, as well as superintending the paving, lighting, and cleansing of the town. The initiative in local government came from outside the corporation of Belfast: town meetings could be called by a public notice instituted by influential inhabitants and published in the newspapers. The parish vestry was the instrument used to assess and collect rates but when some

42 Colonel William Sharman, 1731–1803. Note the Volunteer parade in the background.

people refused to pay, the legality of the rate was questioned. The problem was exacerbated when the economic crises of the 1790s caused an increase in crime and poverty, so that in 1800 Parliament was compelled to pass a special act for the reform of the government of Belfast. The other towns in the province had to await local government reform in the nineteenth century to give expression to the wishes of the townspeople and to free them from landlord domination.[26]

In fact landlord power in Ulster reached its peak in the late eighteenth century. Before that time very few of them had been titled but many were then ennobled and exercised considerable influence in the Dublin Parliament. The zenith of their power coincided with the success of the Irish Volunteers movement when they mobilized the Protestants for the defence of the country against French invasion and for the protection of property rights. Such an assertion, however, would greatly oversimplify the complexities of Ulster society. Although outside Dublin itself Ulster was the great stronghold of the Volunteering movement, it was not the landlords but the new middle class of merchants and professional men who had created it. The landlords did manage to gain control of the leadership of the movement but only at the cost of recognizing the strength, and representing the aspirations of their supporters.[27] It was not a mere coincidence that in 1782, the same year that the Volunteers held their first great convention at Dungannon, the linen drapers of Ulster met at Armagh to compel the withdrawal of new regulations by the Linen Board in Dublin and secured their ends with the support of several great landlords who represented Ulster on the Linen Board.

IV

These years introduced Ulstermen to the techniques of politics – public meetings, resolutions, lobbying – and some of them proved to be enthusiastic students. Even after the close of the American War of Independence when the majority of the Volunteers put away their equipment, some radical spirits continued to diagnose the ills of their own society. They resented the dominance of the landlord interest in politics and in the control of all the organs of government but they could not convince their fellow citizens to break what they viewed as the shackles of oppression.

This continuing movement for reform was consolidated and developed by the foundation of the Society of United Irishmen in Belfast in October 1791. (A similar association was established in the following month in Dublin.) Influenced by the more radical ideas of the French Revolution, the Society, which had initially endorsed a programme of moderate constitutional reform, moved steadily toward the advocacy of a republican constitution, to be established through revolutionary change. By 1796 it had experienced considerable success in establishing branches outside Belfast, particularly in Counties Antrim, Down and Londonderry. Moreover, its alliance with the Catholic agrarian movement had given it a popular base and contributed greatly to its potential force. Its gathering strength, however, convinced the government that Ulster was the centre where rebellion was most likely to begin. Thus in 1797 General Lake was authorized to enforce a policy of severe repression through-out the province. Within a year political opposition in Ulster had been so weakened through Lake's campaign that when rebellion actually broke out elsewhere in the country, the attempts by Henry Joy McCracken and Henry Munro to raise the United Irishmen in Antrim and Down failed miserably.

Blame for the '98 rebellion was in large part laid upon the republican shopkeepers for misleading the countryfolk. Yet several Presbyterian clergymen also played a part. For political dissent in Ulster – even if it was tempered by the spirit of the French Revolution and couched in radical language – represented in essence a further expression of the ancient resentment nursed by certain elements in the Presbyterian congregations against the Anglican aristocratic ascendancy.[28]

Though it is clear that the rebellion of '98 did not impinge greatly upon general life in the province between the 1780s and the early 1800s,[29] it nonetheless convinced the London government of the need for a union between Britain and Ireland in 1800: they had lost confidence in the ability of the Anglican aristocracy to rule Ireland. The union concealed the developing political vacuum but, with hindsight, we realize that it was inevitable that in three provinces the Catholics would succeed to power whereas in Ulster they would not be in a position to challenge the Protestants.

In Ulster it was not just that Catholics were in a numerical minority. They were also at a severe social disadvantage. The sequence of wars in the seventeenth century had deprived not only the native landowners of their freehold property but also the farmers of their leaseholds. Over much of the province, wherever the British landlords were able to attract immigrants, the natives were reduced to the status of subtenants. In such a subservient position they posed no threat to the new social structure and were able to continue in their traditional life-style. Although many of them adapted to the expanding commercial economy by buying and selling around the country or taking up weaving for the linen export market, their lack of capital and business connections prevented them from securing a significant share of the prosperity generated in the middle years of the century. They did benefit, however, from the readiness of the landlords to exploit the potential of their estates by negotiating leases with those who could afford to pay regular rents and many of them obtained leases for 31 years, placing them almost on a par with their Protestant neighbours. Especially in 'the linen triangle' many landlords pursued this policy of dividing up holdings among the original subtenants to such an extent that the class of substantial farmers that could have maintained order, was seriously weakened. In the egalitarian society that ensued, men were forced to band together to cultivate new group loyalties that would protect their local community interests.[30]

The most reliable guide we possess to the relative strength of Catholics and Protestants across the province is the previously mentioned 1766 census of religion by parishes. Contemporaries would have associated Protestant-ism with the descendants of British colonists and Catholicism with the native Irish even where they knew about exceptions to the rule. In order to emphasize the significance of the ratios, it is best to distinguish those districts that were

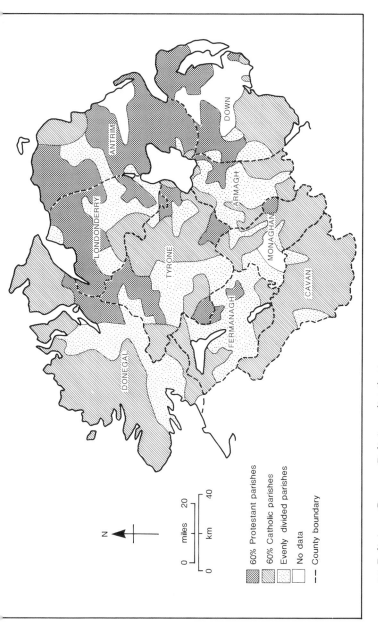

N

0 — miles — 20
0 — km — 40

▓ 60% Protestant parishes
▨ 60% Catholic parishes
░ Evenly divided parishes
☐ No data
– – County boundary

43 1766 Religious Census: Religious distribution.

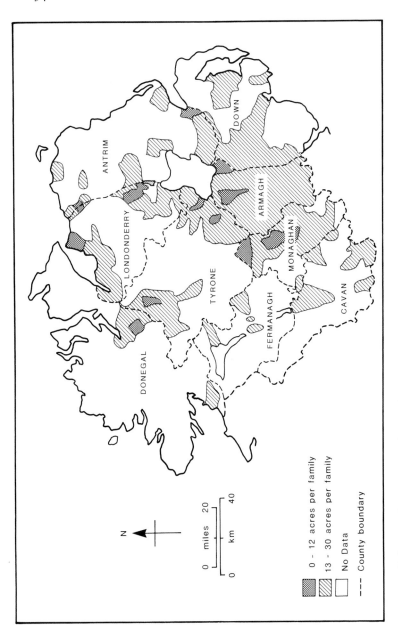

44 *1766 Religious Census: Population density.*

predominantly (i.e. more than 60 per cent) Catholic from those that were predominantly Protestant, and those that were only marginally one or the other. (It might be objected that since the count was made by Anglican clergymen it would be biased either in favour of Protestants or against Catholics: if the census was taken during a period of a Catholic 'scare', then the numbers of Catholics would be inflated, but if it was taken during a period of Protestant confidence, Protestant numbers would be increased. It is likely that Protestant numbers were overestimated simply because the clergy would be more able to identify Protestants than Catholics, especially in those areas where Protestants composed only a small minority.)

Very conspicuous on the map are two Protestant areas: the south Antrim/north Down region straddling the Lagan Valley and the region stretching along the north coast from Lough Swilly in the west to the Giant's Causeway in the east and including the lower half of the Foyle basin: it was from these bases that British colonization had advanced in the seventeenth century. Just as striking is the broad Catholic strip running in depth all along the southern border of Ulster: this indicates that the colonization thrust had been halted and contained before it reached either Leinster or Connaught. If the settlers had exerted serious pressure against Monaghan and Cavan it would have altered the religious balance and character of those two counties also. Pockets of colonization around certain towns illustrated the ability of certain landlords, such as Abercorn and the Brookes, in promoting British tenants on their estates. In contrast is the apparent success of the Irish in the old O'Neill homelands around Dungannon on the Powerscourt, Ranfurly and Charlemont estates in Co. Tyrone.

Special attention should be paid to those districts such as the western shore of Lough Neagh where Catholics and Protestants occupied distinct neighbourhoods. In north Armagh where faction-fighting (endemic in rural society throughout Ireland) first assumed a sectarian form, strong Catholic parishes faced Protestant parishes and the dense populations were well matched. Both parties were composed of weavers whose life-styles differed little but they rarely intermarried. Throughout most of the century Catholics had been prepared to accept a subordinate role in society but by the 1780s they were confident enough to challenge this role and to assert their rights whenever necessary. It is significant that the issue that provoked the trouble concerned claims by both sides to a dying person: the confrontation that ensued involved many more people and led to clashes.

These minor skirmishes were difficult to suppress. In the aftermath of the Volunteer period there were too many guns about the countryside and plenty of provocation to use them. Peace-keeping was in the hands of the local justices of the peace, but they could get little co-operation and in the absence of police or military aid had to depend on the local companies of Volunteers to keep the peace. Finally, the disbandment of the Volunteers in 1793 transferred the responsibility for keeping the peace from the hands of the landlords to government control.[31] As a result both Protestants and Catholics organized themselves more effectively, copying freemasonry lodge structures and emblems, and created respectively the Orange Boys and the Defenders. The skirmishes between them, especially at fairs, continued until late in the nineteenth century.

In eighteenth-century Ulster the pace of change had been very rapid. So swift had been the increase of population that it was almost as large as that of all Scotland by 1821. The domestic linen industry had swept through the province dividing and subdividing the townlands into a myriad of small farms, while cultivation had advanced settlements along the mountain valleys. The new farms were served by thousands of miles of new roads that linked a complex network of market towns and villages and imported the products of the new industrial culture. Urban life with its esteem for education and commercial progress introduced politics, organization and administration that must serve as the hallmarks of nineteenth-century Ulster society. The Anglican ascendancy had been forced to share much of its power with the merchant classes in the towns and the more substantial farmers throughout the countryside, and it was they who set the tone for the new century.

Further reading

Several valuable essays appear in T. Bartlett and D.W. Hayton (eds.), *Penal Era and Golden Age*, Belfast, 1979, and P. Roebuck (ed.), *Plantation to Partition*, Belfast, 1981. Various aspects of the linen industry are explained in W.H. Crawford, *Domestic Industry: the Experience of the Irish Linen Industry*, Dublin, 1972, but this should be supplemented by the same author's 'The evolution of the linen trade in Ulster before industrialization' in *Irish Economic & Social History*, xv, 1988, pp. 32–53. *Arthur Young's Tour in Ireland 1775–1779*, ed. A.W. Hutton, 2 vols., London, 1892, provides a valuable report about several districts in Ulster. To this may be added W.H. Crawford, 'Economy and society in South Ulster in the eighteenth century', *Clogher Record*, viii 3, 1975, pp. 241–58. The best introduction to the practice and history of Ulster agriculture is now J. Bell and M. Watson, *Irish Farming: Implements and Techniques 1750–1900*, Edinburgh, 1986. It should be read with the classic *Statistical Survey of the County of Tyrone* by James McEvoy, Dublin, 1802. It is worth looking also at the career of 'William Starrat Surveyor – Philomath' recounted by J.B. Cunningham in *Clogher Record*, xi 2, 1983, pp. 214–25. The most comprehensive account of the rural unrest of the 1760s and 1770s is provided by J.S. Donnelly, 'Hearts of Oak, Hearts of Steel', *Studia Hibernica*, 21, 1981, pp. 7–73, while D.W. Miller charts 'The Armagh Troubles 1784–95' in S. Clark and J.S. Donnelly (eds.), *Irish Peasants: Violence and Political Unrest 1780–1914*, Manchester, 1983, pp. 155–91. On the role of Presbyterian ministers in the national politics of the 1790s see D.W. Miller, 'Presbyterianism and "modernization" in Ulster', *Past and Present*, 80, 1978, pp. 66–90. Insight into the social history of the period is provided in L.A. Clarkson and E.M. Crawford, *Ways to Wealth: the Cust Family of Eighteenth-Century Armagh*, Belfast, 1985.

6 Ulster society and politics, 1801–1921

Brian Walker

The period covered in this chapter is neatly demarcated by two important pieces of legislation – the Act of Union, 1800, and the Government of Ireland Act, 1920. During this time other acts of parliament, covering a wide range of matters, from education to land tenure and political enfranchisement, had a deep influence on people's lives in Ulster. This extension of parliamentary involvement into so many areas is a major new feature of the period which marks it off clearly from earlier eras. It would be wrong, of course, to concentrate unduly on government legislation. To gain a full picture of changes in this period we must also look at the various social and economic developments which occurred during these years and which often were not related to government planning. Fortunately, the growth in parliamentary enquiries and commissions, which accompanied the rise in government involvement, enables us to obtain a much more accurate picture of life in Ulster at this time than was possible in earlier centuries.

I

Many travellers' accounts of Ulster in the nineteenth century drew particular attention to the development of industry and the growth of towns in the province. J.B. Doyle, for instance, in his *Towns in Ulster* of 1851, talked of 'an intensely industrious manufacturing population'.[1] Compared to the rest of Ireland it is true that there was a high degree of industry in Ulster, but it must be realized that until the early twentieth century the province remained a

*45 New farmhouse with slated roof replaces thatched cottage at
     Carnmoney, Co. Antrim, c. 1890.*

mainly rural society, where the majority of people lived in
the countryside and were engaged in agriculture. The census
reports show that in 1841 under 10 per cent of the Ulster
population lived in towns of 2,000 or over while by 1911
the figure was still under 40 per cent.

For these reasons it is appropriate to begin a survey of
Ulster in this whole period with a look at the countryside.
Of the many changes which occurred on the land in Ulster
during these years the most obvious was the decline in the
importance of the landlords. Until the 1880s rural society
continued to be dominated by landlords whose position was
largely accepted by the bulk of the tenantry. A parliamentary return of 1876 showed that almost 80 per cent of the
land of the province was the property of only 800
landowners. In the same year there were nearly 200,000
occupiers of land, of whom just over 20 per cent formed
holdings above 30 acres.[2] By this time about 18 per cent of

46 Labourer's cottage at Carnmoney, Co. Antrim, 1890. While the position of farmers improved considerably in the nineteenth century, labourers' conditions changed little and as a group they declined rapidly in numbers in the countryside.

the holdings in Ulster were held under leases, while the rest were yearly tenancies. Until the 1880s there were few who publicly demanded abolition as opposed to the reform of the existing land system. Along with their economic position, the landlords enjoyed great social influence. Landlord–tenant conditions have frequently been cast as hostile but recent research has shown that this was not the case and, especially in Ulster where many farmers enjoyed the benefits of the Ulster custom, the leading status of the landlords was accepted by the population at large.[3]

There were, of course, sources of tension in the relationships between landlords and tenants, arising largely out of the insecurity of the tenants. In the late 1840s and early 1850s there was organized opposition among the farmers against the landlords, but only with limited effects, and it was not until the 1870s that a serious rift developed between the two groups. Ill-considered land legislation in 1870 soured landlord–tenant relations and caused the beginning of an organized tenant right movement in Ulster. A downturn in agricultural prices from 1877 and bad harvests in 1879 and 1880 led to widespread organized support in Ulster and in the rest of Ireland for land reform and caused serious questioning of the position of the landlords.[4]

Faced with this protest movement throughout the country the government under Gladstone was obliged to introduce the Land Act of 1881, which gave the tenant definite rights of tenure – fair rents, fixed tenure and free sale – in effect a type of part-ownership. The 1885 Ashbourne Act began a process of peasant proprietorship which, by the early 1920s, resulted in most farmers in Ulster owning their own land. Along with these changes in ownership went an undermining of the social dominance of the landlords. Deference to this group had been seriously undermined in the 1870s and 1880s and the Local Government Act of 1898 established effective local councils on a broad franchise, which gave farmers a major role in running rural affairs.

The demographic structure of the rural population in Ulster over this whole period showed fundamental changes. The numbers of people in the countryside continued to rise until the 1840s. In 1841 the population of the whole province stood at 2,386,373 of whom only 10 per cent lived in towns of 2,000 and over. The Great Famine of the late 1840s, however, had a dire effect on population numbers. Deaths or emigration because of the famine caused an immediate large drop in the population, but thereafter numbers continued to fall until by 1911 the total figures for the province stood at 1,581,696 of whom nearly 40 per cent lived in towns. So the numbers living in the countryside fell dramatically.[5]

The causes for this long-term decline in the rural population are many. Of special significance is the change which occurred in land use. Early in the nineteenth century farming in Ulster was geared primarily to tillage, which created a need for a large labouring population, but market demands for products such as butter led from the 1830s to a shift to pastoral farming with its lower labour requirements.

If we look at the census returns from 1851 onwards we can see a steady fall in the number of agricultural labourers and their families while farmers witnessed a rise in their own proportional strength in the rural population. The increased mechanization in the linen industry and consequent drop in cottage linen work, which had become widespread in the late eighteenth century, also undermined the economic position of many rural people. Those who left the countryside either went to the growing urban centres of Ulster or emigrated. The rural community which had emerged by the early twentieth century was composed mainly of small farmers who now owned their own land.

This period saw other important changes in the countryside. Mechanized farming methods were introduced increasingly from the middle of the nineteenth century. Rural housing conditions improved dramatically. In 1841 nearly

47 Carnmoney Dispensary, Co. Antrim, c. 1890, part of a wide range of medical, social and educational facilities established by the government throughout the Ulster countryside from the 1830s.

one-third of rural families lived in what were called fourth class houses, that is dwellings built of mud, or other perishable material, and with only one room or window. Ten years later, after the famine, the figure had dropped to under 10 per cent. Thereafter, the position improved with a continued decline in poor housing and an increase in the building of substantial farm houses. By 1911 the proportion of families in rural areas who lived in first or second class houses, a category which covers 'good farm houses' with a minimum of five rooms and windows, stood at nearly 70 per cent compared with 1851 when the figure was just over one-third.[6]

II

While Ulster society in the nineteenth century was predominantly rural, there were nonetheless many flourishing towns in the province. The best example was Belfast, which William Thackeray had described in 1842 as 'hearty, thriving and prosperous, as if it had money in its pocket and roast beef for dinner.'[7] The Chambers Encyclopaedia noted in 1868: 'The general aspect of Belfast is indicative of life and prosperity, exhibiting all the trade and commerce of Glasgow and Manchester, with far less of their smoke and dirt.' Twenty years later, Belfast was officially designated as a city. The population increased from just under 100,000 in 1851 to over a third of a million at the end of the century: indeed Belfast grew faster than any other urban centre in the British Isles in the second half of the nineteenth century.

The drive and spirit of Victorian Belfast is well illustrated by R.J. Welch's photograph of the Grand Trades' Arch which was erected in Donegall Place for the visit of the Prince and Princess of Wales in 1885. Around the edge of the arch were the words: 'Man goeth forth unto his work and to his labour until the evening' and 'Trade is the golden girdle of the globe'. Other slogans proclaimed: 'Employment is nature's physician' and 'Temperance is a girdle of gold'. Models of a steam engine, a loom and a ship on the arch represented the great industries of engineering, linen

48 *Trade arch in Donegall Place, Belfast, 1885, with slogans and symbols which capture well the work ethic of nineteenth-century Belfast.*

and ship-building, which were the basis of Belfast's remarkable growth and prosperity.[8] By 1881 there were nearly 75,000 people employed in the manufacturing industries of Belfast.

Although Belfast was exceptional in the extent of its growth, other towns in Ulster, especially in the north-east, also witnessed expansion and rising prosperity, thanks chiefly to the linen industry. By the middle of the nineteenth century linen had ceased to be a domestic industry and was concentrated in large-scale mills and factories. The centres most affected were Ballymena, Lisburn, Lurgan, Portadown, Coleraine, Newry and Derry. Even smaller towns, like Killyleagh and Castlewellan in Co. Down, often had the benefits of a substantial linen mill located in their area. Industrial communities gathered round factories at places such as Drumaness and Shrigley, Co. Down; Bessbrook, Co. Armagh; and Sion Mills, Co. Tyrone. Bessbrook, for example, was a village built by the

49 Ewart's Linen Mill, Crumlin Road, Belfast, 1900.

Richardson family (prominent Quakers) for their mill workers, and it had various amenities such as a school, recreational hall and library, but, thanks to the Richardsons, no public houses.

This economic development in the north of Ireland caused a substantial growth in the number of industrial workers. By the 1880s, however, there was still relatively little trade union organization apart from engineering unions, which seem to have been mainly concerned with protecting their position from other workers. The growth of Belfast and these towns had another important outcome, namely a significant increase in the prosperity and numbers of the middle classes. Some of these merchants and industrialists were from established families such as the Richardsons of Lisburn and Bessbrook, but many were new arrivals, particularly linen manufacturers, who appeared about the middle of the nineteenth century and, like T.A. Dickson of Dungannon, were to prosper greatly in the early 1860s due to the linen boom caused by the American Civil War.

The benefits of manufacturing industry in Ulster, however, affected not only the towns, but also the surrounding countryside. The cultivation of flax for the linen business continued to benefit northern farmers. The growing towns and expanding factories gave the rural population good markets for their produce and alternative means of employment. Little industrial and urban expansion occurred in the rest of Ireland. There were, of course, important centres of population and of commerce such as Dublin and Cork. But there was no industry to compare with the linen and shipbuilding industries in the north. A point worth noting in regard to the economies of Ulster and the other provinces is that in their growth as the major industrial centre in the country, Belfast and north-east Ulster were less connected with the internal economy of Ireland than with raw materials from Great Britain and export markets there and elsewhere in the world.

The physical appearance of the Ulster towns and cities underwent great change. Besides the growth of important new institutions such as hospitals, colleges, schools and poor houses, many urban centres saw the building of town halls to house the town and municipal councils which were established during the nineteenth century. Belfast acquired its magnificent city hall in the early 1900s while Derry city opened its grand new Guildhall in 1890. Reflecting the important developments of the second half of the nineteenth century in urban centres such as Belfast and Derry, the majority of Ulster towns assumed their dominant present-day style in architecture. Charles Lanyon and W.J. Barre were only two of a long list of able architects who helped transform Ulster towns and cities with their fine Victorian buildings.

For all the population of Ulster, both in towns and in the countryside, the nineteenth and early twentieth centuries witnessed a dramatic change in the area of education. Early in the nineteenth century standards of literacy had been low in the province; they remained so until the middle of the century, by which time the situation had been transformed by the new National Schools. These schools were the result

50 The Library, Queen's College, Belfast, 1874. This college was one of three similar institutions set up in Ireland in the 1840s to provide non-denominational higher education.

of an education act of the early 1830s which gave grant-aid to new schools throughout the country. By 1861, 30 per cent of the Ulster population aged five years old and upwards were illiterate but 30 years later the figure was just 15 per cent.[9] In the second half of the century and early in the twentieth century improvements were also made in secondary and university education.

The aims of the National Schools, when they were first set up, had been twofold.[10] Firstly, they were to provide basic education everywhere, and in this they largely succeeded. The second aim, however, was to provide schooling on an integrated basis for all denominations, and in this the scheme largely failed. Attempts to provide non-denominational education, at both primary and higher levels, were not successful, a failure which reflected the denominational divisions in society, which in many ways deepened during this period. These denominational divisions remained very important for life throughout Ulster and were to add a special dimension to the social and political divisions of the province.

III

Ulster is often thought of as a predominantly Protestant region. But the first census analysis of religious belief in 1861 revealed that 50 per cent of the population was Catholic. By 1871, however, the Catholic percentage of the population had fallen to 48.9 and 20 years later it stood at 46.0. This fall in numbers was due to the fact that most industrial expansion was in the east of the province, where Protestants predominated. Of the Protestants in the province, the Presbyterians were the largest single group and members of the Church of Ireland were the next biggest: in 1871, for example, Presbyterians were 26.1 per cent, members of the Church of Ireland 21.5 per cent, Methodists 1.6 per cent, and others 1.9 per cent.[11] There was considerable variation in denominational distribution within the province.

While there were members of each denomination in every

county, the counties can conveniently be divided into several types. First there were the three counties, Antrim, Down and Londonderry, where not only were Protestants a clear majority, but Presbyterians comprised the largest Protestant group. Secondly, there were the three mid-Ulster counties of Armagh, Fermanagh and Tyrone, where Protestants made up around 50 per cent, but members of the Church of Ireland were the most numerous Protestant section. Finally, there were the three counties of Monaghan, Cavan and Donegal where Catholics comprised a substantial majority and members of the Church of Ireland and Presbyterians were similar in numbers in the first two but not the third. In urban areas the denominations were variously distributed, but in Belfast, which had a population of 386,947 in 1911, Protestants were over two-thirds.

A statistical survey of the denominations, such as we have given above, is helpful but at the same time gives little real insight into the importance of religious division in the community. Along with these religious divisions went other social differences. For example, the gentry were nearly all members of the Church of Ireland; the leading merchants tended to be Presbyterian; farm labourers were more likely to be Catholic or Church of Ireland than Presbyterian. Presbyterians dominated the new skilled crafts in Belfast, thanks largely to their educational standards which throughout the nineteenth century were higher than those of other denominations, as the census literacy figures clearly show. These social differences added to the tensions between the denominations, but more important were the changes in attitude and outlook of the denominations in religious matters as they related to each other and to public affairs.

For all the denominations the nineteenth century was a time of considerable organizational growth and spiritual revival. This was especially so for the Catholic Church which sought to rebuild after the deprivation of the penal laws. During this period churches and schools were constructed at an ever increasing rate and membership of the priesthood increased markedly. Important new devotional practices were introduced to Irish Catholicism in the decades after the famine. The authority of the bishops over their clergy and Catholic affairs was strengthened. Changes caused by the Vatican Council of 1870 were taken up enthusiastically by the Irish Catholic Church. Irish bishops had favoured the movement in the council for acceptance of papal infallibility and it was quickly assented to by Irish Catholics.

Exactly what effect these changes had on the attitude of Irish Catholics towards Protestants is difficult to say. The changes in devotional practice no doubt tended to emphasize the differences in spiritual matters between Catholics and Protestants and to give Catholics more of a separate identity. The declaration of papal infallibility probably had an adverse effect on Catholic views concerning a broad Christian church, including different viewpoints. Certainly Catholic tolerance of the Protestant position on theological matters seems to have improved little in this period. The Catholic-owned newspaper, the *Anglo-Celt* of Co. Cavan, in 1868 described the Church of Ireland as 'founded and maintained by swords and bayonets' while the Belfast *Weekly Examiner* in 1886 called it 'the alien Church'.[12]

Specific Catholic grievances against the existing system were several. Many Catholics were concerned about the continued establishment of the Church of Ireland as the state church, because its members were a minority (only 11.96 per cent of the Irish population in 1861). This was seen as part of the earlier system of Protestant domination with its restrictions on the social and political activities of Catholics which had been largely, but not altogether, removed by the late 1860s. Catholics welcomed the disestablishment of the Church of Ireland in 1870 but regarded other facets of 'Protestant ascendancy' as still in existence. In a local context, grievances were felt over various matters such as Protestant dominance of official positions and discrimination against Catholics by some Protestant town councils and poor law boards of guardians. Restrictions against Catholics in a broader sense, within the United Kingdom as a whole, were felt in symbolic things such as the Ecclesiastical Titles

Act. A further cause of bitterness among many Catholics in Ulster and Ireland was the attitude taken by Protestants and the British government towards Catholic temporal affairs in Europe. The local Catholic press gave widespread and sympathetic coverage to the struggle of the Pope and the church authorities in various countries, especially Germany and Italy, against hostile nationalist and state forces, which often had British support. The failure to provide sufficient denominational education at university level was a major Catholic grievance for much of the nineteenth century.

In spite of these problems the second half of the nineteenth century saw the growth of a new, self-confident spirit among Ulster Catholics. This was especially so in Belfast which was under the charge of Bishop Patrick Dorrian of Down and Connor from the mid-1860s. At his funeral service in 1885 glowing reference was made to how 20 years earlier he had taken over a very weak Catholic structure with few priests and churches, and transformed it:

> What do we see now? We see the city dotted over, as it were, by magnificent catholic churches.... We have now, I think, eight catholic churches, which for beauty and magnificence are second to none. We have six convents, in which every want that flesh is heir to is provided for. We have 40 priests in the town instead of three and we have a community of men of the Congregation of the Passion who not only edify the people here, but by their missions throughout the country spread religion and piety among the people elsewhere.[13]

Besides such institutional improvements, which were plainly evident in other dioceses, Catholics benefited in general from the growing prosperity in the countryside and towns. Their numbers among the professional and business community increased. Such changes led to a new confidence and sense of identity.

For Protestants also the second half of the nineteenth century was a time of considerable reorganization and spiritual growth. Two characteristics of Irish Protestantism in this period are especially noticeable. First, all the churches

continued to be distinguished by evangelical fundamental-
ism, a development aided, although not started, by the
religious revival in the north in 1859. Secondly, by this
time the main churches were marked by a fairly conservative orthodoxy; this was seen in the Presbyterian church by
the triumph of Rev. Henry Cooke and his followers and in
the Church of Ireland by the new church constitution of the
early 1870s which set up that body on relatively narrow,
low church principles.

Again, as in the case of the Catholic church, it is difficult
to assess precisely the effect of these developments. Given
that these low church features of Irish Protestantism
emphasized differences between Protestant and Catholic
viewpoints in spiritual matters and that the firm establishment of a conservative religious orthodoxy made people
more opposed to the idea of a pluralist Christian church and
society, it is very likely that these developments made
Protestants less tolerant towards Catholics. It is probable
that the growing conservatism within Irish Protestantism
made Protestants more conservative in general outlook. The
reaction of Protestants to Catholicism could often be harsh.
The Protestant-owned *Ballyshannon Herald* began its editorial
of 19 June 1880 with the question, 'Is the Pope a man of
sin?' It answered in the affirmative. Certain clergymen and
ministers such as Rev. Thomas Drew and Rev. Hugh
Hanna were often very abusive in their sermons about
Catholicism.

Protestants took a different view from Catholics on the
existing social and religious system. Contributory to this
were the disparate social positions between Catholics and
Protestants in Ireland and also the fact that while Protestants
were a minority and Catholics a majority in Ireland,
Catholics were a minority and Protestants a majority in the
United Kingdom of Great Britain and Ireland. This latter
fact was seen as justification for the establishment of the
Church of Ireland. Not only in Ireland but also in Great
Britain, however, many Protestants shared a distrust of
Catholics on religious grounds and this affected their
approach to Catholics in other matters.

At the beginning of the nineteenth century the character of the constitution and government of the United Kingdom had been largely Protestant. During the century this Protestant character of the state was progressively altered by measures such as Catholic emancipation and the admission of Jews to parliament. Among Protestants in Great Britain a more tolerant and pluralist view of society came to be held.

By the 1860s the idea of a pluralist religious society had taken less hold among Protestants in Ireland than among those in Great Britain. Suspicion of Catholicism remained a strong force among Irish Protestants who looked on Catholic claims and the reorganizing Catholic church as part of an aggressive ultramontane movement which was hostile towards them. The declaration of papal infallibility was regarded as a religious and political challenge. The growing power of the Catholic bishops and clergy concerned many Ulster Protestants. For example, Catholic clerical intervention in elections in the 1885–6 period and in the early 1890s greatly aroused Protestant fears. The Ne Temere decree of 1907 which laid down very stringent Catholic conditions for mixed marriages was seen as a serious threat to the religious rights of Protestants. At the same time, besides such

51 Orange parade, 12 July, c. 1905, Coleraine, Co. Londonderry.

concerns, Ulster Protestants experienced a rise in self-confidence, thanks to the social and economic changes in the province.

So far our attention has focused on Protestant–Catholic division, but mention must be made of intra-Protestant conflict. As already noted, there were marked differences in the social profiles of the Presbyterian and Church of Ireland communities. Although Rev. Henry Cooke in the 1830s had urged an alliance of the two denominations, many Presbyterians remained hostile to the Church of Ireland. In part, this hostility arose from religious objections. W.F. McKinney, a Presbyterian tenant-farmer of Sentry Hill, Carnmoney, writing in the late 1870s, remarked on 'the nonsensical, unscriptural customs that are still practised in the Church of Ireland'.[14] It was also caused by radical opposition to an establishment, of which 'the landlord class and the Church of Ireland were seen as two aspects of one thing'.[15]

Relations between the denominations, however, were not all heated. In the late 1860s at Ballynahinch the Catholic

52 Catholic fife and drum band, Strabane, c. 1910.

Bishop of Dromore, J.P. Leahy, thanked the persons 'both Roman Catholic and Protestant' who had generously subscribed towards the new church in the town.[16] J.A. Rentoul, in his biography, recorded the good relations between the different clergy in Donegal in the 1870s and 1880s. He described how in the 1850s Daniel McGettigan, Catholic bishop of Raphoe, had regarded his father, a Presbyterian minister, as 'a co-worker engaged with him in a common war, though fighting under different regimental colours'.[17] A.M. Sullivan (Jnr.) recalled how a Church of Ireland rector forbade the flying of flags on his church, to avoid giving offence to his Catholic neighbours.[18] In the rural community, farmers of all denominations commonly gave each other assistance at harvest time. But still religious divisions were of considerable consequence, not only because of the social divisions which accompanied them, but also because of the differences in attitude of the denominations to each other and to various aspects of society. The significance of these matters spread beyond simple church matters to other areas of importance such as education and politics.

IV

The nineteenth century witnessed important political changes in Ulster. As a result of the Act of Union the province returned 28 MPs, a number which increased to 29 in 1832, 33 in 1885 and 37 in 1918.[19] Laws governing elections altered significantly in this period. The number of people who could vote changed from approximately one per cent in 1832 to four per cent in 1868, 14 per cent in 1885 and 44 per cent in 1918. Only in 1918 were women, over the age of 30, allowed to vote. Other changes included the Catholic Emancipation Act of 1826 which allowed Catholics to sit in parliament. Various acts concerning corrupt practices affected behaviour at elections.

The nature of party politics changed considerably during the period. At the beginning of the nineteenth century, MPs did not belong to parties but either opposed or supported

53 Riots in Belfast, June 1886, following high tension after the rejection at Westminster of the first Home Rule Bill.

the government. With the rise of issues in politics in the 1820s MPs began to be identified with party groupings. By the 1830s the majority of Ulster MPs had emerged as Tories. Most MPs were from a landowning and Church of Ireland background, reflecting the social and economic importance of this group. During the 1870s and the early 1880s these parliamentary representatives were challenged by a liberal section, made up of business and professional people who had the support of many of the tenant farmers, especially among Catholics and Presbyterians.

By 1885–6, however, a new type of politics had emerged in Ulster. Thanks to the franchise extension of 1884 and the growth of good party associations we find the emergence of popular political organizations and involvement. The issue of home rule was now to the fore and politics were divided between unionist and nationalist, a cleavage which correlated closely with the Protestant-Catholic division. The Liberal Party in Ulster, which had drawn on inter-denominational support, was destroyed.

The causes of the division of Ulster politics along unionist and nationalist lines, based on denominational cleavages, are complex. In part the unionist position resulted from economic and social factors. During the period of the union, as we have seen, northern industry had prospered and had enjoyed considerable commercial benefits from the link with Great Britain, while the prevalence of the Ulster custom had mitigated to some degree the local resentment felt over the land issue. Ulster unionists did not feel the same sense of economic and social disillusionment with the Westminster parliament which many nationalists, especially in the south and west of the country, had experienced. These factors alone, however, are not enough to explain the emergence of unionism and nationalism: many Catholics in Ulster also shared the benefits of the union, just as Protestants in other parts of Ireland had economic reasons to question the union. Yet Protestants were nearly all unionist, while Catholics were almost all nationalist.

To gain a fuller understanding of these divisions we

54 Unionist demonstration, Ulster Hall, 27 September 1912.

must appreciate the strength of both religious conflict and denominational bonds in nineteenth-century Ireland. Although most specific religious issues were settled by the 1880s, religion still coloured peoples' views on broader political matters, including the question of the link with Great Britain. Past religious controversies had caused Catholic disillusionment with the connection, a feeling not experienced by Protestants, who now saw the possibility of a majority Catholic, home rule parliament as a threat to them. The strengthening of denominational ties and identities during the nineteenth century meant that for most people in Ulster, and in the rest of Ireland, the links with their respective religious groups overcame other social and economic factors.

By 1885/6 nearly all Ulster Catholics, of every social rank, identified strongly with the political aspirations of their co-religionists elsewhere in Ireland who, for the social and economic reasons mentioned above, as well as because of a sense of religious alienation, now saw their best future in a Dublin parliament and so voted Nationalist. Because of their different experiences in all these areas, Ulster Protestants voted Unionist, a political stance shared with their co-religionists in other parts of Ireland. Another factor linking religion with the political forces of unionism and nationalism in 1885/6 was the way in which the parties of both sides integrated denominational structures with their respective organizations. The Catholic clergy were given a special place in the Nationalist Party structure while the Orange Order was placed in a key position in the Unionist organization.[20]

From 1885/6 these political divisions remained essentially constant in Ulster. The only new factors of importance were changes in support from allies in Great Britain. The backing of Gladstone and the Liberals for the Irish Nationalists led to the introduction of Home Rule Bills at Westminster in 1886 and 1893 but the backing of the Conservatives in both houses for the Unionists prevented the bills passing. In 1912, however, with the Lords now only able to block legislation for a limited period, a third

Home Rule Bill was introduced by a Liberal government. In face of this threat, over 450,000 Ulster unionists in September 1912 signed the Ulster Covenant, which pledged full opposition to home rule. An armed Ulster Volunteer Force was formed to fight it. An Irish Volunteer Force was also formed, to defend the nationalist position. Intense negotiation ensued between the British government and the two Irish parties, with ideas being advanced for the first time for an amendment to the Home Rule Bill which would allow all or some of the Ulster counties to opt out. No firm agreement could be reached and the third Home Rule Bill finally became law in 1914, only to be immediately suspended because of the outbreak of the war in Europe.[21]

By the end of the war, in which thousands of men from the province died, matters had changed dramatically in Ulster and the rest of Ireland. A rising in Dublin at Easter 1916 by a small group of revolutionary republicans was a military failure but in the aftermath, partly as a result of the execution of the leaders, nationalist public opinion swung towards Sinn Féin, the political party of the republicans. At the 1918 General Election the nationalist seats in Ulster were divided between the Nationalist Party MPs and Sinn Féin representatives, who swept the board in the rest of Ireland. A guerrilla war then broke out between the armed wing of Sinn Féin, the Irish Republican Army, and crown forces. The Government of Ireland Act in 1920 finally established two political units in Ireland – six of the Ulster counties would make up Northern Ireland, while the other three formed part of 'Southern Ireland'. Only the part concerning Northern Ireland became fully operational, but as a result of the Anglo-Irish Treaty of 1921, southern delegates accepted a new, semi-independent status for the other 26 counties of Ireland.

Further reading

The basic source for Ulster history in the nineteenth and early twentieth centuries remains the two volumes edited by T.W. Moody and J.C. Beckett, *Ulster since 1800* (i) *A Political and Economic Survey;* (ii) *A Social Survey*, London, 1955, 1957. A wide range of more recent books now supplements several aspects of this work. These include *An Economic History of Ulster, 1820–1939*, Manchester, 1985, edited by Liam Kennedy and Philip Ollerenshaw; J.C. Beckett and R.E. Glasscock (eds.), *Belfast: the Origins and Growth of an Industrial City*, London, 1967. Religion is usefully dealt with in R.F.K. Holmes, *Henry Cooke*, Belfast, 1981, and Ambrose Macaulay, *Patrick Dorrian, Bishop of Down and Connor, 1865–1885*, Belfast, 1987. For politics see A.T.Q. Stewart, *The Ulster Crisis*, London, 1967; Patrick Buckland, *Irish Unionism, 2: Ulster Unionism and the Origins of Northern Ireland, 1886–1922*, Dublin, 1973; Michael Laffan, *The Partition of Ireland*, Dundalk, 1983; and B.M. Walker, *Ulster Politics: The Formative Years, 1868–86*, Belfast, 1989.

7 Northern Ireland: from birth pangs to disintegration, 1920–72

Éamon Phoenix

I

The recent history of Ulster or, more correctly, that part of it which became the political entity known as Northern Ireland, was set in train by the Government of Ireland Act, 1920. This measure represented the political response of Lloyd George's coalition government to the long-smouldering question of Irish self-government, now made more urgent by the victory of the revolutionary Sinn Feín movement in the 1918 general election and the outbreak of the Anglo-Irish War.

The task of finding a solution to the Irish issue was a daunting one for the British coalition whose members had been so bitterly divided on the issue of home rule only six years earlier. However, the need to replace the 1914 Home Rule Act, due to become operative when the last peace treaty was signed, together with growing pressure from the United States, made it imperative that a major Irish initiative should be introduced without further delay. It was inevitable also, given the shift in the balance of power at Westminster from the Home Rule Party to Ulster Unionism after 1918 (thanks to Sinn Feín's 'blessed abstention') that Craig and Carson were well placed to influence Irish policy and it is no exaggeration to say that the Fourth Home Rule Bill – the only Bill to be even partially implemented – was drawn up in close collaboration with them.

But while partition was the major aim of the government, the Cabinet was agreed that if American and Dominion opinion was to be satisfied, the Bill should pave the way for an all-Ireland parliament when both north and south were willing to accept it. Another major problem which faced the drafting committee in late 1919 and early 1920 was the crucial question of the area to be included in the new 'Ulster'. The Government felt that the choice lay between the six-county *bloc*, accepted by Carson in 1916, and the historic nine-county province. It was strongly urged in Cabinet that if the ultimate aim of the Bill was the unity of Ireland, it would be desirable to place the whole province, with its large Catholic minority (43 per cent) in the northern area. In the end, however, the Cabinet acquiesced in James Craig's pragmatic view that a six-county *bloc* would provide a more 'homogeneous' and viable area for Unionist control.[1]

On the principle that 'self-determination' for all Irishmen would best find favour with world opinion, the Government of Ireland Act (1920) divided Ireland politically into two areas, 'Northern Ireland' embracing the six counties, and 'Southern Ireland' covering the rest. Each area was to have its own local parliament and government. This marked a new offer to Ulster unionists who had never sought home rule but while the disillusioned Carson gave it a frigid reception, Craig and his followers quickly grasped the value of a parliament of their own as a further bulwark against any threat to subject them to a Dublin parliament.[2]

The new Northern legislature was based on the Westminster model with two chambers, a 52-member House of Commons to be elected by proportional representation (P.R.) and a Senate which was to be elected by the Lower House. The new Parliament was subordinate to the British Parliament, and like its projected southern counterpart, was empowered to make laws for the peace, order and good government of the six counties but not in the vital areas of foreign policy, defence and external trade. Other matters, including major taxation, were 'reserved' to the Imperial Parliament.

In its second major provision, the Bill seemed to foreshadow eventual Irish unity by providing 'a bond of union' in the shape of a Council of Ireland, to consist of 20 representatives elected by each Irish parliament. A number of relatively minor matters, such as railways and fisheries, were placed under the remit of the Council but the hope was firmly expressed at the time that this body might evolve into an all-Ireland parliament.

The relationship between Belfast and London, already a complex one under the Act, was further complicated by its financial provisions which were tightly restrictive. Thus, the future Northern Ireland government lacked control over revenue – four-fifths of which was controlled by the sovereign parliament, including major sources of taxation. The inevitable result was that Northern Ireland was always dependent on special payments from the British Treasury to make ends meet. Nor could the regional government develop distinctive policies attuned to the particular economic and social problems of the province.

The 1920 Act represented a major triumph for the Ulster unionists, much as they might declare their acceptance of it 'as a final settlement and a supreme sacrifice in the interests of peace'. As one of their spokesmen, Captain Charles Craig, pointed out in the House of Commons in March 1920: 'the Bill gives us practically everything we fought for, everything we armed ourselves for . . . in 1913 . . . '. They would be 'in a position of absolute security' for the future.[3]

Sinn Féin, the motive force in nationalist Ireland with growing support among Ulster Catholics, remained intent on the achievement of an all-Ireland republic. On the nationalist side, only Joe Devlin, the leader of the northern Home Rulers and a solitary figure at Westminster, saw the dangers of the 'Partition Act' and inveighed against it as portending both 'permanent partition' and 'permanent minority status' for northern Catholics. Not without justification Devlin attacked the glaring lack of safeguards in the Act for the minority. Apart from a clause forbidding discrimination and the retention of proportional representation for a three-year period, the Act was deficient in this vital respect. To nationalist anger, the northern Senate was to be a mirror-image of the lower house rather than part of a system of checks and balances in a divided society.

55 Joe Devlin.

Devlin's appeal for minority safeguards, however, was disregarded by the government which assumed that majority rule would operate as satisfactorily in Northern Ireland as it did in Britain.[4]

The passage of the 1920 Bill through Westminster coincided with the outbreak of serious sectarian and political violence in Ulster itself, as the tensions of the Anglo-Irish War and the spiralling IRA (Irish Republican Army) campaign spilled over into the province. The worst episode occurred in Belfast in the summer of 1920 when the assassination of an Ulster-born RIC (Royal Irish Constabulary) officer in the South resulted in the mass expulsion of some 8,000 Catholic workers from the shipyards and other industries. These events were a foretaste of the serious sectarian disturbances which were to scar the face of Belfast and other northern towns during the next two years, for it was not until late 1922 that murder, arson and expulsion from homes ceased to be a factor in the everyday life of Northern Ireland. Over 450 people, a majority of them Catholics, were killed during this period.[5]

This upsurge of violence had two important effects. First, it seemed to confirm nationalist fears of being subjected to the rule of the unionist majority in a separate state. The black days of 1920–22 made it certain that the new entity of Northern Ireland would find the politico-religious minority difficult to govern, let alone assimilate. Secondly, the mounting unrest in the six counties led the government to endorse Sir James Craig's plans for the enrolment of an auxiliary police force which might both 'curb rebel influences' in Ulster and pave the way for the speedy implementation of partition. Thus was born in October 1920 the 'Ulster Special Constabulary'. It consisted of three classes of constables, largely drawn from the ranks of the former UVF (Ulster Volunteer Force) and was to swell to 32,000 men by 1922. In nationalist eyes, this all-Protestant force was perceived 'with a bitterness exceeding that which the Black and Tans inspired in the South'.[6] But the Ulster Special Constabulary played a vital role in establishing the new state in the face of IRA resistance and was to become a permanent feature in the political landscape.

In February 1921, James Craig succeeded the ailing Carson as leader of the Ulster Unionists and, therefore, effectively as the future Prime Minister of Northern Ireland. The first election for the new parliament was held in May and Craig's supporters won a victory even more sweeping than they had expected. All 40 Unionists were returned while the Nationalist and Sinn Feín parties, united on an abstentionist platform, secured six seats apiece. However, the polling figures reflected graphically the politico-religious balance of the new state, with the Unionists securing two-thirds of the vote to the anti-partitionist parties' one-third.

Partition, however Sinn Feín or the northern nationalists might view it, had now become a fact and the Unionists lost no time in establishing their new government and parliament. Craig became Prime Minister and his choice of Cabinet reflected a desire to balance the various geographic and sectional interests within unionism. Two appointments were of particular importance. The choice of Dawson Bates at the critical post of Home Affairs was a most unfortunate

56 Opening of Parliament, 1921.

57 Northern Ireland Cabinet, 1921.

one, since his narrow vision and total insensitivity to minority views over the next 22 years did little to reconcile Catholics to the new state. On the other hand, as first Minister of Education, the aristocratic and 'ecumenical' Lord Londonderry brought wider British experience to an otherwise provincial team and showed himself capable of broader vision.

The new Parliament was opened by King George V in June 1921 and the Ulster Unionists soon had reason to be grateful for their new-found constitutional security. As expected, Sinn Féin refused to work the 1920 Act in the south. However, 'in the spirit of the King's words' a truce to hostilities was arranged in July 1921 and the remainder of the year saw protracted negotiations between the representatives of Dáil Éireann and the British government on a final Irish settlement.[7]

II

The resulting Anglo-Irish Treaty, with its grant of Dominion status for the south, came as a bitter shock to the northern government, however. Under its terms, Northern Ireland was automatically included in the new Irish Free State and although its right to 'opt out' was carefully guarded, Article 12 provided that she must purchase such immunity at the expense of a revision of her frontiers by a Boundary Commission. This formula, invented by Lloyd George to prevent a breakdown of the negotiations, seemed to hold out the prospect of the subtraction from Northern Ireland of such nationalist majority areas as Fermanagh, Tyrone and Derry City. Indeed, many nationalists hoped that this might produce Irish unity by a process of 'contraction'. To Craig, however, the proposal to tamper with the north's 1920 frontiers was a perfidious breach of faith on the part of the British government and he made clear his government's intention to ignore the Commission. Thus, it is impossible to underestimate the de-stabilizing effect of the Boundary Commission in the northern state during its early formative years.

The Treaty was accepted by the Dáil in January 1922, but the subsequent drift towards civil war had a profound effect on the already unstable situation in the North. Two major problems confronted Craig's administration in 1922: the attitude of the minority towards the state and its institutions, and the continuing problem of IRA and sectarian violence, especially in Belfast. The northern nationalists had refused to recognize the new state since 1921 and were now supported in this policy by the pro-Treaty government of Michael Collins. This 'non-recognition' found expression in a number of ways: for ten months, Catholic teachers refused to accept their salaries from the Craig government and were paid by Dublin; Nationalist councils pledged their allegiance to the Dáil and were dissolved for their pains; and Nationalist and Sinn Féin MPs enforced a strict boycott of the new parliament.

Secondly, the IRA, now secretly assisted by Collins, continued its campaign of burning and disruption within the six counties in an effort to undermine the Unionist government's authority. This was matched by an upsurge of sectarian warfare in Belfast where 73 Protestants and 147 Catholic civilians were killed between December 1921 and May 1922.

The Unionist government's response to this concerted threat to its existence was to revert to stringent measures. These included the introduction of the draconian Civil Authorities (Special Powers) Act, passed in 1922 and subsequently made permanent, and the introduction of internment and the strengthening of the Ulster Special Constabulary.

It was against this background that two agreements were signed by Craig and Collins in 1922. Both men had much to gain from the restoration of settled conditions, north and south, while Craig recognized the need to conciliate his own resentful minority. However, the two pacts took too little account of the realities of the political situation in both parts of Ireland at this time. Their prospects of success were blighted by the violent activities of the anti-Treaty IRA in the south and the unhelpful attitude of the northern Ministry of Home Affairs. It was not until the outbreak of open civil war in the Free State and the adoption of a 'peace policy' towards Ulster by the new Irish government of William T. Cosgrave in the summer of 1922 that the violence which had plagued the north for two years finally ended.[8]

It was during these first years that the basic local government and educational framework of Northern Ireland was laid down. Moreover, the strict nationalist boycott ensured that policy in these areas was worked out without any constructive criticism from the minority population. Notwithstanding this factor, however, the fact remains that on all matters over which the regional parliament had real control – especially education, representation and law and order, policy, in Dr Buckland's words, 'was determined by the majority with scant regard for the interests and susceptibilities of the minority'.[9]

The 1923 'Londonderry' Education Act provided for a state system of non-denominational primary schools, based on a series of Regional Education Committees. Under it, there were to be three classes of schools. The Ministry undertook to pay teachers' salaries in all three classes of school but while the first group – 'transferred schools' –

received the full cost of building and maintenance from public funds, the 'voluntary' schools – those schools mainly Catholic, which for religious reasons stood outside the system – got no building or maintenance grants. The new Act, however, provoked a vigorous campaign by the Protestant Churches and Orange Order to have 'Bible teaching' and 'Protestant teachers for Protestant pupils' included in the educational code. The Government's surrender found lasting expression in the 1930 Education Act. This amounted to the 'virtual endorsement of Protestantism' by the state and was thus contrary to the religious safeguard in the Government of Ireland Act. Finally, faced with a Catholic threat to ask Westminster to rule on the validity of the legislation, the Unionist government agreed to make 50 per cent grants towards the building and equipping of voluntary schools.[10]

In the sphere of local government, the regional government by an Act of 1922 abolished proportional representation for local elections and set in train the re-drawing of electoral wards. This decision, taken under pressure from the border loyalist grass-roots, was bitterly resented by the nationalist population who saw P.R. as a safeguard and feared an attempt to paint the nationalist border counties with 'a deep Orange tint' in anticipation of the Boundary Commission. These measures, together with the nationalist boycott of the enquiry, ensured the effective domination of local government by unionism and underlined the indifference of the Craig government to minority interests. The overhaul of local government provoked angry nationalist charges of gerrymandering, charges which were to be upheld by the Cameron Commission almost 50 years later. By 1924, only two major councils were controlled by nationalists.[11]

Nationalist resentment was also sharpened by the adoption of 'a sectarian security policy' during the troubles of the early 1920s; internment and floggings, for example, tended to be directed only at the 'disaffected and disloyal' section of the population, convincing many that they could not expect impartial treatment from the new regime.[12]

Other important steps were taken during these early years. In May 1922, a new police force, the Royal Ulster Constabulary, replaced the RIC. One third of the places in the new force were reserved for Roman Catholics, but its Catholic membership was to decline from an initial 16 per cent to 12 per cent by the 1960s. In the vexed sphere of finance, the Colwyn Committee (1922–5) eased Northern Ireland's burden by making the imperial contribution a last charge upon the regional exchequer. Craig also pledged his government to a step-by-step policy of keeping pace with British welfare benefits. But perhaps the most positive strides were made in the field of agriculture. Here, a series of Acts was passed by 1925, affecting livestock breeding, the marketing of eggs, and drainage, while the upgrading of agricultural education was a step of major long-term significance.

By 1925 one major constitutional threat still faced Northern Ireland. Owing largely to the civil war in the South and the recalcitrance of Craig, it was not possible to constitute the Boundary Commission until 1924. Early in 1925, the three Commissioners – the Chairman, Judge Richard Feetham of the South African Supreme Court, Professor Eoin MacNeill, representing the Free State, and Joseph Fisher, appointed by the British government to uphold the interests of Northern Ireland – perambulated the frontier, taking evidence from nationalists and unionists. Craig seized the opportunity to hold a 'border' election which faithfully reflected unionist feeling on the issue. It soon became clear that the Chairman, whose role was vital, was committed to 'mere rectification' of the boundary line rather than large-scale changes. This view was confirmed by the leak of the Commission's report in November 1925, which revealed that only a few uneconomic areas of Northern Ireland were to go to the South whereas an important area of east Donegal was to be transferred to the North. The result was the Irish Boundary Agreement of December 1925, signed by Craig, Cosgrave and, for the British government, Baldwin. By this new treaty, the Free State government finally recognized the 1920 border in return for certain financial concessions. Craig rejected the suggestion of safeguards for the northern nationalists but succeeded in having the 1920 Council of Ireland – the last formal bridge between the two Irelands – dissolved by general consent. His much-vaunted suggestion of joint Cabinet meetings was never implemented and 40 years were to pass before a Northern Ireland Prime Minister again met his Dublin counterpart. Craig had won a notable victory, a fact recognized by the Northern Ireland Parliament which presented him with a silver cup with the memorable phrase 'Not an Inch' inscribed on it.[13]

The 1925 pact came as a bitter disappointment to the border nationalists – mostly former supporters of Sinn Feín – and by 1928 this section had joined with Devlin and the constitutional nationalists in a new united movement, the 'National League', dedicated to pursue Irish unity by peaceful means. Devlin, a seasoned parliamentarian, was now leading a party of 10 MPs in the Belfast House of Commons. But his appeals for the redress of nationalist grievances were repeatedly rejected by the unionist majority. His hopes that stability would bring about a new political alignment in Ulster along class lines were finally dashed by the abolition of P.R. for parliamentary elections in 1929. In championing this measure, Lord Craigavon (Craig had become a viscount in 1927) signalled his determination to eliminate the various 'deviationists' who had embarrassed unionism under P.R., as well as the prospects of the fledgling Labour Party. In the Prime Minister's words, there was room only for two political parties in Northern Ireland, 'men who are for the Union, on the one hand, or who are against it and want to go into a Dublin Parliament, on the other'.[14] The unionist monopoly of power was now complete and politics became so predictable that many parliamentary seats ceased to be contested.[15] Thus, after 1929, the Unionists usually held 36–39 seats and the Nationalists 9–11 seats. Finally, in 1932, Devlin, dispirited and ill, led his followers out of the northern Parliament, declaring that the Unionist government was determined to 'rivet sectarianism'[16] to the political system for the future.

59 Eddie MacAteer and Eamon De Valera with members of the Northern Ireland Nationalist Party.

Devlin died in 1934 and for the next decade his followers abstained for the most part from parliament, allowing the League to atrophy and preferring instead to enlist the support of de Valera – now returned to power in the south – in their efforts to end partition. This policy, however, merely entrenched the Northern Ireland government in its lack of generosity to the minority.

During those early years the consolidation of the state was marked by the establishment of an Inn of Court for Northern Ireland in 1926 and, above all, by the state opening of the new lavish Parliament buildings at Stormont by the Prince of Wales in 1932.

III

Thus 'Stormont' became the symbol, for Unionists as well as Nationalists, of 'a Protestant Parliament and a Protestant state'. There was no sign of a rapprochement between the two communities or between north and south, despite the hopeful 'Irish Locarno' of 1925, as Cosgrove had termed the Boundary Agreement. 'Instead, the divisive pattern of government and politics sketched out in the angry early months was confirmed and became even more deeply entrenched ...'.[17] The government 'became the instrument of the Unionist Party' which drew its strength from the Orange Lodges and never produced a Catholic MP in the 50 years of Stormont rule. Indeed, the dominance of unionists over public life generally was summed up by the fact that Craig remained Prime Minister until his death in 1940, while all but one of his cabinet 'soldiered on' well into the 1930s.[18] The same pattern recurred in Westminster representation where ñionists could usually rely on holding 10 of the 13 seats. Above all, the use of government patronage to reward its supporters meant that discrimination, long a feature of Ulster life, 'became built into the processes of government and administration as the government pandered to unionist whims, large or small' in such diverse fields as local government, employment, education and civil service recruitment. To unionists, of course, this policy was easily justified by the claim that 'proven loyalty' was a prerequisite for government employment. Political considerations contributed to the minority's reluctance to serve a 'foreign' government in the early decades, but the tendency of government ministers to regard 'all Catholics as nationalists and all nationalists as enemies' was also a factor.[19]

The minority, on the other hand, equipped with its own social infrastructure of Church, schools, hospitals, sporting activities, newspapers, businesses, and sectarian Ancient Order of Hibernians, virtually opted out of the state, forming a kind of 'state within a state'. Unlike unionism, however, nationalism did not form a solid monolith and there was constant rivalry between the constitutional advocates of Irish unity and an intractable republican element which favoured abstentionism and physical force.

One of the first casualties of the bitter divisions in Northern Ireland was the Labour Party. Despite the existence of a large unionized workforce, and the social and economic difficulties of the inter-war years, it could never command more than three or four seats at Stormont. A major factor here in the early decades was Labour's irresolute attitude towards partition, which alienated unionist voters, whilst nationalists and Catholics distrusted its socialism and largely Protestant leadership.

The inter-war period and the 1930s, in particular, were years of depression and persistently high unemployment in Northern Ireland. Unemployment afflicted on average 19 per cent of the insured labour force between 1923 and 1930, and in the thirties the figure was 27 per cent; of all the United Kingdom regions, only Wales had a worse record. In the Free State, by contrast, de Valera's attempt at self-sufficiency was marked by a sharp increase in industrial employment in these years, though this was offset by a slump in agricultural exports due to the 'Economic War' with Britain. The high unemployment rate in the north stemmed largely from the inexorable decline of the region's three staple industries: shipbuilding, linen and agriculture, which during the period accounted for over 40 per cent of the working population. All three fell victim, after a brief post-war boom, to worldwide economic trends which neither local industrialists nor government could control. Additionally, there was a marked failure to attract 'new' rapidly growing industries, such as motor vehicle production and chemicals.

The main problem for the Belfast shipyards was worldwide over-capacity and new competition. Yet, given these difficulties, the yards performed creditably in the 1920s, launching the largest tonnage in the world in 1929. Thereafter, however, the industry was badly hit by the slump of world trade. In 1935, the smaller Workman Clark shipyard ceased operations and, despite efforts to diversify, the larger partner, Harland and Wolff, failed to recover as well as British shipyards which benefited to a larger extent from government contracts.

These years also witnessed a permanent decline in the output and export of linen, again largely due to a worldwide fall in demand not unrelated to changes in fashion and the production of cheaper fibres. Depression and unemployment resulted. Agriculture, which employed a quarter of the total labour force in 1926, also faced difficulties between the wars. As in the 1920s, the regional government's intervention was valuable in this sphere. Marketing schemes for milk and pig production, geared to local conditions, were introduced by the Belfast government, while farmers benefited from financial subsidies, funded by the British Treasury.

It is arguable that the Northern Ireland government could have done more to attract the newer, growth industries to offset the decline of traditional ones. Yet it is clear that due to the combination of low revenue, stemming from the 1920 Act, and the Stormont policy of maintaining 'parity' with Britain in social services, there was little money left for bold economic initiatives after the Northern exchequer had met its commitments. Some aid was given to shipbuilding in the 1920s but 'all in all, the contribution of the Northern Ireland government to economic activity was marginal.... Financial penury prevented any lavish subsidies to attract new firms to the province.'[20] With the exception of the Short and Harland aircraft factory, whose establishment in 1937 was the result of fortuitous circumstances rather than Stormont subsidies, few 'new' jobs were created before World War II.

Social conditions in Ulster also lagged behind the rest of the United Kingdom during the inter-war years. Housing conditions were particularly poor. Only 7,500 public-sector houses were built before 1939, while a government report of 1937 characterized the poorer classes as 'mostly residing in homes more or less unfit for habitation'.[21] Health conditions were also poor and while it is true that the pre-war years saw a marked improvement in medical provision and life expectancy, the indices for infant and maternal mortality and deaths from tuberculosis were significantly higher than those for Britain – the latter a reflection of the poorer standards of nutrition, housing and treatment. Educational provision also left much to be desired. New primary schools were built and the quality of teachers improved, but little was done to assist needy children and the numbers in secondary schools remained low, while the number of assisted places at university level was derisory.[22]

Yet despite these serious defects, the quality and variety of life in the six counties improved in several ways between the wars. The number of motor vehicles quadrupled; rural electrification was extended in the 1930s; people's leisure activities were much more varied by 1939. Cinema-going proved a great draw with all social classes, as did radio, after the opening of the BBC transmitter in Belfast in 1924. Sports flourished by the thirties, with the working classes flocking to the Irish League soccer grounds and greyhound stadia. Motor sport was particularly popular and the Ards Tourist Trophy race was the greatest sporting spectacular in Ireland in these years (1928–36). Gaelic games, following a dip in the troubled twenties, underwent a dramatic revival. And for the middle classes, there was rugby, golf, yachting and cricket. The theatre also proved popular, with the Ulster kitchen comedy of George Shiels vying with the more probing plays of Joseph Tomelty. In the field of visual arts, William Connor emerged as the representative painter of the depression years through his graphic images of shawled mill-girls and shipyard workers.

But the high unemployment of the 1930s did not produce any sense of working-class solidarity apart from a brief moment in 1932 when Protestant and Catholic workers rioted in unison against inadequate unemployment relief. Two died in this unprecedented and unrepeated upsurge. In general, sectarian rioting and sectarian rhetoric were more diagnostic hallmarks of the 'hungry thirties'. 1932 saw attacks on Catholic pilgrims travelling to the Eucharistic Congress in Dublin and the rise of the avowedly sectarian 'Ulster Protestant League'. But the worst outbreak of violence since the 1920s occurred in July 1935 when 11 people were killed and over 300 families, mostly Catholic, expelled from their homes in an orgy of rioting, sniping and arson. Nationalist and Catholic leaders demanded a British inquiry into the disturbances but the Prime Minister, Baldwin, refused this on the grounds that the matter was one which came solely within the jurisdiction of the

Northern Ireland government. This state of affairs stoked minority resentment and led the British-based National Council for Civil Liberties to publish a scathing indictment of the Unionist regime.

Inter-communal tension was not eased by the gratuitously offensive speeches of politicians and churchmen. In this regard, the public exhortation of Sir Basil Brooke, a future Prime Minister, to Protestants not to employ Roman Catholics, 'who were really out to cut their throats if opportunity arose', was particularly unfortunate.[23] Similarly, Cardinal MacRory's remark that the Protestant churches were 'not even a part of the Church of Christ' offended many Protestants.[24] There was much force in the words of the Belfast coroner at the inquest on the victims of the 1935 disturbances: 'The poor people who commit these riots ... are influenced almost entirely by the public speeches of men in high and responsible positions ...'.[25]

The British government, of course, retained ultimate responsibility for affairs in Northern Ireland, but while concern was expressed in official circles in the 1930s about minority grievances there, the Imperial Parliament took the steady view until the 1960s that events in Northern Ireland were 'no business of ours'.[26] The rise of de Valera in the south after 1932, his success in dismantling the 1921 Treaty and, especially, his 1937 constitution with its territorial claim over Northern Ireland and his renewed pressure on London for an end to partition tended to heighten Unionist defensiveness while raising false hopes among northern nationalists. Craigavon took advantage of the Anglo-Irish negotiations of 1938 to hold yet another 'border' election, which returned a larger than usual Unionist majority.

IV

'We are King's men' declared the visibly ailing Prime Minister when the Second World War broke out in September 1939. While the Imperial government prudently decided not to extend conscription to the six counties, Northern Ireland played a vital part in the ensuing struggle

60 Men at the home front, *by William Connor.*

which did much to strengthen her constitutional position and boost the economy. Northern Ireland ports helped to protect the crucial sea-lanes between Britain and the United States while her ports and bases served as shelter for British and later American forces. Agricultural production and heavy industries, such as shipbuilding and aircraft manufacture, were stretched to full capacity to meet Britain's war needs.

Moreover, Northern Ireland suffered in common with the rest of the United Kingdom, sending volunteers to the fronts and being subjected to four German air-raids on Belfast in 1941. More than 700 died and extensive damage was caused in the most serious of these in April 1941. The North's contribution to Britain's war effort and her share of death and devastation was in sharp contrast to de Valera's policy of neutrality during 1939–45. The South's neutrality, however 'benevolent' and sensible from a Southern standpoint, widened the gulf between the two parts of Ireland

61 Lord Brookeborough.

and ensured the North's claim on Britain's gratitude in the post-war years.

Craigavon died in 1940, having long since 'run out of steam' and was replaced by J.M. Andrews. However, his lack of commitment to the war effort resulted in his replacement in 1943 by Sir Basil Brooke (later Lord Brookeborough), a Fermanagh landowner and a traditional unionist of narrow views. He was destined to remain the state's Prime Minister until 1963, years which confirmed his limitations as a political leader for the entire Northern Ireland community.[27]

The return of a Labour government at Westminster in the British general election of July 1945 had a catalytic effect on politics in Northern Ireland. Labour was generally perceived as being friendly towards Irish unity and this factor, plus the fear of 'creeping Socialism', led the Brooke Cabinet briefly to consider Dominion status for the north before it finally decided to work in harness with Attlee and his colleagues. For the Nationalists, the revival of Labour was the signal for a major upsurge of anti-partitionist activity as the various strands of nationalism coalesced in a new mass movement, the Anti-Partition League (APL). Supported by all the major parties in Dublin and a vocal element in the British Labour Party, the APL waged a world-wide campaign against 'the evil of partition' in the late 1940s and early 1950s. But the movement's single focus on the constitutional issue, rather than on well-founded grievances, drew no encouragement from the Labour government. The accession to power of a coalition government in the south in 1948, which included a strongly republican element, assisted the Nationalist campaign, though the decision of the Costello ministry to 'take the gun out of Irish politics' by declaring a republic in 1949 was to redound to the Unionists' advantage. Following a further Unionist triumph in the 1949 Northern Ireland election, the British Parliament passed the Ireland Act (1949) which strengthened partition by stipulating that the north's constitutional status could not be changed without the consent of the Parliament of Northern Ireland. And in the same year, the Northern Ireland Labour Party finally declared itself pro-union, thus shedding many of its Catholic supporters without broadening dramatically its appeal to Protestants.[28]

But if the old issues were rekindled after 1945, the immediate post-war period witnessed a veritable revolution in the north. These years saw the coming of the modern welfare state and major educational reform, changes which were to bind Northern Ireland even more closely to Britain and to give Unionists a 'bread and butter' incentive for opposing Irish unity. In the sphere of social services, a series of financial agreements (1946–51) enabled the 'step-by-step' policy to be maintained while resolving the financial problems which had dogged earlier Belfast governments. In return for the province's acceptance of more rigorous financial scrutiny by the Treasury, Britain agreed to finance the massive increase in expenditure required to enable Northern Ireland to enjoy the full range of cash social services 'from the cradle to the grave'. As a result, the archaic Poor Law system was swept away and replaced by a comprehensive system of National Assistance, family allowances and non-contributory pensions on a par with Britain.

A Health Services Act of 1948 followed the British Act in establishing the National Health Service in the north. Under this legislation, a new General Health Services Board administered the new, free comprehensive health service while a Hospitals Authority supervised hospital services. Steps were also taken to eradicate tuberculosis. The net result of these reforms was that the death rate, from being the highest, became the lowest in the United Kingdom.

In education, the Stormont Act of 1947 implemented the revolutionary changes wrought across the water by the 1944 'Butler Act'. This provided for free post-primary education for all children and a new system of primary, secondary and further education, while generous university grants put real equality of opportunity within the grasp of all pupils, regardless of social background. The Act also introduced a 'conscience clause' for the protection of teachers in state schools and increased grant aid to voluntary schools from 50 to 65 per cent. This concession was bitterly attacked by the more extreme loyalists while the Catholic Church still demanded full grants on the 'separate but equal principle'. The dramatic expansion of third-level education was fraught with great significance for the future since it was to throw open the universities and the professions to a whole generation of Catholics, previously excluded from such opportunities for socio-economic reasons.[29]

These strides were not taken without friction, however, and sectarian controversy obtruded itself both in educational reform and in the health services, where the Catholic-controlled Mater Hospital, a respected acute and teaching hospital, remained for conscientious reasons outside the National Health Service. This issue festered until 1972, when in a rather altered political climate, the 'Mater' finally came in as 'a member of a bright constellation'.[30] Another controversial measure of these years was a politically-loaded Safeguarding of Employment Act (1947), passed by Stormont to prevent large-scale immigration of workers from the South. Also in the same year, the regional government sowed the seeds of much future discord by its blatant refusal to follow the British example in adopting 'one man, one vote' for Stormont and local government elections; the retention of Unionist control in border areas was the chief determinant here.

Other important measures were taken to stimulate the Northern Ireland economy and improve its infrastructure. A new Housing Trust was charged with the provision of workers' houses at the government's expense and by 1963 the government had achieved its target of 100,000 new homes. Agriculture saw dramatic modernization and, while employment contracted, the region enjoyed a flourishing trade with Britain throughout the 1950s and 60s. Industrial expansion was promoted by generous inducements for new firms. However, this policy tended to neglect the less-favoured (and predominantly nationalist) areas of the south and west. To nationalists, it seemed that 'the government's policy was clearly to denude the west and enrich the east'. By 1966, only 16 of the 111 advance factories built by the Ministry of Commerce were sited west of the Bann. The decline of the traditional industries accelerated rapidly after the war, with the consequence that unemployment reached 9 per cent in the late fifties. Moreover, the government's nationalization of public transport in 1948 did not make the services profitable, as a series of rail closures in the 1950s confirmed.

Notwithstanding the 'welfare revolution' and increased urbanization, however, Northern Ireland passed through the 1950s as the most divided as well as the poorest region of the United Kingdom. The Roman Catholic proportion of the population showed a slight rise during these years – from 33.5 per cent in 1926 to 34.9 per cent in 1961 – but Catholics continued to account for a disproportionate number of those leaving the north. Brookeborough's policy of ignoring the minority, and opposing every proposal for broadening the basis of unionism to include members of the Catholic community, tended to drive many

62 Arms found during IRA campaign, 1956–62.

nationalists into the arms of a revived republican movement by the mid-1950s. In the Westminster election of
1955, the Nationalist Party stood aside, enabling Sinn Feín,
with its emphasis on armed force, to win a massive 152,000
votes and two seats. This was largely a protest vote by a
frustrated community but it was seen by the IRA leadership
as providing necessary moral sanction for a renewed
campaign of violence.

The resulting IRA campaign of 1956–62, aimed at
expelling a 'British Army of Occupation' from the six
counties, had never any prospect of success. But by the time
it was finally abandoned in desultory fashion in 1962 it had
cost 16 lives and considerable material damage. Its failure
was due to a combination of several factors, amongst them
vigorous security measures, including the use of internment
by both Irish governments, the strong condemnation of the
Catholic Church, and perhaps most importantly the factor
stressed by the IRA itself, the lack of any sizeable support
for the campaign from the minority population.

This was partly related to the impact of the 1947
Education Act on middle-class Catholics. A new group of

63. Terence O'Neill and Sean Lemass meet in Belfast, 14 January 1965.

graduates and professionals, articulate and unwilling to settle for a position of second-class citizenship, and affected to some degree by liberalizing influences within Catholicism, now preferred 'to use their own efforts to achieve a tolerable present rather than wait behind the barricades for a heavenly Nationalist hereafter'.[31] Ulster Catholics, declared Dr G.B. Newe, a leading lay Catholic, in 1958, had a duty 'to co-operate with the *de facto* authority' (the Northern Ireland state) and must forsake the traditional Nationalist policy of passivity and abstentionism in political and social life.[32] Encouraged by the more conciliatory northern policy of Sean Lemass, who was Taoiseach (Prime Minister of the Irish Republic) in 1959–66, a new graduate movement had emerged by the early 1960s. This was soon transformed into the National Democratic Party, pledged to work for Irish unity by the consent of the northern majority – a considerable shift in traditional anti-partition policy.

These political developments, together with the successful

attraction of such new industries to Northern Ireland as the giant Courtaulds textiles plant at Carrickfergus (1950) and Du Pont's synthetic rubber plant near Derry (1960), seemed to point to a better future for the state as the inflexible Brookeborough finally relinquished the reins of office in March 1963.

The post-war period was not one of stagnation in the arts. The 1950s saw the emergence of Ulster-born playwrights such as Brian Friel – soon to gain international status – and Sam Thompson, while Brian Moore, Benedict Kiely and Sam Hanna Bell produced novels of distinction. At the turn of the decade, two important developments occurred in the broad field of culture. First came the establishment of the Belfast Lyric Theatre, perhaps the most exciting development in Ulster drama since the war. 'The Lyric' was to be the stimulus for a whole series of local plays, while encouraging poets such as Seamus Heaney and John Hewitt, both of whom ominously struck 'a note of communal menace'. The second development was the foundation in 1963 of the Ulster Folk Museum, truly illustrative of Ulster life, culture and the arts and of the imprints left on the North by both traditions.[33]

V

Brookeborough was succeeded by his Minister of Finance, Captain Terence O'Neill, a former Irish Guards officer and, like his predecessor, a scion of a Unionist landed family. O'Neill's first task was to tackle the economic problems neglected by the Brookeborough government. A firm believer in economic planning, the new Prime Minister quickly adopted the recommendations of the Wilson Report (1964) for the creation of 30,000 new jobs in manufacturing industry. His abler and more astute rival, Brian Faulkner, as Minister of Commerce, threw his formidable skills into the task and was able to secure the establishment of some 60 new factories over the next six years.

But more striking was O'Neill's attitude towards the one-third minority. Whilst sharing many traditional Protestant assumptions about Catholics and their cultural tradition, the new premier broke virgin soil by setting out to reduce sectarian bigotry and end the 40 years' 'cold war' with the south. His new 'era of good feeling' was marked by symbolic visits, notably to Catholic schools, while his policy of *détente* with the Republic found dramatic expression in Sean Lemass's historic visit to Stormont in January 1965, and O'Neill's return visit to Dublin the following month.[34]

O'Neill's policy at first earned the goodwill of the Nationalist parliamentarians led by Eddie McAteer (in 1965, they accepted the role of official opposition for the first time). However, it confused and divided Unionists and evoked a hostile reaction from the right wing of his Cabinet and, outside Parliament, from the Reverend Ian Paisley, 'a stoker of anti-popery fires' and a magnetic demagogue, then commencing a meteoric political career. To Paisley and others well-placed in the government and Unionist Party, O'Neill was 'betraying Ulster's British and Protestant heritage'.[35]

In fact, O'Neill gave nothing away to the South. Indeed, a major aim of his strategy was to entrench the North's constitutional position by winning significant Catholic support. Little of practical significance was done in the early O'Neill years to improve the position of the minority. In all major respects, Northern Ireland remained a Protestant state. To the long-standing nationalist resentment of such practices as discrimination, gerrymandering and government neglect of the depressed border counties was added uncontrolled anger at the decision to site the region's new university, not in predominantly Catholic Derry city with its long tradition of learning, but in the Protestant market town of Coleraine. Thus, while the Prime Minister had gone too far for many Unionists, Nationalists fumed at 'the betrayal by O'Neill of hopes falsely raised'.[36] Outside Parliament, the Catholic 'eleven-plus generation', epitomized by the young Derry schoolmaster, John Hume, were demanding equality of citizenship. It was their impatience with O'Neillism and mobilization in the Northern Ireland

Civil Rights Association (NICRA or CRA), formed in 1967, which proved the most potent threat ever mounted to the system of Unionist ascendancy.

The programme of the CRA, a broad-based, mainly Catholic pressure group, may be reduced to a single objective: British rights for British subjects. As a result it quickly secured British, especially Labour Party, support. In October 1968, a civil rights march in Derry – chosen as 'the citadel of discrimination'[37] – resulted in a police baton-charge in support of a government-imposed ban. The resulting bloody scenes, relayed throughout the world by the electronic media, marked a major turning-point in the North's history. The 'Troubles' had begun.

No longer could the Westminster government stand idly by. Under pressure from the Labour government, O'Neill announced a reform package. This conceded most of the marchers' demands, including a 'points system' for the allocation of houses, the reform of local government and the replacement of the Unionist-dominated Derry Corporation, but did not include the basic demand for 'one man, one vote'. A radical student movement, 'People's Democracy',

64 People's Democracy demonstration in Lurgan, April 1969.

now captured the headlines with a controversial civil rights march from Belfast to Derry in January 1969. The marchers were viciously attacked by loyalists at Burntollet, and it was against a background of mounting violence on the streets that O'Neill, beleaguered by the challenges from his own right-wing, and the target of much bitter abuse from Paisley and his paramilitary satellite, the Ulster Protestant Volunteers (UPV), finally called an election in February 1969. Much as O'Neill represented this in solemn tones as a 'crossroads election', he failed to win a decisive mandate for his reformist programme. Amid a series of bomb explosions by the outlawed loyalist Ulster Volunteer Force (UVF), aimed at his overthrow, O'Neill finally resigned in April, to be succeeded by the benign but ineffectual Major James Chichester-Clark.[38]

On the minority side, the 1969 election saw the eclipse of the old-style Nationalist Party by new civil rights MPs such as John Hume and Ivan Cooper, reflecting Catholic support for the new style of political action.

It was during Chichester-Clark's two-year premiership that the problem of violence became acute, with the eruption of naked sectarian warfare in Derry and Belfast in August 1969. In Belfast six died and 150 Catholic homes were burned. Not since the 1920s had such vicious mob violence disgraced the streets of Northern Ireland. As the Dublin government of Jack Lynch hovered on the brink of a risky military intervention on behalf of 'our people', the British Cabinet sent troops to hold the peace in the two cities. From now on, Westminster gradually took over responsibility for security in Northern Ireland, while in the 'Downing Street Declaration' of 19 August 1969, the British government re-affirmed the constitutional position while enjoining Stormont to maintain the momentum of reform.[39]

Events moved rapidly during the years 1969–72. At first, the people of the Catholic ghettoes fêted the British Army as their saviours from a merciless pogrom. But the rise at the end of 1969 of the Provisional IRA, formed by a group of Northern activists angry at the republican movement's notorious failure to defend the embattled nationalist areas

65 *Back-to-back housing in Belfast.*

during the August upsurge, transformed the entire situation. Financed and armed by elements in the south and, increasingly, by the Irish in America, the Provisionals were able to mount a major bombing offensive by the spring of 1971. The implementation by the Chichester-Clark government of 'one man, one vote', O'Neill's last political bequest, and proposals to disarm the RUC and disband the Ulster Special Constabulary made no difference to the republican militants, now bent on consummating the struggle for a 32-county republic. And as Catholic relations with the army soured in the face of a new 'forward' security policy, loyalist resentment at the erosion of Unionist supremacy found ominous expression in the formation of the paramilitary Ulster Defence Association (UDA) in 1971, and the verbal attacks of Paisley, now in the Stormont Parliament. On the constitutional front also, 1970 witnessed the formation of two new political parties – the non-sectarian, pro-union Alliance Party and, of great significance for the future, the amalgamation of the various civil rights and more progressive nationalist MPs in the Social Democratic and Labour Party, under the leadership of the Westminster parliamentarian, Gerry Fitt.

The replacement of Chichester-Clark by the more resolute and experienced Brian Faulkner (one of the chief architects of O'Neill's downfall) signalled the last phase in the disintegration of devolved government in Northern Ireland. Notwithstanding his reputation as a Unionist 'hard-liner', Faulkner saw the need to involve the opposition more actively in the system of government, but his efforts were dashed by the impact of the IRA's mounting campaign of violence. This led Faulkner in August 1971 to commit the fatal blunder of re-introducing internment without trial. Based upon poor intelligence and directed at only one section, this measure was viewed as an act of war by almost the entire Catholic population. As violence escalated frighteningly in the latter months of 1971, the nationalist community embarked on a massive campaign of protest and civil disobedience while the nationalist opposition abandoned Parliament. This secession was a fatal blow to the

Stormont system which had always depended on a degree of Catholic consent, no matter how resentful. But nationalist anger and British impatience towards the Faulkner regime reached breaking-point following the events of 'Bloody Sunday' in January 1972, when 13 civilians were shot dead by troops during an anti-internment march in Derry. The Conservative government of Edward Heath moved swiftly and, on 30 March 1972, the Northern Ireland Parliament was suspended. Direct rule from Westminster was now imposed under the direction of a Secretary of State, William Whitelaw, with a seat in the British Cabinet. Over 400 people had died violently since 1969, 173 in 1971 alone.[40]

As the last session of the prorogued Stormont closed on that March day, it was clear to unionists and nationalists alike that the old system of virtually untrammelled one-party rule had gone forever. Perhaps, given Northern Ireland's violent birth-pangs and the chronic difficulties posed by 'a divided society, a decaying economy and an irredentist neighbour',[41] the wonder is not that the 1920 settlement dissolved into violence in the 1960s and early 1970s but that it endured so long. But as IRA violence continued unabated and the forces of loyalist militancy prepared for the long-awaited 'backlash', it remained to be seen whether some form of cross-community consensus might yet emerge from the surrounding chaos.

Further reading

Despite the daunting spate of publications on Northern Ireland since the outbreak of the present disturbances in 1968, several works are essential reading for the student and general reader. The relevant chapters of F.S.L. Lyons, *Ireland Since the Famine*, Glasgow, 1973, provide a balanced survey of the period reviewed in this chapter. Equally valuable are Patrick Buckland, *A History of Northern Ireland*, Dublin, 1981, and David Harkness, *Northern Ireland Since 1920*, Dublin, 1983. Michael Farrell's *Northern Ireland, the Orange State*, London, 1976, provides a detailed account, albeit from a strong anti-Unionist perspective. All these works contain useful bibliographies.

Patrick Buckland's *Irish Unionism ii: Ulster Unionism and the Origins of Northern Ireland 1886–1922*, Dublin, 1973, contains a wealth of detail on the birth-pangs of the new state. The same author's *The Factory of Grievances: Devolved Government in Northern Ireland 1921–39* deals with the critical formative decades. There is a dearth of published material on northern nationalist politics in the post-partition era, although E. Rumpf and A.C. Hepburn, *Nationalism and Socialism in Twentieth Century Ireland*, Liverpool, 1977, is useful.

On the economy, D.S. Johnson's chapter in Liam Kennedy and Philip Ollerenshaw (eds.), *An Economic History of Ulster, 1820–1939*, Manchester, 1985, is indispensable. There is no published cultural history of Northern Ireland though John Boyd's article in the *Belfast Telegraph Centenary Edition*, 1 September 1970, is helpful here. Again, little has been written about the role of the churches, a gap partly filled by Eric Gallagher and Stanley Worrall's *Christians in Ulster, 1968–80*, Oxford, 1982. On the vexed issue of education, D.H. Akenson, *Education and Enmity: The Control of Schooling in Northern Ireland, 1920–50* is invaluable.

Among the plethora of books published since 1968, Terence O'Neill's *Autobiography*, London, 1972, and Henry Kelly's *How Stormont Fell*, Dublin, 1972 stand out. For documentary material, the reader may refer to A.C. Hepburn, *Conflict and Nationality in Modern Ireland*, London, 1980 and John Magee, *Northern Ireland: Crisis and Conflict*, London, 1974.

8 Living with the troubles: Northern Ireland since 1972

David Harkness

The devolved government experiment in Northern Ireland ended and direct Westminster rule began on 1 April 1972, a year described in the *Annual Register* as 'the worst year in Northern Ireland's history'. It was a year of violence and despair, with a record number of 467 politically-related killings, already well under way by April and horrifyingly augmented in July in the village of Claudy, in an incident hauntingly and poignantly commemorated in James Simmons's ballad of that name. It was the year of the destruction of Belfast's largest store, the Co-op, at the cost of £10m, and of worsening economic conditions, and it was the year when the Unionist paramilitary UDA emerged to match the Nationalist IRA, and of the Diplock Report, which soon led to non-jury courts to prevent the intimidation of jurors. It was also a year marked, in spite of four earlier years of turmoil, by a growth in productivity higher than in Great Britain, by Ulster poet Seamus Heaney's *Wintering Out*, by an Olympic gold medal for Ulster pentathlon star Mary Peters, and by Alex Higgins's first world snooker title.

Thirteen years later, 1985 was notable for a dazzling array of sporting achievements associated with the province. It was Dennis Taylor this time who became world snooker champion, while Joey Dunlop won the world motorcycling championship for the fourth time at Formula One, and Brian Reed for the first time in Formula Two, and world indoor bowls champion Jim Baker added his share of the world triples championship. The Northern Ireland football team clinched its place in the 1986 world cup finals,

66 The Opera House, Belfast.

the province claimed seven members of the Irish rugby fifteen, were winners of the Triple Crown and Five-nations Championship, and could surely claim, too, a share in the world featherweight boxing victory of Barry McGuigan.

During these years Northern Ireland's cultural life boomed: appropriately, given the restoration and recommissioning of the major theatre in Belfast (the Grand Opera House) in 1980, dramatists led the way: Stewart Parker, Brian Friel and Graham Reid gained national prominence with television commissions on top of their stage successes, and Martin Lynch and Frank McGuinness followed close behind; in poetry Seamus Heaney stood out above all rivals, but Paul Muldoon and Tom Paulin were given the accolade of editing separate modern anthologies, while in 1983 the freedom of Belfast was conferred on John Hewitt; novelists Brian Moore and Bernard McLaverty remained prominent. In the field of music James Galway made early headlines with his flute, while later on Barry Douglas edged towards the Tchaikovsky piano prize he would win in Moscow in

1986, and the Ulster Orchestra triumphed over financial difficulties to emerge as one of the best in the United Kingdom. At the popular level, success in the Eurovision song competition attended singer Dana and songwriter Phil Coulter, while Van Morrison continued to extend his international following. Comedian Frank Carson became a nationally known entertainer, as much for the manner of his expression as the quality of his material.

The years since 1972, then, have been years of distinction for some Ulster men and women, and years of achievement of a more ordinary kind for many unreported individuals who have succeeded in living normal lives, in rearing their children, doing a good job of work, being considerate neighbours, useful citizens. These have not just been years of political and paramilitary activity, by men of little learning and no wit and without any claim to distinction who have nevertheless captured media attention and dominated the province's image. Television footage, statistics of savagery, press column inches may not be the best indication of what is of lasting significance. This closing

67 'Operation Motorman', 31 July 1972: British troops occupy barricaded areas in Belfast and Derry.

chapter is, after all, the unfinished business at the end of a historical survey. It is true that a discouraging list of major industrial enterprises closed in Northern Ireland between 1972 and 1985: Rolls Royce, STC Larne, and International Engineering, Belfast, in 1975, British Enkalon, ICI, Courtaulds, Chemstrand, Du Pont's Orlon plant and Grundig in 1980 being but a selection. It is true, too, that hope blazed briefly with the Peace People from 1976 to 1978, and despair marked the hunger strike months of 1980 and 1981; that the total of deaths from violence mounted inexorably even if the annual destruction of persons and property declined steadily (annual statistics for violent deaths in 1972–85 were as follows; 467, 250, 214, 245, 295, 111, 81, 113, 75, 101, 97, 74, 64, 55); and constitutional initiatives failed consistently to overcome the gulf of bitter hatred and suspicion between communities. Inevitably, an account now of these years can only be a subjective one. For the historian too, 'the way I tell them' implies a personal selection and in so recent a period, without the perspective of distance; the historian's judgement may have no more

68 Aftermath of bomb explosion at a Belfast police station, 6 November 1974.

validity than anyone else's. Dramatic events and political initiatives may dominate the paragraphs that follow, and it is a fact that such things will have touched the lives of all the people of Northern Ireland. Nevertheless it should also be recalled that for most of the people, for most of the time, ordinary life proceeded and the mundane held sway.

I

Attempts after the fall of Stormont to find an alternative form of devolved administration in the province can be briefly outlined. In the first instance Stormont had been merely suspended and a search began immediately for a

69 *Parliament buildings at Stormont, opened 1932, designed by Arnold Thornely.*

local government body in which representatives of the minority could share power. Success almost attended this search; indeed, it became a fleeting reality, and it has remained since an elusive and popular ideal.

A green paper on the province's future, dated 30 October 1972, led to the publication, on 20 March 1973, of *Constitutional Proposals for Northern Ireland.*[1] It should be noted here that a referendum on Northern Ireland's constitutional position (promised to occur at not less than ten-yearly intervals) had taken place on 8 March, and that, despite a boycott called by its opponents, a 59 per cent turnout had been achieved, with 591,820 in favour of continued membership of the United Kingdom and only 6,463 voting for union with the Irish Republic. Elections by proportional representation followed on 28 June for an assembly which opened on 31 July. From the deliberations of this 78-member body, a mixed team of Unionists (U), the Social Democratic and Labour Party (SDLP) and the Alliance Party came together to announce, on 21 November, their willingness to share power. After discussions at Sunningdale on 6–9 December with representatives of the British and Irish governments, in which they agreed to embody the newly accepted 'Irish dimension' to the Northern Ireland situation in a future Council of Ireland, the first Power-sharing Executive took up office on 1 January 1974. Under Chief Executive Brian Faulkner (U) its members were: Deputy Chief Executive, Gerard Fitt (SDLP); Legal Minister and head of law reform, Oliver Napier (Alliance); Minister of Information, John L. Baxter (U); Minister of Environment, Roy Bradford (U); Minister of Housing, Local Government and Planning, Austin Currie (SDLP); Minister of Health and Social Services, Patrick Devlin (SDLP); Minister of Commerce, John Hume (SDLP); Minister of Finance, Herbert Kirk (U); Minister of Education, Basil McIvor (U); and Minister of Agriculture, Leslie Morrell (U). The Ministers outside the executive were Ivan Cooper (SDLP), Community Relations; Robert Cooper (Alliance), Manpower Services; Edward McGrady (SDLP), Planning and Co-ordination; and L. Hall Thompson (U), Chief Whip.

70 Northern Ireland Executive, 1974.

The Sunningdale concessions had alienated the bulk of Unionist opinion in the province, however, and with the Official Unionists, led by Harry West from 22 January, joining with Ian Paisley's Democratic Unionist Party (DUP) and William Craig's Vanguard Unionists to form a United Ulster Unionist Council (UUUC), opposition became formidable. Just how formidable became clear in the snap general election called and lost by Edward Heath in February, the results on the 28th revealing 11 UUUC victories, with the remaining seat being retained by the SDLP. The new Labour government appointed Merlyn Rees Secretary of State for Northern Ireland in place of Francis Pym, who had only replaced William Whitelaw, the province's first Secretary of State, the previous November. But when in May 1974 the power-sharing executive reaffirmed its commitment to Sunningdale, UUUC anger exploded and Rees could not mobilize support to combat a province-wide strike organized by the Ulster Workers Council to begin on the 15th. The executive proved unable to carry on in the face of sustained hostility and collapsed on the 28th, the strike being called off the next day. Direct rule resumed.

Next a Constitutional Convention was tried. Announced on 4 July, its progress was delayed by the need for a second general election to reaffirm Labour's mandate (an election in which Harry West lost his seat) but its own elections took place on 1 May 1975 and its 78 members met at Stormont on the 8th. Dominated by the 47-strong UUUC group, it rejected Westminster's insistence on power-sharing and sent its report in favour of a return to strong majority devolved rule to Rees on 7 November.[2] This was rejected by Government and although the Convention was recalled on 3 February 1976, it refused to alter its stance and was therefore dissolved formally on 5 March.

Roy Mason replaced Rees on 10 September 1976. Although he could say at the end of 1977 that 'the atmosphere has undergone a change for the better and I am determined that it will improve still further. The message for 1978 is one of real hope',[3] and although he talked of establishing an assembly without legislative powers to run local departments he was no more successful than the Conservative Humphrey Atkins (who replaced him in turn on 5 May 1979) in translating discussions into institutional reality. Atkins did initiate constitutional talks in January 1980, set out alternative options based on power-sharing or a majority-dominated committee system in July, and suggested an advisory council of already-elected representatives a year later, in July 1981, but he obtained no support. It was not until the coming of Secretary of State James Prior, on 13 September 1981, that steps were at last taken to restore a forum for local political debate.

Prior's plans were more ambitious but in the end scarcely more successful. A complex scheme for 'rolling devolution' was launched on 20 April 1982,[4] with elections for another 78-member assembly on 20 October following, after the Royal assent had been given on 23 July. This Assembly was bedevilled from the outset, however, by the abstention of the minority representatives, principally the SDLP, with 14, but also Provisional Sinn Feín (PSF) which had won 5 seats (the Official Unionists having won 26, DUP 21, Alliance 10 and other Unionists 2). Designed to acquire real power once genuine cross-community support could be demonstrated, the Assembly began life simply as a scrutinizing body, examining government legislative proposals and setting up a series of committees to oversee the principal areas of economic and social life. In this capacity it did excellent work but it was destined not to move further, and after periods of dissension which reflected the deep divisions within the broad Unionist camp, and after a brief flurry of Unionist solidarity in the face of the Anglo-Irish Agreement of 15 November 1985, it was finally dissolved by Secretary of State Tom King on 23 June 1986 (Prior had been replaced by Douglas Hurd in September 1984 and he in turn by King a year later).

II

The Anglo-Irish Agreement was itself the culmination of yet another process of exploration, this time between the London and Dublin governments. After a preliminary meeting between Charles Haughey and Margaret Thatcher in May 1980, a formal summit was arranged to bring the two prime ministers together in Dublin on 8 December.

71 'Ulster says No' campaign: Rev. Ian Paisley and Mr James Molyneaux campaigning against the Anglo-Irish Agreement.

On this occasion it was announced that 'the totality of the relationship within these islands' would be reviewed,[5] a somewhat ambiguous statement variously interpreted and utilized for short-term gain in a London under hunger-strike pressures and a Dublin facing economic crisis and fearing electoral defeat. Defeat duly followed for Haughey in June 1981, but the process was taken forward by his successor, Garret FitzGerald, and Mrs Thatcher on 6 November, when proposals for an Anglo-Irish Inter-governmental Council were announced.

By the time of Haughey's return to power in February 1982, differences of interpretation of the northern problem between the major parties in the Republic had become evident, but, as relations between Thatcher and Haughey worsened over the Falklands War, it was not until Garret FitzGerald in turn had regained power in November 1982 that further discussions occurred. FitzGerald met Thatcher in Brussels in March 1983 and two months later embarked on the New Ireland Forum, the most elaborate exercise ever conducted by elected nationalist representatives to envisage what shape a united Ireland might take. The deliberations and eventual *Report*[6] of the Forum took longer than expected, and served to postpone Anglo-Irish meetings or London initiatives, but once it had been completed in May 1984 it made some response from London essential. Although this response, in December 1984 was (in line with broad Unionist opinion) apparently dismissive, in due course a bolder reply proved possible.

Recognizing Dublin's fear of Provisional Sinn Feín growth at the expense of the SDLP, and itself anxious to break the deadlock in the Stormont Assembly, to find ways both to bring constitutional nationalists into the devolutionary process and to give expression to their cultural tradition and political aspirations, and also, if possible, to 'drain off the water of passive nationalist support in which the PSF and IRA fishes swim', the British government shocked Unionists of all colours by signing an agreement with Dublin at Hillsborough on 15 November 1985. Though asserting at the start of the joint undertaking that 'any change in the status of Northern Ireland would only come about with the consent of a majority of the people of Northern Ireland',[7] the terms of the Agreement, which established an Inter-governmental Conference of Ministers, backed by a secretariat (to be housed in Northern Ireland), and with wide-ranging responsibilities (political, legal, economic, social and cultural, and for security), outraged Unionist susceptibilities. The failure to consult their representatives, while those of their opponents were fully involved, proved the final straw. Ignoring its sensitive preface and interpreting its terms in the worst possible way, Unionist politicians to a man declared the Union in peril and in December converted the Assembly into a Grand Committee with the sole purpose of examining the Agreement. The province entered a new phase of tension and divided counsel and in a bid to recover the initiative the elected Unionist Members of Parliament resigned *en bloc* on 15 December. Presenting the 15 by-elections of 23 January 1986 as a referendum on the Agreement, and aiming for a massive half-million Unionist votes, the combined Unionists' vote fell somewhat short (with 418,239), and suffered the humiliation of losing the Newry-Armagh seat to the SDLP deputy leader, Seamus Mallon. Nevertheless the total vote, in a 62.2 per cent turnout on a wet winter Thursday, was an impressive popular display of solidarity and irritation.

The province had profited from the close parliamentary rivalry at Westminster in April 1978 when the hard-pressed Labour government agreed to a revision of Northern Irish constituency sizes to bring them into line with those of the rest of the United Kingdom. The boundary revision then set in motion increased the total of seats from 12 to 17, a measure which first came into effect in the election of June 1983 when the Official Unionists (OUP) won 11 seats, DUP 3 and UUUP (James Kilfedder) 1, the remaining two going to SDLP and PSF.

This bald outline of constitutional experiment hints only towards the end at the political turmoil at the centre of Northern Irish life in these years. The old Unionist solidarity, assisted by access to state power and by a self-image of superiority and privilege, quickly fragmented once direct rule from Westminster was imposed. The divisions apparent under O'Neill hardened and multiplied. To the Democratic Unionists, established by Ian Paisley and Desmond Boal in September 1971, was added Ulster Vanguard early in 1972, a ginger group to promote unity, oppose any suggestion of direct rule and demand tougher security policies. Led by William Craig, Vanguard became an alternative political party in 1973, a focus for those discontented with the leadership of Brian Faulkner. But Craig's willingness to form an emergency alliance with the SDLP during the 1975 Constitutional Convention precipitated further division, the bulk of his Vanguard Unionist Progressive Party breaking away, under Ernest Baird, to form the United Ulster Unionist Movement, which itself in 1977 became the short-lived United Ulster Unionist Party (UUUP).

Meanwhile the rejection of the Sunningdale proposals[8] by the Ulster Unionist Council in January 1974 had led to the resignation of Brian Faulkner and his replacement as leader by Harry West. Faulkner then founded his own Unionist Party of Northern Ireland, leaving the popular label 'Official Unionists' to adhere to the party he had left. From the manoeuvrings for advantage during the Constitutional Convention (1975–6) the Official Unionists and the Democratic Unionists again emerged as the principal vehicle of popular unionism with Harry West (after a brief appearance during 1974 as MP for Fermanagh-South Tyrone) finally resigning his leadership to James Molyneaux in 1979. Rivalry between these parties has continued, but there has also been acute division within the Official Unionists over the desirability of devolved government, on the one hand, and of full integration into the United Kingdom – the course championed especially by Enoch Powell after becoming MP for South Down in October 1974 – on the other. In elections for the European Parliament, in 1979 and 1984, the more visible, dynamic and apparently single-minded leader of the DUP has outclassed his OUP rivals, but in the less exciting fields of local government and assembly polls, apart from a fractional reverse in voting numbers (but not seats) in the 1981 local elections, the Official Unionists have maintained superiority. The Westminster elections of 1983 showed a 34 per cent share of the poll for the OU against 20 for the DUP, with 1985 local government figures being 29.4 against 24.3.

The Democratic Unionists, vehemently opposed to power-sharing in 1974 and enthusiastic backers of the Workers Council strike which undermined the executive in May of that year, became forceful exponents of a return to majority-rule and devolved government in the Constitutional Convention in 1975 and 1976. In the Westminster elections of May 1979 the party added two more members to the North Antrim seat held by Paisley since 1970, most notably that of Peter Robinson in East Belfast, a success topped by that of Paisley himself in the June 1979 European election. The party's popularity continued to grow until 1981, since when its voting strength has diminished somewhat, though its leader has retained his image as the most intransigent critic of the government's direct rule policies and in particular its programme of talks with Dublin leaders. Paisley was perhaps the politician most prepared to make something of the scrutinizing role of James Prior's 1982 Assembly but was also the most outspoken opponent of the Anglo-Irish Agreement of 15 November 1985, taking a lead in the transformation of the Assembly into a forum of opposition to that Agreement, a development that led to its early dissolution. Under the strain of these events, members of the DUP, as of the OUP, have toyed with the concept of 'independence' for Northern Ireland, in this instance voiced by the deputy party leader, Peter Robinson. Little inclination has been shown to accept the Anglo-Irish framework created in 1985, or to contemplate round-table talks while the Agreement is still in being, though a glance at the economic and political circumstances of the feared Republic might have pointed to the unreality of any threat of Irish unity.

The Alliance Party, born in 1970 in an effort to bridge the

sectarian community divide, has not succeeded in reaching ten per cent of the votes cast since the Westminster election of 1979 (when it polled 11.8 per cent), despite a distinguished record under its leader Oliver Napier and his successors John Cushnahan (in 1984) and John Alderdice (1987). Alliance still retained a middle-class image, even though its members must have included at least some of those who had belonged to the NI Labour Party and some former Nationalists who had come to identify their interests as lying within the United Kingdom, satisfied, presumably, by the real advances in equality of citizenship and, no doubt, worried by the major problems facing a Republic in economic distress and politically unable to adopt social measures which are taken for granted in the north.

III

Amongst the nationalist community there was also division and change of direction during this period. The SDLP, created in 1970 by the combination of seven Stormont politicians, represented a broad spectrum from the start. It lost its best known Labour figure, Paddy Devlin, in 1977; its founding leader, Gerry Fitt, resigned over policy in 1979; and a third founder member, Senator Paddy Wilson, had become a victim of sectarian murder in 1973. Since 1979 it has been led by John Hume, the one politician in the province who has continued to grow in international stature and political skill. Elected MEP in 1979, and Westminster MP for Foyle in 1983, he has developed his party from an essentially pragmatic stance within Northern Ireland (seeking both equality of opportunity and input into decision-making for members of the nationalist/Catholic community, with a long-term goal of Irish unity) to a still pragmatic approach in the broader context of north–south relationships and Irish–British relationships, with a clear preference for a Northern Ireland with special safeguards within an Irish rather than a British state. Prepared to play a full part in the power-sharing Executive, and prepared to pursue that objective for some further time, despite growing Unionist rejection, Hume eventually tired of Britain's apparent lack of will to deal with Unionist intransigence and shifted his party's perspective. Damaged by the 1981 hunger-strikes which so polarized the province, and electorally threatened from behind by Provisional Sinn Féin (PSF), he and his colleagues have looked to Dublin to speak for constitutional nationalism, in an effort to widen the context from that 'narrow ground'[9] of Northern Ireland where numbers alone traditionally ensure nationalist defeat.

In 1982 the SDLP rejected Prior's rolling devolution as being condemned to failure in advance by Unionist refusal to share power. The elections were fought, nonetheless, on an abstentionist ticket, taking on PSF for the first time at the polls and taking 18.8 per cent of the vote against PSF's 10.1 per cent. John Hume had already begun to articulate his demand for the wider debate of Northern Ireland's problem and he coupled his rejection of the Assembly in 1982 with a specific call for a Council for a New Ireland to enable politicians, north and south, to discuss the implications of Irish unity. In this call lay the genesis of the New Ireland Forum and the 1985 Anglo-Irish Agreement and although there were other voices within the SDLP, John Hume held the reins firmly in his hands. While awaiting a positive response from Unionism, he rejects equally the mere pursuit of an end to the Irish border as a policy for his own party and, with more vehemence, the 'ballot and bullet' strategies of PSF.

Provisional Sinn Féin, which like the Provisional IRA (PIRA) dated from the December 1969 split in the movement, also underwent major change. Initially dominated by old guard southern leaders, it effectively abandoned their four-province, federal policy in 1980 and adopted instead a demand for a unitary 32-county Irish state, a demand which became official policy in 1982 under the newly consolidated northern leadership of Gerry Adams. Fully committed to supporting 'the armed struggle', Sinn Féin ran candidates for the 1982 assembly and won 5 seats, with 10.1 per cent of the votes cast; and in the Westminster elections of 1983 it improved this percentage to 13.3. Party leader Gerry Adams also won West Belfast in this election, though the party lost Fermanagh-South Tyrone, first held by hunger-striker Bobby Sands in April 1981 and, after his death, by Owen Carron. In the local elections of 1985 its vote was reduced to 11.8 per cent, but its organizational and financial resources maintain the party as a credible threat to the SDLP's leadership of the nationalist community in a way that the brief Independent Irish Party (1977–83) did not and the more interesting Workers Party does not. The Workers Party, operating to the south as well as the north of the border, grew out of the Official IRA in the north, in 1982, incorporating the former Republican Clubs. Under the northern leadership of Seamus Lynch, vice-president of the all-island party, it seeks an eventual Irish socialist republic but is prepared for the moment to work within the northern state. As yet it has small electoral support.

Of those prepared to operate without reference to popular support, the PIRA must be treated first, if only because of its great destructive impact. In its record of killings, bombings, destruction of businesses and jobs, sums raised through robbery and intimidation, it must take pride of place. It can claim part credit for the ending of the Stormont administration but it is hard to imagine that it can contribute to a healthier society in the future by way of replacement. It may seek 'Brits Out' and a new Ireland that is Gaelic and free, but its methods are more likely to bring a desert to be inhabited by a people economically reduced and dependent upon other nations for survival. The PIRA record from 1972 is one of fluctuating fortunes, times of confidence and increased destruction alternating with losses through security force action, informing and internal feuding. Boosted at home and abroad by the deaths of hunger strikers in 1981, the organization has continued into the 1980s by combining a reduced pressure within Northern Ireland with occasional forays into Britain itself. It has occasionally been surpassed in ruthlessness by members of the Irish National Liberation Army, the military wing of

72 IRA gunmen operating in the Markets area of Belfast,
11 August 1971.

the Irish Republican Socialist Party, which gained recruits
during a protracted PIRA truce in 1975 and which has ever
since paralleled PIRA activity on a smaller if sometimes
more spectacular scale. For each it is easier to compile the
record of past atrocity than future vision.

Not that the record of the main Unionist paramilitary
organization is much better: the Ulster Defence Association
and its suspected ancillaries such as the Ulster Freedom
Fighters and the Protestant Action Force may not be
predisposed to effect economic destruction, but protection
and other rackets, the sectarian killings of Catholics and
further exercises in intimidation are not any more attractive
for claiming
to be 'reactive' or 'defensive'.

IV

All in all, th3 years since 1972 are a sorry record of
incompatible aims and incapacity to live and let live, to find

the shared ground and expand through negotiation and working compromise a shared management of this small and lightly-populated corner of the island of Ireland. The problem persists because sovereignty lies at the heart of the divisions between nationalist and unionist and because so far no unionist is prepared to risk what he has – full British citizenship and membership of the United Kingdom – for the slightest step towards what might become an unmanageable, slippery slope into the Irish Republic. Nationalists, in turn, retain an all-island aspiration. Meanwhile deadlock and impasse and violent deeds disfigure the political landscape, and inexorable, relentless decline spreads across the province's economy.

The impressionistic picture given by the list of closures at the beginning of this chapter is only too readily confirmed by the regular analyses, conducted by accountants, businessmen and academics alike, of Northern Ireland's 'economic situation and prospects'.[10] Not a separate economy as such, more a depressed region of the United Kingdom economy, Northern Ireland nevertheless keeps a full record of employment and production statistics. They are deeply disheartening.

'Political developments have created considerable uncertainty about the course of events in the province over the next few years', begins the Coopers and Lybrand *Survey of the Northern Ireland Economy* for January 1986, and it proceeds to point out the extent of recent economic decline: industrial output down 17 per cent since 1978, 21 per cent since 1973; manufacturing jobs down 43 per cent since 1970; unemployment continuing to rise. Indeed early hopes of a stable if 'unacceptable' unemployment level of around 20 per cent were dashed as a total of 124,717 (21.5 per cent) was reached by May 1986 (grown to 129,432 by July). Jobs in manufacturing industry fell below 100,000 for the first time, in March 1986 (98,270), while jobs in the construction industry fell by 10 per cent in the first quarter of the year. Tables of employment by sector, and a breakdown of manufacturing as an example, give the extent and direction of change since 1981 (see below).

TABLE 1   *Numbers employed by sector*

Sector	1981	1982	1983	1984	1985	% change 1981-5
Agriculture, forestry & fisheries*	8,750	8,910	9,510	9,710	9,740	+11.3
Manufacture	119,750	107,110	102,600	102,160	100,690	−15.9
Construction	25,800	25,790	24,710	23,790	22,850	−11.4
Energy & water	10,100	9,560	9,310	9,250	9,150	− 9.4
Services	320,500	321,260	320,710	319,650	320,830	+ 0.1
TOTAL	484,900	472,690	466,840	464,740	463,260	− 4.5

*Excluding self-employed
Source: Coopers & Lybrand, *NI Economy: Review of the Economic Situation and Prospects,* Jan. 1986.

TABLE 2   *Manufacturing industrial employment in Northern Ireland*

	1979	1986	% change
Engineering and allied trades	41,600	29,650	−28.7
Textiles	30,000	11,030	−63.3
Food, drink & tobacco	22,600	18,720	−17.2
Clothing	18,900	16,220	−14.2
Other	26,900	22,650	−15.8
TOTALS	140,000	98,270	−29.5

Source: *TSB Business Outlook & Economic Review,* Sept. 1986.

Further analysis of jobs by region and religion could show that in November 1985 in the more depressed, and more solidly Catholic – if more lightly populated and more remote – area west of the Bann, unemployment was 28.8 per cent of the population, compared with 18.2 per cent east of the Bann, at a time when the overall figure stood at 21.8 per cent. According to the calculations of the Fair Employment Agency, using 1981 statistics, the burden of unemployment was noticeably uneven between Catholic and Protestant, the former community being then 25.5 per cent unemployed, the latter 10.2 per cent. Since then both communities have suffered severe job losses but new jobs

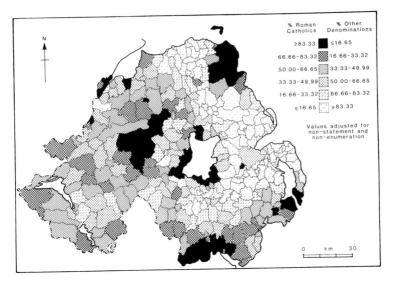

% Roman Catholics	% Other Denominations
≥83.33	≤16.65
66.66-83.32	16.66-33.32
50.00-66.65	33.33-49.99
33.33-49.99	50.00-66.65
16.66-33.32	66.66-83.32
≤16.65	≥83.33

Values adjusted for
non-statement and
non-enumeration

0   km   30

73 Religious distribution, 1981.

have been easier to create in predominantly Protestant areas
so that the disparity is likely to have increased.

   1981 was a census year. The *Report*[11] revealed a
workforce of 629,759, of which 105,465 were unemployed.
Compared to that of the previous decade it showed a
number of changes. Population figures indicated a slight
drop only, from an accepted figure in 1971 of 1,536,065 to a
corrected 1981 total of 1,532,200, but movement of
population was more considerable with Belfast reducing
from a total of 416,679 in 1971 to 314,270 ten years later,
reflecting a short-distance move to satellite towns, as well as
steady urban renewal at lower population densities. With
people migrating out, the province as a whole is assumed to
have lost some 134,000 over the decade (compared to only
60,000 between 1961 and 1971). 1985 figures suggest that
emigration in the eighties has slowed again, and that the
population may have risen once more, to 1,578,500 by the
end of 1984.

   Production, employment and population statistics over
the past 15 years reflect the hammer blows inflicted on the

province by the oil crises of 1973 and 1979 which wiped out almost completely the artificial fibre industry and which had such an extensive and damaging impact on a wide range of local firms, as well as contributing to the malaise in UK manufacturing industry in general. They also reflect fluctuations in construction; failures of judgement, such as the De Lorean and Lear Fan enterprises (closed in 1982 and 1985 respectively); and latterly the contraction of tobacco production. All of these, combined with the image projected by violence and communal strife, have made it impossible to achieve an adequate replacement supply of new jobs and inward investment, even though levels of productivity have been high and labour relations good.

Sadly, the heroic efforts in the 1950s and 60s to replace decayed industries, that had served the province for a century and a half, have seen but short-lived success. After two decades the peripheral units of multi-national companies, enticed to the province at considerable cost, were closed down as world recession and oil-induced price rises called for retrenchment. Only growth in service sector employment has served to counter this sorry trend and with 45 per cent of jobs in the mid-1980s within the public sector, employment remains acutely vulnerable to government cuts. When it is realized that some 30,000 jobs are involved in the security industry (including the Ulster Defence Regiment and RUC) the picture is seen to be gloomy indeed. The discovery by the Geological Survey in 1984 of extensive deposits of lignite in Co. Tyrone may have the happy repercussion of lowering the cost of electricity production in the province but is of itself insufficient to induce much optimism. If proceeded with it will be offset by social costs and will serve in the end only to reduce existing subsidies from the national exchequer.

So what of the agricultural sector, the underlying strength of the old economy? Here, too, post-war shrinkage has been dramatic. A total workforce of 101,000 in 1950 had by 1983 reduced to 54,000, all but 8,950 being self-employed. While it remains the most important single employer (with direct and ancillary employment of some 13 per cent) and

74 New and old housing in Belfast.

contributes some 6 per cent of the United Kingdom's gross
domestic product from its 45,000 farms (half of them very
small), it has followed the same employment decline as the
province's industrial sector.

In the realm of everyday life – in health and housing,
education and leisure, welfare, the arts and science – much
has been achieved in the period under review. Northern
Ireland always had an admirable ratio of population to area
and to outdoor amenity, especially sailing and golf, fishing
and hill-walking, and in the 15 years of direct rule a string
of leisure centres has amplified this provision. The BBC
regional headquarters, Queen's University and the University
of Ulster, the province's two national museums (The Ulster
Folk and Transport Museum at Cultra and the Ulster
Museum in Belfast), the Arts Council, and the Ulster

Orchestra, as well as a host of local societies for drama and local studies, language and speech and music, ensure the vitality of cultural activity at every level, and a continued contribution to scientific research, theoretical and applied.

The Northern Ireland Housing Executive (NIHE), criticized by some for wastefulness and insensitivity to the individual householder, has a proud record of housebuilding achievement. In Belfast alone it has done much to modernize a Victorian boom city, so that from ashes that were in the main the result of planning decisions there have arisen new dwellings at less density, realigned streets and a range of facilities, for the aged as for the young. Since 1972 it is probably true to say that half the average house completions have been achieved by the public sector NIHE. Total numbers have fluctuated from 11,650 (1972) to 6,084 (1982) per annum, with the NIHE building some 62,589 houses between 1972 and 1984.

On the other hand, very little has occurred to bring the children of the province into closer contact than is permitted by an educational system divided by religious allegiance. Efforts to rationalize teacher training foundered in 1980 on charges of interference in Roman Catholic rights, and private enterprise efforts to create integrated schools have made slow progress: Lagan College, a mixed ability secondary school, was founded in 1981, and in 1985 another, Hazelwood College, and two primary schools, Hazelwood's own and Forge – all in the Belfast area. It should also be said, however, that much initiative has been shown in a variety of ways to bring children into contact, in debates, projects and social and community work, and that it is in such areas as these, and in the burgeoning voluntary work field (literally in the case of the Farset farm project) that the unsung successes occur. Corrymeela, or PACE (Protestant and Catholic Encounter), or the Churches Central Committee for Community Work may momentarily hit the headlines, but the quality of everyday life, for adults as for children, is affected much more by a host of small groups giving time and care across and within community boundaries.

75 *Mrs Thatcher and Dr Garret FitzGerald signing the Anglo-Irish Agreement, November 1986.*

Common membership of the United Kingdom and the Republic of Ireland in the European Economic Community, from 1 January 1973, was expected to provide an improving climate in which to overcome national and local differences. While much remains to be resolved there is no doubt that, within the EEC itself, member countries are now much better informed of Northern Ireland's problems and have proved very sympathetic towards proposals for assistance and development (even to the extent of making exceptions to general rules in order to include a region technically outside the scope of particular Community schemes). Support for both integrated urban and rural development initiatives has been given, urban renewal and communication networks have been funded and invaluable cultural initiatives made, in particular 50 per cent grants from the Regional Fund which have led to the building of heritage interpretation centres, such as that at the Giant's Causeway, and leisure facilities, such as the Ardhowen Theatre, Enniskillen. These latter grants, apart from improving the quality of contemporary life, are in addition to help given to improve the tourist infrastructure of an area now well equipped to increase its visitors, once peace and tranquillity are secured.

As is so often the case in societies under stress, the impossibility of complacency induces, in some at least, a determination to seek better things. Northern Ireland, in the last decade and a half, has witnessed considerable activity amongst, for example, women's groups, welfare associations, environmentalists and law reformers, out of all proportion to its small population. It is because of this activity, and because of this alone, that an open-ended survey can pause on a note of guarded optimism.

Further reading

For a contemporary period there can be no established corpus of further reading, but the following books, self-explanatory in title, should prove useful to those seeking greater depth.

P. Arthur, *Government and Politics in Northern Ireland*, London, 1984.

R.H. Buchanan & B.M. Walker (eds.), *Province, City and People: Belfast and its Region*, Antrim, 1987, was the handbook for the British Association visit to Belfast, summer 1987, and is a thorough survey of current matters.

P. Compton, *Demographic Trends in Northern Ireland*, Northern Ireland Economic Council Report, 57, Belfast, 1986.

John Darby (ed.), *Northern Ireland: Background to Conflict*, Belfast, 1983.

D. Harkness, *Northern Ireland since 1920*, Dublin, 1983.

Ed. Moloney and Andy Pollak, *Paisley*, Swords, 1986.

P. O'Malley, *The Uncivil Wars: Ireland To-day*, Belfast, 1983.

Notes

Chapter 1 pp. 13–41

1 M. Herity and G. Eogan, *Ireland in Prehistory*, London, 1977, p. 37.
2 ibid., pp. 238–40.
3 T.F. O'Rahilly, *Early Irish History and Mythology*, Dublin, 1946, pp. 1–42.
4 idem.
5 K.H. Jackson, *The Oldest Irish Tradition: a Window on the Iron Age*, Cambridge, 1964.
6 The most recent survey of the problem is by N.B. Aitchison, 'The Ulster Cycle: heroic image and historical reality', *Journal of Medieval History*, 13, 1987, pp. 87–116; cf. also, J. Carney, 'The history of early Irish literature: the state of research', in G. MacEoin, A. Ahlqvist and D. Ó hAodha (eds.), *Proceedings of the Sixth International Congress of Celtic Studies*, Dublin, 1983, pp. 113–30.
7 F.J Byrne, 'Introduction', in T. O'Neill, *The Irish Hand*, Dublin, 1984, pp. xvi–xviii; J.P. Mallory, 'The sword of the Ulster Cycle', in B.G. Scott (ed.), *Studies on Early Ireland*, 1981, pp. 99–114; J.P. Mallory, 'Silver in the Ulster Cycle of Tales', in D. Ellis Evans, J.G. Griffith and E.M. Jope (eds.), *Proceedings of the Seventh International Congress of Celtic Studies*, Oxford, 1986, pp. 31–78.
8 See for example, F.J. Byrne, 'Introduction', in T. O'Neill, *The Irish Hand*, Dublin, 1984, pp. xvi–xviii.
9 cf. also N.B. Aitchison, 'The Ulster Cycle: heroic image and historical reality', *Journal of Medieval History*, 13, 1987, pp. 109–110; F.J. Byrne, *Irish Kings and High Kings*, London, 1973, pp. 106–7.
10 H.W. Lett, 'The Great Wall of Ulidia commonly known as "The Dane's Cast", or "Gleann-na-muice-duibhe"', *Ulster Journal of Archaeology*, series 2, 3, 1896–7, pp. 23–9 and 65–82.
11 W.F. De Vismes Kane, 'The Black Pig's dyke: the ancient boundary fortification of Uladh', *Proceedings of the Royal Irish Academy*, C, 27, 1909, pp. 301–28, 'The Dun of Drumsna: a frontier fortification of the Kingdoms of Aileagh and Cruaghan', *Proc. Roy. Ir. Acad.*, C, 32, 1915, pp. 324–32; 'Additional researches on the Black Pig's Dyke', *Proceedings of the Royal Irish Academy*, C, 33, 1917, pp. 539–63.
12 O. Davies, 'A summary of the Archaeology of Ulster', *Ulster Journal*

of Archaeology, series 3, 11, 1948, p. 32. Incidentally in this article Davies appears to accept a theory of climatic determinism when he states that 'the warm moist climate which prevails to-day has covered the mountains with a blanket of peat which makes them practically valueless, has made the plains damp and marshy, and has created a heavy atmosphere which produces mental stagnation and laziness, which form a drag on the natural capabilities of the people' (cf. p. 1). This type of determinism was also espoused by the archaeologist R.A.S. Macalister. Quoted by E. Estyn Evans in *The Personality of Ireland*, Cambridge, 1973, p. 20.

13 O. Davies, 'The Black Pig's Dyke', *Ulster Journal of Archaeology*, series 3, 18, 1955, pp. 1, 35.

14 E. Estyn Evans, *The Personality of Ireland*, Cambridge, 1973, pp. 26–7.

15 C.J. Lynn, 'The Dorsey and other linear earthworks', in B.G. Scott (ed.), *Studies on Early Ireland*, Belfast, 1981, pp. 121–8; C.J. Lynn, 'Navan fort: a draft summary of D.M. Waterman's Excavations', *Emania*, 1, 1986, pp. 11–19; R.B. Warner, 'Preliminary Schedules of Sites and Stray Finds in the Navan Complex', *Emania*, 1, 1986, pp. 5–9.

16 M.G.L. Baillie, 'The Central Post from Navan Fort: the first step towards a better understanding of the Early Iron Age', *Emania*, 1, 1986, pp. 20–21.

17 Ian Adamson, *Cruthin: the Ancient Kindred*, Newtownards, 1974, p. 12.

18 See also Ian Adamson, *Bangor: Light of the World*, Bangor, 1979; *The Identity of Ulster, the Land, the Language and the People*, Newtownards, 1982; Michael Hall, *Ulster: the Hidden History*, Belfast, 1986; Michael Sheane, *Ulster and the Lords of the North*, Stockport, 1980. 'Where Cúchulainn is still a hero', *Irish Times*, 6 April 1987, p. 13, indicates how paramilitary groups have made use of this interpretation.

19 T.F. O'Rahilly, *Early Irish History and Mythology*, Dublin, 1946. For criticisms see below.

20 F.J. Byrne, 'The Ireland of Saint Columba', *Historical Studies*, 5, 1965, p. 38.

21 For an enlightened discussion of this general problem with pertinent examples see D. Ó Corráin, 'Historical need and literary narrative', in D. Ellis Evans, J.G. Griffith and E.M. Jope (eds.), *Proceedings of the Seventh International Congress of Celtic Studies*, Oxford, 1986, pp. 141–58.

22 T.F. O'Rahilly, *Early Irish History and Mythology*, Dublin, 1946, p. 194.

23 For a recent summary and analysis see B. Raftery, *La Tène in Ireland, Problems of Origin and Chronology*, Marburg, 1984, pp. 324–35; S. Piggott, 'The coming of the Celts, the archaeological argument', in G. MacEoin, A. Ahlqvist and D. Ó hAodha (eds.), *Proceedings of the Sixth International Congress of Celtic Studies*, Dublin, 1983, pp. 139–40.

24 J. Bannerman, *Studies in the History of Dál Riada*, Edinburgh, 1974; M.O. Anderson, *Kings and Kinship in Early Scotland*, Edinburgh, 1973; F.J. Byrne, *Irish Kings and High Kings*, London, 1973.

25 F.J. Byrne, op.cit. p. 108.

26 T. Charles-Edwards and F. Kelly, *Bechbretha*, Dublin, 1983, pp. 68–9, 123–31.

27 F.J. Byrne, op. cit., pp. 73, 82–3.

28 D. Ó Corráin, 'Historical need and literary narrative', in D. Ellis Evans, J.G. Griffith and E.M. Jope (eds.), *Proceedings of the Seventh International Congress of Celtic Studies*, Oxford, 1986, pp. 151–2.

29 ibid., pp. 150–51.

30 F.J. Byrne, op. cit. ff pp. 114,

31 ibid., p. 127.

32 The foregoing is based largely on 'Ulster kings', chapter 7 in F.J. Byrne's *Irish Kings and High Kings*.

Chapter 2 pp. 44–76

1 Cenél nEóghain means the people; Tír Eóghain the land they occupied, wherever that might be. English usage concentrated on the latter name, but contemporary Irish writers refer to the kingdom as Cenél nEóghain.

2 The incoming people are known to modern scholars by several names, usually as 'Anglo-Normans', in order to avoid the modern linguistic and nationalistic connotations of the word 'English'. They called themselves 'English', however, in the sense of 'men owing allegiance to the king of England'. It is in this sense that I use it here.

3 Giraldus Cambrensis, *Expugnatio Hibernica: the Conquest of Ireland*, eds. A.B.. Scott and F.X. Martin, ch. XVI; *Annals of Ulster*, 1181, 1182.

4 *Calendar of Documents relating to Ireland*, vol. II, nos. 929, 1918, 2073.

5 D.A. Chart (ed.), *The Register of John Swayne*, Belfast, 1935, pp. 56, 61, 114, 118.

6 *Annals of the Four Masters*, 1433, 1434, 1442, 1444.

Chapter 3 pp. 77–103

1 Good surveys of social and economic conditions in Ulster and elsewhere in Gaelic Ireland can be found in K.W. Nicholls, 'Gaelic society and economy in the high-middle ages', in Art Cosgrove (ed.), *A New History of Ireland: ii Medieval Ireland*, pp. 397–438 and Mary O'Dowd, 'Gaelic economy and society', in C. Brady and R. Gillespie (eds.), *Natives and Newcomers: Essays on the Making of Irish Colonial Society*, Dublin, 1986, pp. 129–47; see also Further Reading for ch. 3.

2 Political changes in Monaghan and Breifne (Cavan) are traced in P. Livingstone, *The Monaghan Story*, Enniskillen, 1980, and C. Brady, 'The O'Reillys of East Breifne and the problems of surrender and regrant', *Breifne*, xxiii, 1985, pp. 233–62. A different process of development is traced for Tyrconnell by Brendan Bradshaw, 'Manus the Magnificent: O'Donnell as Renaissance prince' in A. Cosgrove and D. MacCartney (eds.), *Studies in Irish History Presented to R. Dudley Edwards*, Dublin, 1979, pp. 15–36.

3 Among the principal texts of this nature are Fynes Moryson, *An Itinerary* (1617), 4 vols, Glasgow, 1907–8, supplemented in Charles Hughes (ed.), *Shakespeare's Europe*, London, 1903; William Farmer's 'Chronicles of Ireland', ed. C.L. Falkiner, *English Historical Review*, xxii, 1907, pp. 104–30, 537–52; and the survey of Captain Nicholas Dawtrey and Sir Richard Bingham in *Calendar of State Papers, Ireland, 1594–6*, p. 247 and 150. D.B. Quinn, *The Elizabethans and the Irish*, Ithaca, 1966, provides a good review of this literature.

4 For different views on the development of Tudor policy toward Gaelic Ireland see B. Bradshaw, *The Irish Constitutional Revolution of the Sixteenth Century*, Cambridge, 1979; N.P. Canny, *The Elizabethan Conquest of Ireland: a Pattern Established*, Hassocks, 1976, and C. Brady, 'Court, castle and country' in C. Brady and R. Gillespie (eds.), *Natives and Newcomers*, pp. 22–49.

5 Bradshaw, *The Irish Constitutional Revolution of the Sixteenth Century*. For the continued application of the policy, its problems and implications, see W.F.T. Butler, *Gleanings from Irish History*, London, 1926.

6 For a fuller discussion see C. Brady, 'The government of Ireland *c.* 1540–1593', PhD Thesis, Dublin University, 1980, ch. 5.

7 On Perrot's Ulster policy see Hiram Morgan, 'The Origins of the Nine Years War', PhD Thesis, Cambridge, 1987, ch. 2.

8 On the O'Reillys see C. Brady, 'The O'Reillys of East Breifne and the problem of surrender and regrant', *Breifne*, xxiii, 1985, pp. 233–62; on the Maguires see D. Green (ed.), *Duanaire Mheig Uidhir* ['The Poem Book of the Maguires'], Dublin, 1972.

9 Sean O'Domhnaill, 'History of Tir Conaill in the sixteenth century', MA Thesis, University College, Dublin, 1946; see also n. 5, Bradshaw.

10 The best work on Tyrone remains unpublished, see T.B. Lyons, 'Shane O'Neill: a biography', MA Thesis, University College, Cork, 1947, and Joseph Costello, 'Turlough Luineach O'Neill', MA Thesis, University College, Dublin, 1973.

11 G.A. Hayes McCoy, *Scots Mercenary Forces in Ireland*, Dublin, 1937; the estimates of numbers are derived from D.P. Dorrian, 'The cockpit of Ireland: north-east Ulster 1540–1603', BA dissertation, Trinity College, Dublin, 1985.

12 Dorrian op. cit. (see n. 11) and T.P. McCall, 'The Gaelic background to the Ulster plantation', MA Thesis, Queen's University, Belfast, 1983.

13 On Smith's abortive enterprise in the Ards see D.B. Quinn, 'Sir Thomas Smith and the beginnings of English colonial theory', *Proc. American Philosophical Society*, lxxxix, 1945, pp. 543–60 and Hiram Morgan, 'The colonial venture of Sir Thomas Smith in Ulster, 1571–1575', *Historical Journal*, xxviii, 1985, pp. 261–78; Essex's adventure in Clandeboy is recounted with copious documentation in W.B. Devereux, *Lives and Letters of the Devereux, Earls of Essex*, 2 vols., London, 1853.

14 Some notice of Piers's operation is given in Samuel McSkimmin,

History of Carrickfergus; 2nd ed., Belfast, 1909, chs. 2–3 and in G. Hill, *An historic account of the MacDonnells of Antrim*, Belfast, 1873; on Bagenal see, P.H. Bagenal, 'Sir Nicholas Bagenal, Knight-Marshall', *Royal Soc. Antiquaries Ireland, Journal*, series 6, vol. v, 1915, pp. 26, 298–311.

15 Pauline Henley, 'The treason of Sir John Perrot', *Studies*, xxi, 1932, pp. 404–22.

16 Hugh O'Reilly died late in 1583, Cuchonnacht Maguire and Sir Ross MacMahon both died in 1589.

17 The most balanced account of Fitzwilliam's administration remains Richard Bagwell, *Ireland under the Tudors*, vol. iii, London, 1890, chs. 43–4; for a contemporary English view highly critical of the viceroy, Thomas Lee, 'A brief declaration of the government of Ireland, 1594' in John Lodge, *Desiderata Curiosa*, Dublin, 1792, pp. 87–150.

18 See Morwenna Donnelly, 'Red Hugh's return home', *Donegal Annual*, iii, 1954–5, pp. 24–30; Lucius Emerson, 'The campaigns of Red Hugh O'Donnell', ibid., iv, 1960, pp. 233–57; J.J. Silke, 'Red Hugh O'Donnell: a biographical survey', ibid., v, 1961, pp. 1–19.

19 See J.J. Silke, 'The Irish appeal of 1593 to Spain: some light on the genesis of the nine years' war', *Irish Ecclesiastical Record*, xcii, 1959, pp. 279–90, 362–71; see also Further Reading for chapter 3.

20 N.P. Canny, 'The treaty of Mellifont and the re-organisation of Ulster', *The Irish Sword*, ix, 1970, pp. 249–62.

21 N.P. Canny, 'The flight of the earls, 1607', *Irish Historical Studies*, xvii, 1971, pp. 380–99.

Chapter 4 pp. 104–133

1 *Calendar of State Papers, Ireland (Cal. S.P. Ire.)*, 1603–6, p. 26.

2 Brendan Jennings, *Wild Geese in Spanish Flanders, 1582–1700*, Dublin, 1964, p. 201.

3 John Hanly (ed.), *The Letters of Saint Oliver Plunkett, 1625–1681*, Dublin, 1979, p. 318.

4 *Cal. S.P. Ire.*, 1603–6, p. 111; *Cal S.P. Ire.*, 1608–10, p. 16.

5 George Storey, *A Continuation of the Impartial History of the Wars of Ireland*, London, 1693, pp. 270–1.

6 For example, the exports listed in Kent Record Office, Sackville Ms ON 4806 (1616); Public Record Office, London, CO 388/85/A15 (1625).

7 Nicholas Canny, 'Hugh O'Neill and the changing face of Gaelic Ulster', *Studia Hibernica*, 10, 1970, pp. 7–35.

8 Bernadette Cunningham and Raymond Gillespie, 'The east Ulster bardic family of Ó Gnímh', *Éigse*, 20, 1984, pp. 106–14.

9 Bernadette Cunningham, 'Native culture and political change in Ireland, 1580–1640', in Ciaran Brady and Raymond Gillespie (eds.), *Natives and Newcomers: Essays on the Making of Irish Colonial Society*, Dublin, 1986, pp. 169–70.

10 Raymond Gillespie, 'The end of an era: Ulster and the outbreak of the 1641 rising', in Brady and Gillespie (eds.), op. cit., pp. 191–213.

11 Raymond Gillespie, 'Scotland and Ireland in the Interregnum', in Peter Roebuck and Rosalind Mitchison (eds.), *Economy and Society in Scotland and Ireland, 1500–1939*, Edinburgh, 1988, pp. 38–47.

12 Raymond Gillespie (ed.), *Settlement and Survival: the Brownlow Leasebook and the Development of the Lagan valley 1660–1700*, Belfast, 1988.

13 J.T. Gilbert (ed.), *A Jacobite Narrative of the Wars in Ireland*, Dublin, 1892, pp. 55–6.

14 *Cal. S.P. Ire.*, 1660–2, p. 164.

15 This is based on an analysis of *A list of the Names of the Popish Parish Priests . . . in the Kingdom of Ireland*, Dublin, 1705.

16 Historical Manuscripts Commission (H.M.C.), *Ormond Mss*, vii, pp. 59–60.

17 Raymond Gillespie, 'The Presbyterian Revolution in Ulster 1660–1690', in W.J. Shiels and D. Wood (eds.), *The Churches, Ireland, and the Irish: Studies in Church History*, 25, Oxford, 1989, pp. 159–70.

18 Hanly, *Letters of Saint Oliver Plunkett*, p. 74.

19 Tomás Ó Fiaich, 'The appointment of Bishop Tyrell and its Consequences', *Clogher Record*, 1, no 3, 1955, pp. 1–14.

20 Padraig Ua Duinnín, *Me Guidhir Fhearmanach*, Dublin, 1917, pp. 69–70.

21 R.M. Young (ed.), 'An account of the barony of Oneilland', *Ulster Journal of Archaeology*, 2nd ser. 4, 1898, pp. 240–41.

22 Raymond Gillespie, 'The making of the Montgomery manuscripts', *Familia*, 2, no. 2, 1986, pp. 23–9; Bernadette Cunningham and Raymond Gillespie, 'An Ulster settler and his Irish manuscripts', *Éigse*, 21, 1986, pp. 27–36; Joan Trimble, 'Carolan and his patrons in Fermanagh and neighbouring areas', *Clogher Record*, 10, 1979–80, pp. 26–50.

23 Cosmo Innes (ed.), *Munimenta alma universitatis Glasquensis*, 3, Glasgow, 1854, pp. 75, 82, 90, 93, 116, 121, 133, for example. In the sixteenth century the term Scots Irish was used only of the Catholic Scots of the Isles.

Chapter 5 pp. 134–157

1 W.H. Crawford, 'The origins of the linen industry in north Armagh and the Lagan valley', *Ulster Folklife*, xvii, 1971, pp. 42–51.

2 W.H. Crawford, 'Drapers and bleachers in the early Ulster linen industry', in L.M. Cullen and P. Butel (eds.), *Négoce et Industrie en France et en Irlande aux xviiie et xixe siècles*, Paris, 1980.

3 A. L'Amie, 'Chemicals in the eighteenth-century Irish linen industry', MSc Thesis, Queen's University, Belfast, 1984, p. 174.

4 Royal Irish Academy Haliday Collection, vol. 151, no. 5, *The distressed state of Ireland considered, more particularly with respect to the North, in a letter to a friend*, 1740, p. 4.

5 L. Slater, *The advantages which may arise to the people of Ireland by raising of flax and flaxseed*, Dublin, 1732.

6 W. Harris, *The antient and present state of the county of Down*, Dublin, 1744, p. 108.

7 Public Record Office of Northern Ireland (hereafter PRONI), Mic. 198, 'Hints towards a natural and topographical history of the counties of Sligo, Donegal, Fermanagh and Lough Erne by Rev. William Henry ... 1739'.

8 W.H. Crawford, 'Landlord–tenant relations in Ulster 1609–1820', *Irish Economic and Social History*, ii, 1975, pp. 5–21.

9 PRONI, Abercorn papers, D.623/A/1771.

10 A summary of the argument in Crawford, 'Landlord–tenant relations'.

11 PRONI, Massereene-Foster MSS, D.562/1270, 'Scheme of R. Stevenson 1795'.

12 D. McCourt, 'The decline of rundale, 1750–1850' in P. Roebuck (ed.), *Plantation to Partition*, Belfast, 1981, pp. 122–6.

13 National Library of Ireland, O'Hara Papers, Charles O'Hara's account of Sligo in the eighteenth century.

14 Armagh Public Library, Lodge MSS, 'County Monaghan by Archdeacon Cranston and Mr Lucas, January 8th, 1738–9'.

15 J. Blackall, *Some Observations and Reflections on the State of the Linen Manufacture in Ireland*, Dublin, 1780.

16 L.M. Cullen, *An Economic History of Ireland since 1660*, London, 1972, pp. 67–72; J. Fitzgerald, 'The organisation of the Drogheda economy 1780–1820', MA Thesis, University College, Dublin, 1972, p. 25.

17 PRONI, T.808/14900, 15261, 15264, 15266, 15267, 'Religious returns of 1766'.

18 J. McEvoy, *Statistical Survey of the County of Tyrone*, Dublin, 1802, p. 32.

19 R. Barton, *A Dialogue Concerning Some Things of Importance to Ireland, Particularly to the County of Ardmagh (sic)*, Dublin, 1751, p. 14.

20 W.H. Crawford, 'Economy and society in eighteenth century Ulster', PhD Thesis, Queen's University, Belfast, 1982, pp. 110–2.

21 ibid., pp. 121–7.

22 See McEvoy, *Statistical Survey of Tyrone*, pp. 53, 158–60, 207–9.

23 *Belfast News-Letter*, 11 November 1746.

24 PRONI, Abercorn papers, D.623/A, Nathaniel Nisbitt to Earl of Abercorn, 20 April 1758.

25 See the publications of the Ulster Architectural Heritage Society, 181a Stranmillis Road, Belfast 9.

26 W.H. Crawford, 'Economy and Society in Eighteenth Century Ulster', ch. 6.

27 P.D.H. Smyth, 'The Volunteers and parliament, 1779–84' in T. Bartlett and D.W. Hayton (eds.), *Penal Era and Golden Age*, Belfast, 1979, pp. 113–36; W.H. Crawford, 'The influence of the landlord in eighteenth century Ulster', in L.M. Cullen and T.C. Smout (eds.), *Comparative Aspects of Scottish and Irish Economic and Social History, 1600–1900*, Edinburgh, 1977, pp. 193–203.

28 W.H. Crawford, 'Change in Ulster in the late eighteenth century', in T. Bartlett and D.W. Hayton, *Penal Era and Golden Age*, pp. 199–202.

29 P. Jupp, 'County Down elections 1783–1831', *Irish Historical Studies*, xviii, no. 70, Sept. 1972, pp. 177–206.

30 For a fuller treatment of this theme see W.H. Crawford, 'The Ulster Irish in the eighteenth century', *Ulster Folklife*, 28, 1982, pp. 24–32.

31 See T. Bartlett, 'An end to moral economy: the Irish Militia disturbances of 1793', *Past and Present*, 99, May 1983, pp. 41–64, as well as D.W. Miller, 'The Armagh Troubles, 1784–95' in S. Clark and J.S. Donnelly (eds.), *Irish Peasants: Violence and Political Unrest 1780–1914*, Manchester, 1983, pp. 155–91.

Chapter 6 pp. 158–181

1 J.B. Doyle, *Tours in Ulster: a Handbook to the Antiquities and Scenery of the north of Ireland*, Dublin, 1854, pp. 1–2.

2 *Summary of the returns of owners . . .* , pp. 21 and 25, H.C. [House of Commons] 1876 (422), 55 and 59; *Agricultural statistics of Ireland for the Year 1876*, [Cmnd 1749], H.C. 1877, 535.

3 See W.E. Vaughan, *Landlords and Tenants in Ireland 1848–1914*, Dublin, 1984.

4 See B.M. Walker, 'The land question and elections in Ulster, 1868–86', in Samuel Clark and J.S. Donnelly (eds.), *Irish Peasants: Violence and Political Unrest, 1780–1914*, pp. 230–70.

5 W.E. Vaughan and A.J. Fitzpatrick (eds.), *Irish Historical Statistics: Population 1821–1971*, Dublin, 1978.

6 *Census of Ireland: general report, 1851* [2134], H.C. 1856, xxxi, pp. 28–9, *Ulster Census, 1911* [Cmnd 6051], H.C. 1912–13, pp. 4–5.

7 William Thackeray, *The Paris Sketch Book and Irish Sketch Book*, London, 1877, p. 508.

8 See E.E. Evans and B.S. Turner, *Ireland's Eye: the Photographs of R.J. Welch*, Belfast, 1977, p. 22.

9 *General census report, 1891*, pp. 474–6 [Cmnd 6780], H.C. 1892, XC, pp. 320–2.

10 See D.H. Akenson, *The Irish Education Experiment: the National System of Education in the Nineteenth Century*, London, 1970.

11 *Ulster census, 1871* [Cmnd 964–I to X], H.C. 1874, lxxiv, pt. 1, table XXXI from each report; Vaughan and Fitzpatrick, *Irish Historical Statistics: Population 1821–1971*.

12 *Anglo-Celt*, 18 July 1868; *Weekly Examiner*, 6 March 1886.

13 *Belfast Morning News*, 7 Nov. 1885.

14 B.M. Walker, *Sentry Hill: an Ulster Farm and Family*, Belfast, 1981, p. 54.

15 Quote is from Alan Megahey, 'The Irish Protestant Churches and social and political issues, 1870–1914', PhD Thesis, Queen's University, Belfast, 1969, cited in Richard McMinn, 'Presbyterianism and politics in Ulster, 1871–1906', *Studia Hibernia*, 21, 1981, pp. 127–46.

16 *Down Recorder*, 4 July 1868.

17 J.A. Rentoul, *Stray Thoughts and Memories*, Dublin, 1921, pp. 32–5.

18 A.M. Sullivan, *Old Ireland: Reminiscences of an Irish K.C.*, London, 1927, p. 37.

19 See B.M. Walker (ed.), *Parliamentary Election Results in Ireland, 1801–1922*, Dublin, 1978; B.M. Walker, 'Parliamentary Election results

from 1801',in T.W. Moody, F.X. Martin and F.J. Byrne (eds.), *A New History of Ireland*, vol. ix, Oxford, 1982, p. 635.

20 See B.M. Walker, 'The land question and elections in Ulster, 1868–86', in Samuel Clark and J.S. Donnelly (eds.), *Irish Peasants: Violence and Political Unrest, 1780–1914*, pp. 230–70.

21 See Michael Laffan, *The Partition of Ireland 1911–25*, Dublin, 1983.

Chapter 7 pp. 182–215

1 Michael Laffan, *The Partition of Ireland 1911–25*, pp. 62–3, 67.

2 Ian Colvin, *Life of Carson*, v. iii, London, 1936, p. 381.

3 Laffan, op. cit., p. 65.

4 Patrick Buckland, *A History of Northern Ireland*, Dublin, 1981, p. 23; *Hansard, House of Commons Debates*, 5 series, v. 136, cols. 882–7.

5 Michael Farrell, *Northern Ireland: The Orange State*, London, 1976, p. 6.

6 Michael Farrell, *Arming the Protestants: the Formation of the Ulster Special Constabulary and the Royal Ulster Constabulary 1920–27*, Brandon, 1983, p. 15.

7 F.S.L. Lyons, *Ireland Since the Famine*, Glasgow, 1973, pp. 426–7.

8 Ronan Fanning, *Independent Ireland*, Dublin, 1983, p. 36.

9 Buckland, *A History of Northern Ireland*, pp. 50–1.

10 Buckland, *The Factory of Grievances: Devolved Government in Northern Ireland 1921–39*, Dublin, 1979, p. 263.

11 David Harkness, *Northern Ireland since 1920*, Dublin, 1983, pp. 28–9; Michael Collins to Winston Churchill, 31 July 1922, University College Dublin, H. Kennedy papers, P4/V/10.

12 Buckland, *A History of Northern Ireland*, p. 51; *The Factory of Grievances*, p. 206.

13 St John Irvine, *Craigavon, Ulsterman*, London, 1949, p. 507.

14 Buckland, *A History of Northern Ireland*, p. 62.

15 ibid., pp. 67–8.

16 *Irish News,* 7 November 1932.

17 Buckland, *A History of Northern Ireland*, p. 55.

18 ibid., p. 60.

19 ibid., p. 63.

20 D.S. Johnson, 'The Northern Ireland Economy, 1914–39' in Liam Kennedy and Philip Ollerenshaw, *An Economic History of Ulster, 1820–1939*, Manchester, 1985, p. 208.

21 ibid., p. 213; Buckland, *A History of Northern Ireland*, p. 76.

22 Buckland, *A History of Northern Ireland*, p. 78.

23 A.C. Hepburn, *The Conflict of Nationality in Modern Ireland*, London, 1980, p. 164.

24 *Irish News*, 18 December 1931.

25 Andrew Boyd, *Holy War in Belfast*, Belfast, 1987, p. 229.

26 Hepburn, op. cit., pp. 169–70.

27 Buckland, *A History of Northern Ireland*, p. 83.

28 John A. Murphy, *Ireland in the Twentieth Century*, Dublin, 1975, pp. 126–7; Harkness, op. cit., p. 123.

29 Ian McAllister, *The Northern Ireland Social Democratic and Labour Party*, London, 1977, pp. 5–6.
30 Speech by Northern Ireland Minister of Health, W.K. Fitzsimmons, as reported in *Belfast Telegraph*, 1 December 1971.
31 Desmond Fennell, *The Northern Catholic: An Inquiry*, Dublin, 1958, pp. 22–3.
32 McAllister, op. cit., pp. 9–10.
33 John Boyd, 'The Arts' in *Belfast Telegraph Centenary Edition*, 1 September 1970, p. 18.
34 Harkness, op. cit., pp. 141–3.
35 Murphy, op. cit., p. 163.
36 Frank Curran, *Derry: Countdown to Disaster*, Dublin, 1986, p. 60.
37 Buckland, *A History of Northern Ireland*, p. 122.
38 Terence O'Neill, *Ulster at the Crossroads*, London, 1969, p. 140.
39 Buckland, *A History of Northern Ireland*, pp. 131–3.
40 Harkness, op. cit., pp. 172–3; Cornelius O'Leary, 'Northern Ireland, 1945–72', in J.J. Lee (ed.), *Ireland 1945–70*, Dublin and New York, 1979, p. 164.
41 Buckland, *A History of Northern Ireland*, p. 41.

Chapter 8 pp. 216–240

1 *Northern Ireland Constitutional Proposals*, Cmnd 5259, London, HMSO, 1973.
2 *Northern Ireland Constitutional Convention Report*, H.C.1, London, HMSO, 1975.
3 *Annual Register, 1977*, London, 1978, p. 49.
4 *Northern Ireland: a framework for devolution*, Cmnd 8541, London, HMSO 1982.
5 See *Belfast Newsletter (BNL)*, 9 December 1980.
6 *New Ireland Forum Report*, Dublin, 1984.
7 *Anglo-Irish Agreement*, Article 1(a). See for example *Irish Times*, 16 November 1985, p. 6.
8 'Sunningdale Conference' agreed communiqué, Belfast, N.I. Information Service, 1974, and see *BNL*, 10 December 1973.
9 For a long-term survey of Ulster history see A.T.Q. Stewart, *The narrow ground: aspects of Ulster, 1609–1969*, London, 1977.
10 See, for example, Coopers and Lybrand Associates, *The Northern Ireland Economy: Review of the Economic Situation and Prospects*, August, 1986.
11 *Northern Ireland census of population, 1981, General Report*, Belfast, HMSO, 1983.

Index

[Because of space constraints this index is selective. Minor place and personal names have been omitted.]